Anti-social Behaviour

Anti-social Behaviour

Andrew Millie

 McGraw Hill   Open University Press

Open University Press
McGraw-Hill Education
McGraw-Hill House
Shoppenhangers Road
Maidenhead
Berkshire
England
SL6 2QL

email: enquiries@openup.co.uk
world wide web: www.openup.co.uk

and Two Penn Plaza, New York, NY 10121—2289, USA

First published 2009

A catalogue record of this book is available from the British Library

ISBN-13: 978-0-33-5229161 (pb) 978-0-33-5229154 (hb)
ISBN-10: 0-33-522916-6 (pb) 0-33-522915-8 (hb)

Typeset by Kerrypress, Luton, Bedfordshire
Printed and bound in the UK by Bell and Bain Ltd, Glasgow.

Fictitious names of companies, products, people, characters and/or data that may be used herein (in case studies or in examples) are not intended to represent any real individual, company, product or event.

Illustrations

All images © the author except the following:
Chapter 8, images of Youth Spaces in Box 8.3, © MADE
Chapter 9, photo of Banksy's graffito in Box 9.1, © Nick Murison

The **McGraw·Hill** Companies

for Joan

with thanks

Contents

List of boxes, figures and tables

Figures

Tables

Foreword

Over the last decade 'anti-social behaviour' has become a hugely important topic in political, media and public debates, particularly in Britain where it has become something of an obsession. For Prime Minister Gordon Brown, the government is 'committed to doing everything in our power to tackle anti-social behaviour'. This book provides an overview of anti-social behaviour, including consideration of theory, concepts and alternative approaches to tackling the problem. It includes case study material from my own research as well as drawing on other academic and policy sources.

Much of the current focus on anti-social behaviour takes as its inspiration the North American literature on incivilities. Other nations have similarly targeted such 'quality of life crime', notably Australia where some states have been looking closely at British developments. Consequently, while the topic is most relevant to Britain, it will be of interest to those elsewhere with a concern for incivility, or for that matter an interest in disorder, deviancy and social control more generally. As a subject, 'anti-social behaviour' cuts across a number of disciplines, including criminology, social policy, sociology, housing policy, politics, law and urban social geography.

The book has evolved from a combination of empirical research and from teaching undergraduates about 'anti-social behaviour'. In terms of research, over the past few years I have been involved in two major studies on anti-social behaviour funded by national charities, the Joseph Rowntree Foundation (Millie et al. 2005a) and Nuffield Foundation (Jacobson et al. 2005, 2008). I have also conducted research for a local Crime and Disorder Reduction Partnership in a Midlands city, and was part of a team that worked on a larger study of anti-social behaviour in London. This was funded jointly by the Government Office for London, Greater London Assembly and the Housing Corporation and informed a pan-London strategy (GLA 2005; Millie et al. 2005b). Where relevant, this book draws on all these sources. Alongside this work I have been exploring practical and theoretical issues relating to anti-social behaviour, resulting in a range of journal articles and chapters (Millie 2006, 2007a, b, 2008a). I have used these texts as starting points for further and deeper exploration.

In terms of teaching, I've recently run an undergraduate module on anti-social behaviour. While there are some excellent books on the market (notably Burney 2005; Squires and Stephen 2005a: Flint 2006a; and Squires 2008) I found a need for a text that gave an overall picture of ASB in terms of theory, policy and practice. This book is designed, in part, to fill that gap. I hope it is of use to students as well as to other scholars with an interest in anti-social behaviour, incivility, disorder and deviancy. It should also be of interest to those exploring the limits of social control. The book is of use to practitioners who want to delve a bit deeper into the problems that go with trying to enforce or negotiate standards of behaviour.

The book's structure

The book is simply structured and consists of nine chapters. The first two chapters consider contested definitions of anti-social behaviour and the extent and nature of the problem in Britain. This is followed in Chapter 3 by consideration of theoretical perspectives that can inform contemporary debates about what is acceptable or anti-social. Chapters 4 and 5 focus on possible causes and rationales for tackling anti-social behaviour. It may seem straightforward that anti-social behaviour should be tackled because it is a menace to society. As shall be seen, things are more complicated. The book then focuses on the various enforcement and preventative options. In Britain the highest profile measure has been the Anti-Social Behaviour Order, or ASBO. The ASBO gets its own chapter in Chapter 6, with other enforcement options explored in Chapter 7 and preventative approaches in Chapter 8. Finally, conclusions are presented in Chapter 9, including possible ways forward for governing and negotiating behavioural expectations. Where appropriate the discussion is illustrated by appropriate case study and photographic evidence.

Acknowledgements

Thanks are of course due to all those I have interviewed on the subject of anti-social behaviour over the past few years, and the people who took part in various focus group discussions. Thanks also to those who agreed to be photographed, especially the young couple at Elephant and Castle (I hope you got the photos ok), and the free runners at South Bank who were more than happy to put on a show for me.

I'd like to thank Open University Press for agreeing to publish the book. I hope what I have delivered matches your expectations! Parts of the book draw on empirical research conducted over the past few years. I wish to thank my colleagues who collaborated on these projects, namely Mike Hough, Jessica Jacobson, Eraina McDonald and Anna Paraskevopoulou. It was a pleasure to work with all these people. Anything within this book that the reader finds disagreeable is entirely my fault and not theirs. Thanks too to Rosie Erol and Victoria Herrington. I am of course indebted to the various project funders, the Joseph Rowntree Foundation, Nuffield Foundation, Greater London Authority, Government Office for London and Housing Corporation. I also wish to thank Nicci Southard-Stuart, the Anti-Social Behaviour Reduction Co-ordinator at the Safer Swansea Partnership, for providing additional data, Julia Ellis and Stephanie Basher at Midlands Architecture and the Designed Environment (MADE) for providing the images of 'Youth Spaces' and Nick Murison for the Banksy photo.

Finally, thanks are due to Chris Cudmore and Jack Fray at Open University Press for their help and guidance through the publication process, and to the anonymous reviewers for their helpful and insightful comments. If there's anyone I have left out, thanks to you too!

1 What is anti-social behaviour (ASB)?

> One knows that it is not a cow or pig, but defining an elephant in precise terms is a little more difficult, at least in legal language. The application of common sense leads to a practice that is well understood by all. (Alun Michael, MP, 2005)

To some, trying to answer the question 'what is anti-social behaviour?' is a wasteful academic exercise; like the elephant in the above quote, you know what it is when you see it. Alun Michael, MP, used a similar argument in a debate on the Crime and Disorder Bill in 1998, stating that 'it is for the police, the local authority and the courts to recognise what has been described as the elephant on the doorstep, which is easier to recognise than to define' (see also Rutherford 2000; Hough and Jacobson 2004; Millie 2007a). Louise Casey, the senior civil servant who was later in charge of the Home Office's campaigns to tackle anti-social behaviour (ASB)[1] held a similar position. In minutes recording a meeting she attended of the Anti-Social Behaviour Scrutiny Panel of the London Borough of Camden (2004), it is stated that Casey, 'did not feel that a group of people sitting around a table analysing definitions was the right way to deal with anti-social behaviour ... We know what the problems are. We know what is needed. Now we have to do it'. Such a 'no nonsense' approach is certainly popular with some politicians. In an after-dinner speech Casey is also reported as saying, 'Topic for the evening, "Research: help or hindrance?" "Hindrance", thanks very much' (*Guardian* 2005). Aspects of this speech were later quoted by Baroness Linklater (2007) in a House of Lords debate:

> The Anti-Social Behaviour Unit [at the Home Office] was created to promote and develop a crackdown on such behaviour – with enormous enthusiasm and a zero-tolerance enforcement approach. However, the rigorous evidential tests more usually required by the

Treasury for funding other Home Office policy initiatives were not applied. Indeed, Louise Casey, now head of the Prime Minister's respect task force, was reported as saying to a senior police audience in 2005: 'If No. 10 says bloody "evidence based policy" to me one more time, I'll deck them.' One can only infer from that extraordinary remark that No. 10 was indicating that at least some research would be desirable, even if the head of the task force had no time for it.

For fear of causing further 'hindrance', this book examines the available evidence concerning the contemporary obsession with ASB in Britain. Rather than accepting at face value that ASB is a menace that needs to be stopped, the extent and nature of ASB is questioned, as well as the policy responses to it. For Louise Casey – a high profile civil servant with very close ties to Tony Blair – to be so publicly anti-evidence is illustrative of a shift from New Labour's earlier pragmatic emphasis on evidence-based practice, that 'what matters is what works' (Blair 1998: 4). The focus had become one of action, not about evidence, and certainly not about definitions. These are, of course, old arguments. For instance, in discussing vandalism back in 1973 Stan Cohen stated that:

> I want to start by considering some of the problems involved in defining vandalism. At first sight, this might sound like an arcane theoretical exercise with no reference to a real world in which 'everyone knows' what vandalism is and clearly recognises it as a problem, threat or menace. Let us imagine, though, having to explain to a foreigner what vandalism is. (p. 23)

Like Cohen's view of vandalism – and contrary to Alun Michael or Louise Casey – in this chapter it is argued that it is *very* important to have tighter definitions and limits to behaviour regarded as anti-social. Rather than everybody knowing what it is, ASB is seen as a contested concept; that one person's ASB may be another's criminality. Similarly, what to one person might be anti-social may be tolerable to another or even celebrated as a valued contribution to contemporary life. Definitional limits to ASB are also important because the consequences of censure can be severe. The highest profile measure designed to tackle ASB is the Anti-Social Behaviour Order (or ASBO), as introduced with the 1998 Crime and Disorder Act. The ASBO is explored in detail in Chapter 6; however, in brief, it acts as a form of hybrid law (Gardner et al. 1998; Pearson 2006) or two-step prohibition (Simester and von Hirsch 2006). It is two step in that it is a civil order in the first instance; however, breach of the order is a criminal offence carrying with it criminal censure in the form of a maximum five years in prison. The consequences of subjective 'common sense' decision making can therefore be very severe indeed.

That said, pinning down what is currently meant by ASB is not easy (e.g. Bland and Read 2000; Harradine et al. 2004; Ramsay 2004; Millie et al. 2005a) with common understandings characterized by vagueness and subjectivity. While criminologists and legal philosophers have been debating the precise nature and limits of criminal activity for decades (e.g. Feinberg 1984, 1985; Muncie 2001; Garland 2002), determining what exactly makes certain behaviours anti-social may be just as difficult – despite everyone apparently 'knowing it when they see it'. Without tighter definitional limits ASB could be anything from the mildly annoying through to the seriously criminal. For instance, if I am rude I am being anti-social, but so too if I steal your car. Most people would exclude both behaviours from definitions of ASB, as being either to trivial or adequately covered by criminal law. ASB lies somewhere in between, but what exactly is it that makes this behaviour unacceptable?

ASB as a political and media invention

There is of course the possibility that the label 'ASB' has simply been invented by politicians and by the media to describe a loose collection of neighbourhood problems (Burney 2005; Millie 2007a). Just as categories of 'crime' can be regarded as inventions of the criminal justice system (e.g. Hulsman 1986), 'ASB' can be regarded as a label of convenience for non-criminal and minor criminal neighbourhood concerns. It would be wrong to suggest that people do not behave anti-socially and that some people and neighbourhoods do not suffer the consequences of this behaviour. Nonetheless, it is certainly possible that politicians and the media have over-sold the problem. For instance, in 2004 a documentary about terrorism was shown on British television, *The Power of Nightmares* by Adam Curtis – broadcast over three nights from 20 October. In this, Curtis claimed that current terrorist threats were exaggerated or illusionary with *fear* of terrorism being used as a powerful political tool. Although on a different scale, it could be argued that ASB was similarly created (e.g. Burney 2005). UK crime rates had been falling from the mid-1990s onwards (e.g. Thorpe et al. 2007) and so ASB provided an opportune 'menace' to target for political rhetoric and action. By keeping the definition of ASB as vague as possible it also made it easier to claim successes. This is, of course, a dangerous game as it can draw people's attention to ASB-type problems and increase worries (Bannister et al. 2006). It seems unlikely that politicians have been quite as calculating, although there has almost certainly been a degree political packaging of ASB (Millie 2007a). Serious forms of ASB do exist, although perhaps not to the scale that we have been led to believe (see Chapter 2). Drawing on evidence from *Factiva, Lexis Nexis* and from the *Economist*,[2] Stuart Waiton (2005: 23) has claimed the following:

> The catch all term 'antisocial behaviour' has today become so widely used it seems strange to find it was rarely used [in the media] until the 1990s. In the 1980s a couple of articles a year were printed in the UK discussing antisocial behaviour, whereas in January 2004 alone, there were over 1000 such articles. Not even the most pessimistic social critic would suggest a parallel increase in problem behaviour.

Origins of the term 'anti-social behaviour'

Before going any further, it is useful to consider the origins of the term ASB. Within a public order enforcement context ASB is a comparatively recent addition to the common lexicon. However, within psychosocial literature 'anti-social behaviour' has been a term used for many years as a label for unwanted behaviour as the result of personality disorder and is the opposite of pro-social behaviour (e.g. Lane 1987; Farrington 1995a; Millon et al. 1998). For instance, writing from a psychosocial perspective, David Farrington (1995a: 84–5) has stated that teenage anti-social behaviour in particular, 'covers a multitude of sins ... such as theft, burglary, robbery, violence, vandalism, fraud and drug use ... bullying, reckless driving, heavy drinking and sexual promiscuity ... heavy smoking, heavy gambling, employment instability and conflict with parents'. This is an exceptionally broad remit. Relatedly, sociopathy and psychopathology are now more commonly regarded under the umbrella term 'Anti-Social Personality Disorder' (ASPD) (see e.g. Eysenck 1994; Squires and Stephen 2005). To avoid any confusion, this is *not* what this book is focused on. Instead a much narrower conception of ASB is considered, with the focus entirely on ASB as understood within a public order enforcement context.

People suffering from ASPD may find themselves the subject of such enforcement measures; however, ASB has greater overlap with conceptions of deviancy and delinquency – including some minor forms of criminality (see Chapter 3). ASB also has a lot in common with incivilities, disorder and 'quality of life crimes'; terms that describe a 'cocktail of social unpleasantness and environmental mess found in decaying neighbourhoods' (Burney 2005:

2). Of these labels the most useful is perhaps 'incivilities'. According to Bottoms (2006: 239), 'incivilities can sometimes consist simply of behaviour that lacks civility and consideration for others … on occasion [they] become genuinely *offensive* to reasonable people, in ways that may also constitute a *wrong* against them.' Just as 'disorder' is the opposite to 'order', 'incivility' is the opposite to 'civility'. The term relates to people's behavioural expectations for a 'civilized' or civil society, characterized by 'consideration for others'. The overlap with ASB is clear, in that someone who is anti-social is, by definition, not being 'social' and similarly lacks consideration or is unaware of the impact of their behaviour on others. In fact, although ASB is a peculiarly British obsession, it owes a great deal to US literature on incivilities and, in particular, Wilson and Kelling's (1982) 'broken windows' perspective. A fuller discussion is given in Chapter 5; but in simple terms, this takes a view that low level issues (such as broken windows) need to be tackled, otherwise there can be detrimental impact on fear, neighbourhood decline and criminality. It was an attractively simple concept to politicians (e.g. Blair 2001).

It is often assumed that ASB is a label created by New Labour. And while New Labour has certainly embraced the concept enthusiastically, it in fact pre-dates Labour coming to power in 1997 and featured in earlier Conservative legislation. Of course, some of the problems commonly regarded as anti-social are very old indeed (see Elias 1978; Pearson 1983, 2006; Burney 2005). However, in legislative terms the origin of what became known as ASB can be seen as the Conservative 1986 Public Order Act. The term ASB is not in fact used in this instance, but what is of significance is the focus on 'harassment, alarm and distress', what became the three pillars of later New Labour legislation to address ASB. According to the 1986 Public Order Act (s.5(1)):

> A person is guilty of an offence if he (a) uses threatening, abusive or insulting words or behaviour, or disorderly behaviour, or (b) displays any writing, sign or other visible representation which is threatening, abusive or insulting, within the hearing or sight of a person likely to be caused harassment, alarm or distress.

A person guilty of causing unintentional 'harassment, alarm or distress' could be given a fine. If intentional (s.4(a)), then the maximum sentence was six months' imprisonment or a higher fine. What is immediately apparent is the subjectivity of the terminology used. For instance, I can be harassed, alarmed or distressed by quite different things to someone else. Similarly, threat, abuse, insult or even disorderly behaviour are concepts open to interpretation. To give an example, between 2005 and 2007 a range of people associated with the pro-hunting 'Countryside Alliance' were arrested or given on-the-spot fines[3] for wearing and selling t-shirts emblazoned with the logo 'Bollocks to Blair' (*Horse and Hound Magazine* 2005; *The Times* 2006). According to *Horse and Hound Magazine* (Butcher 2007), a case was dropped against a man 'for brandishing a placard that read "Bollocks to Blair" above the M4 motorway'. He had originally been charged under the 1986 Public Order Act with 'displaying any writing, sign or other visible representation which is threatening, abusive or insulting'. The subjectivity of what causes harassment, alarm or distress is clear, and, in this instance, had a lot to do with the perception of offensiveness (see Feinberg 1985). As reported in *The Times* (2006), a stallholder noted the bizarre situation where he could be charged for selling 'Bollocks to Blair' t-shirts, while the clothing company French Connection could sell t-shirts with their logo 'FCUK' across them: 'We're continuing to display [the shirts] at shows and they are selling really well. It is a bit of a punchy slogan but I personally find it offensive for young girls to go round in t-shirts with FCUK written on them. Perhaps we should spell it Bollokcs to Blair.' The case is reminiscent of QC Sir John Mortimer's famous defence in 1977 of the Sex Pistols album, 'Never Mind the Bollocks, Here's the Sex Pistols' (see Cloonan 1995). It seems that notions of offence and 'civility' have not moved on as far as may have been thought.

As noted, the 1986 Public Order Act did not use the term ASB, but it covered much in common with what later became labelled as anti-social. One of the first definitions was put forward by the Chartered Institute of Housing (1995), as: 'Behaviour that unreasonably interferes with other people's rights to the use and enjoyment of their home and community'. This highlighted the importance of housing in ASB discourse. It has been noted elsewhere (Burney 2000, 2002; Brown 2004; Flint 2006a) that much of the current focus on ASB originated in a housing context in an effort to address issues of 'problem neighbours' or 'neighbours from hell' (cf. Field 2003) – something quite different to the public order targeted by the 1986 Act. At the Chartered Institute of Housing's annual conference in 1995 a lobby group was formed called the 'Local Authority Working Group on Anti-Social Behaviour', later to become the 'Social Landlords Crime and Nuisance Group' (see Burney 1999). Their influence on Labour Party policy, then in opposition, was immediate. In the same year Labour published their paper *A Quiet Life: Tough Action on Criminal Neighbours*. This outlined proposals for a 'Community Safety Order', which evolved into the ASBO when introduced in 1998. However, the term ASB was not adequately defined in any of these discussions, although it had become synonymous with neighbour disputes and people's rights to 'the use and enjoyment of their home and community'; or to a 'quiet life' – whatever that meant.

This emphasis was apparent in the 1996 Housing Act introduced by the Conservative government. This was the first time ASB was mentioned in legislation, here relating to powers for social landlords to grant injunctions against anti-social tenants.[4] According to the Act (s.152), a person is guilty of ASB if she or he is:

> (a) engaging in or threatening to engage in conduct causing or likely to cause a nuisance or annoyance to a person residing in, visiting or otherwise engaging in a lawful activity in residential premises to which this section applies or in the locality of such premises (b) using or threatening to use residential premises to which this section applies for immoral or illegal purposes, or (c) entering residential premises to which this section applies or being found in the locality of any such premises.

This definition was certainly not the shortest. In this case what was deemed to be ASB centred on 'nuisance' or 'annoyance', as opposed to the 'harassment, alarm or distress' of the 1986 Public Order Act. But these are similarly subjective concepts, meaning there was a lot of scope for interpretation of other people's behaviour. For pragmatic reasons, the injunction powers also included persons using or threatening to use premises for immoral or illegal purposes – principally to cover drug dealing or prostitution.

'Harassment' was also a feature of the 1997 Protection from Harassment Act, one of the last pieces of Conservative legislation enacted before the general election in May that year. 'Harassment' was defined as follows:

> A person must not pursue a course of conduct (a) which amounts to harassment of another, and (b) which he knows or ought to know amounts to harassment of the other. (s.1(1))

Here, according to Finch (2002a, cited in Ramsey 2004: 911) the definition is left vague as it, 'enables the victim to determine the parameters of acceptable interaction on an individualistic basis ... [with] primacy given to the victim's interpretation of events when attributing liability'. Not only was acceptability of behaviour a subjective decision made by the victim, it is stated that the perpetrator 'ought to know' that it is harassment. In effect, the perpetrator is in the peculiar position of having to understand how someone *may perceive* their actions. That said, there was some elaboration as the behaviour had to have occurred at least twice (s.7(3)) and could include speech (s.7(4)) (see Finch 2002b: 423). Still, this left considerable scope for interpretation.

The 1998 Crime and Disorder Act definition of ASB

When Labour came to power following election success in 1997 one of the first pieces of legislation passed was the 1998 Crime and Disorder Act seeing, among other things, the introduction of the ASBO. While the ASBO was their 'baby', Labour had inherited much legislative language from the Conservatives, a fact made clear by the definition of ASB used in the 1998 Act (s.1(1a)). Here the definition relates to when ASBOs are appropriate, with ASB being defined as acting:

> in a manner that caused or was likely to cause harassment, alarm or distress to one or more persons not of the same household as [the perpetrator].

Unfortunately, Labour also inherited the Conservative's lack of legislative clarity. The phrase 'not of the same household' excludes incidents of domestic violence as these were already covered by the 1996 Family Law Act (Thorp 1998: 23). Nonetheless, what is left is *everything else* that causes or is likely to cause 'harassment, alarm or distress'. By including the phrase 'likely to cause', the definition creates further problems in that it includes behaviour *perceived* to be a threat, rather than focusing solely on actual behaviour; put another way, a focus is on the supposed consequences of perceived threat (e.g. Armitage 2002). This was acknowledged in a Home Office report (Harradine et al. 2004: 3), that 'by describing the consequences of behaviour rather than the behaviour itself, the definition lacks specificity and measurability'. As noted, 'harassment' had already been covered by the 1997 Protection from Harassment Act; however, for the 1998 Act 'harassment' is only part of the picture. By including harassment, alarm *or* distress, behaviour that is perceived to lead to *any one* of these effects could be censured as anti-social. A local authority worker interviewed for a recent study (see also Millie et al. 2005a) summed up the problem with ASB definition thus:

> What's the definition? The police's is anything which causes alarm or distress, large groups wandering around the streets. Goodness me, I mean I used to do it and mostly everyone else did, used to wander around with their mates on the street once the youth club's shut. But they cast that as anti-social behaviour, a bit of fun, a bit of malarkey ... I think anti-social behaviour, the term of it, is very much abused if you like, I really do.

Defining a problem so loosely and subjectively means most unwanted behaviour can be regarded as anti-social. It has been well documented (e.g. Ashworth et al. 1998; Burney 2000a; Whitehead et al. 2003; Ramsey 2004; Millie et al. 2005a; Macdonald 2006) that this vagueness has led to the inclusion of both criminal and non-criminal behaviour – or as Home Office guidance (1999) put it, criminal and *sub*-criminal behaviour. This blurring of boundaries in criminal justice is something that Cohen (1985) had anticipated and can clearly cause problems (see Brown 2004; Squires 2006). In effect, behaviour that had previously been regarded as unpleasant, but tolerated, can be 'up tariffed' or criminalized. To use Cohen's (1985) famous fishing analogy, it is an example of 'net widening', where behaviour – and perpetrators of this behaviour – previously outside the scope of criminal law get caught in an ever expanding criminal justice net. For example, ASBOs have been granted to disruptive teenagers with the condition not to congregate with other youths. Congregating with other youths is, understandably, for the vast majority of young people a perfectly acceptable part of daily life. However, in order to deter future ASB, for a select few it can lead to a breach of ASBO conditions, with the breach carrying the possibility of criminal censure. One of the principles of criminal law is *equality* before the law; however, ASBOs break this principle and can be regarded as personalized penal codes, 'where non-criminal behaviour becomes criminal for individuals who have incurred the wrath of the community' (Gil-Robles 2005: 37). Similarly, ASBOs have been given to street sex workers and street drinkers (e.g. Jones and Sager 2001; Fletcher 2005; Macdonald 2006; Moore 2008), not for criminal acts, but for the perceived effect of their behaviour.

Following the 2002 Police Reform Act, ASBOs could also be granted post-criminal conviction in an attempt to prevent future criminal behaviour (what have become known as criminal ASBOs or CrASBOs). In such cases, the risk is one of 'down tariffing', with offences that are clearly criminal being treated in legal language as though they were an anti-social problem.

An elastic definition of ASB

A vague definition runs the risk of infringing rule of law principles by '[failing] to give fair warning to citizens of what kind of conduct may trigger these powers' (von Hirsch et al. 1995: 1501). That said, it has been argued that the there are distinct advantages to having an elastic definition. In a government report on ASB the difficulties with definition were avoided by claiming '[t]here is no single definition of anti-social behaviour. It covers a wide range of behaviour from litter to serious harassment' (SEU 2000a: 14). According to Carr and Cowen (2006: 59) the resulting political and policy discourse has been that 'we do not know what it is, although it is sometimes said in response that we all know what it is when we see or experience it'. For those studying ASB this is not a satisfactory position. However, for practitioners this vagueness has given them a considerable degree of local discretion.

Speaking as the Home Office's 'Respect Coordinator', Louise Casey (2005) has stated 'the legal definition of antisocial behaviour is wide. And rightly so'. It is claimed that a wide definition allows for the identification and prioritization of local concerns. Whether local discretion is a good thing is another matter as there is a risk that outsider groups (cf. Becker 1963) may be discriminated against. According to Ashworth et al. (1998: 9) early proposals included provisions to mitigate against discrimination 'on grounds of race, religion, sex, sexual orientation or disability in applying for or enforcing ASBOs'. These provisions did not reach the 1998 Crime and Disorder Bill (although they later reappeared in a Home Office classification of anti-social behaviours (Harradine et al. 2004)). Ashworth et al. (1998: 9) have noted:

> Even if the police and local authorities can be trusted to be scrupulous in avoiding discrimination on these grounds – and we are not sure that they can – this is no obstacle to these orders being used as weapons against other unpopular types, such as ex-offenders, 'loners', 'losers', 'weirdos', prostitutes, travellers, addicts, those subject to rumour and gossip, those regarded by the police or neighbours as having 'got away' with crimes, etc.

According to Donoghue (2007:418) having such local discretion leads to 'inconsistency in application and administration'. A vague definition has also allowed civil powers associated with ASB legislation to be used for more serious criminal activity in an attempt to speed up the criminal justice process – as with the use of CrASBOs. In the Labour Party's early consultation paper on ASB, *A Quiet Life* (1995), this was a justification for introducing the new measures, that there was 'intense dissatisfaction [among practitioners] with the extent and speed of existing procedures'. According to Tony Blair: 'though many of these [anti-social] things are in law a criminal offence, it is next to impossible for the police to prosecute without protracted court process, bureaucracy and hassle, when conviction will only result in a minor sentence. Hence these new powers to take swift, summary action' (Blair 2003a).

The trouble with this perspective is that, although the court process can be painfully slow, much of the 'bureaucracy and hassle' is there to ensure a sound conviction. There is well-documented concern that such ASB measures circumvent due criminal process (e.g. von Hirsch 1995; Ashworth et al. 1998; Gil-Robles 2005; Macdonald 2006). According to Burney (2002: 474) the result can be ASBO applications where, 'we know you boys committed that crime but we can't prove it to criminal standard'. Of course, some of the more 'unusual' ASBO applications may not make it past the courts. As Donoghue (2007: 428) has observed: 'While it is the local authorities and the police who are instructive in determining ASBO *applications*, it is the judiciary who primarily define their legitimacy, their purpose and scope, and their function in law.' Having said this, there are still some quite bizarre ASBO applications that do get through (see Chapter 6).

Typologies of ASB

As a response to a lack of a legislative clarity, the Home Office initially produced a list of behaviours deemed to be anti-social (Home Office 2003b; Harradine et al. 2004). This was part of a one-day count of ASB in an attempt to determine the scale of the problem (10 September 2003 – see Chapter 2). Up until that point the government was quite happy introducing new legislation without any knowledge of the extent and nature of the problem. The behaviours included were:

- Litter/rubbish
- Criminal damage/vandalism
- Vehicle-related nuisance
- Nuisance behaviour
- Noise
- Rowdy behaviour
- Abandoned vehicles
- Street drinking and begging
- Drug/substance misuse and drug dealing
- Animal-related problems
- Hoax calls
- Prostitution, kerb crawling, sexual acts.

This was a useful start, but left some ambiguity. For instance, at what level does 'noise' become intolerable? Is this the same in an urban block of flats as it is in a rural village? Similarly 'animal-related problems' is vague enough to include any animal concerns, although most cases were presumably related to 'dog mess' or uncontrolled pets. An example here is when, in 2004, a farmer was given an ASBO that stipulated he was not to let his pigs and geese escape (Macdonald 2006). In terms of the nature of the problem and impact, this is quite a different concern to the 'prostitution', 'street drinking' or 'rowdy behaviour' also listed. ASB seemed to be anything that would be *really* annoying, but was either a very minor criminal offence or not criminal at all.

To gain some clarity various typologies of behaviour thought to be anti-social have been suggested, as shown in Box 1.1. The first was a 'spectrum of anti-social behaviour' produced by Bannister and Scott (2000) in work commissioned by the Scottish Office.[5] This was chiefly concerned with ASB within social housing and divided ASB into neighbour problems (such as noise), area or neighbourhood problems (litter, graffiti, etc.) and also criminal behaviour (such as burglary).

In 2004 the Home Office published a typology (Harradine et al.) that covered similar ground, but divided ASB into (1) acts directed at people; (2) environmental damage; (3) misuse of public space; and (4) disregard for community/personal well-being. The category 'misuse of public space' was a useful development as it emphasized the public nature of ASB; as noted, the 1998 Crime and Disorder Act definition excluded domestic incidents. Where the Home Office typology failed was in its inclusion of clearly criminal acts. For instance, included under the heading 'acts directed at people' is intimidation and harassment on the grounds of race. This is quite rightly treated as a serious criminal offence in section 32 of the 1998 Crime and Disorder Act (racially aggravated harassment). Calling racially aggravated harassment 'anti-social' runs the risk of 'down tariffing' the offence.

Box 1.1 Typologies of anti-social behaviour

- Bannister and Scott (2000: 7) **Spectrum of anti-social behaviour**
    1 *Neighbour*: A dispute arising from nuisance, e.g. noise.
    2 *Neighbourhood*: Incivilities within public spaces, e.g. rubbish.
    3 *Crime*: All forms of criminal activity, e.g. housebreaking.
- Harradine et al. (2004: 4) **Home Office typology of anti-social behaviour**
    1 *Acts directed at people*: Intimidation/harassment (including on the grounds of race, sexual orientation, gender, religion, disability or age).
    2 *Environmental damage*: Criminal damage/vandalism, litter/rubbish.
    3 *Misuse of public space*: Drug/substance misuse and dealing, street drinking, begging, prostitution, kerb crawling, sexual acts, abandoned cars, vehicle-related nuisance and inappropriate vehicle use.
    4 *Disregard for community/personal well-being*: Noise, rowdy behaviour, nuisance behaviour, hoax calls, animal-related problems.
- Millie et al. (2005b: 9) **A typology for the London ASB Strategy 2005–08**
    1 *Interpersonal or malicious ASB*: Directed at individuals, groups or organizations, such as threats to neighbours, hoax calls or vandalism directed at individuals or groups.
    2 *Environmental ASB*: Such as noise nuisance, abandoned vehicles, graffiti or fly tipping.
    3 *ASB restricting access to public spaces*: Including intimidating behaviour by groups on the street, aggressive begging, street drinking and open drug use.

- www.respect.gov.uk (accessed 2007) **Types of anti-social behaviour**
  1   *Nuisance neighbours*: Rowdiness, excessive noise and animal-related problems are all examples of anti-social behaviour caused by nuisance neighbours.
  2   *Environmental crime*: such as graffiti and fly tipping, has a huge impact on our communities and on how happy we are in them. It can ruin public spaces and is expensive to clean up.
  3   *Street problems*: Intimidation, begging, public drug dealing, and the reckless driving of mini-motorbikes are all street problems that fall under the definition of anti-social behaviour.

Note: Some ordering has been changed to ease comparison.

In 2005 I was involved in work associated with the pan-London ASB Strategy, working with Mike Hough, Jessica Jacobson and others at King's College London (GLA 2005; Millie et al. 2005b). As part of this we produced a typology of anti-social behaviours (as shown in Box 1.1). This also isn't perfect; but unlike the earlier Home Office classification it attempts to restrict behaviours to those that are *just* anti-social, and excludes the seriously criminal. ASB is divided between (1) interpersonal or malicious ASB; (2) environmental ASB; and (3) ASB restricting access to public spaces. A more recent Home Office categorization (Respect website 2007a) is very similar, with problems divided between (1) nuisance neighbours; (2) environmental crime; and (3) street problems. Classification can only go so far in determining the exact nature of ASB. To take 'street problem ASB', or 'ASB restricting access to public spaces', as an example, which groups have legitimacy in using, and in some instances dominating, shared spaces is going to be contested. Retail spaces and city centres are clearly populated by shoppers; yet others will have equal claim to these spaces, including groups of young people often deemed to be anti-social just by their presence. Another example is shown in Box 1.2 which gives two uses of public space; after-work drinking by city workers in London and a street homeless man encamped outside Waterloo Station. Both activities restrict access to shared spaces and both would tick some of the boxes in the Home Office list of anti-social behaviours; but are any *really* anti-social? Or at what point does their behaviour become anti-social?

Box 1.2 Contested uses of shared spaces in London

City workers drinking in Farringdon

Street homeless man begging outside Waterloo

Public understandings of anti-social behaviour

In a recent national survey (Millie et al. 2005a), respondents were asked what they thought the government meant by ASB (see Table 1.1). Half answered an open-ended question and half had to choose from a checklist of problems, including some from the Home Office typology (Harradine et al. 2004) and some not usually thought of as ASB. Most thought the government's focus was on youth problems (71% given the checklist). However, two-fifths of those given the checklist chose mugging or burglary – clearly criminal activity rather than anti-social. Others chose 'drug use of dealing' (63% of those given the checklist, although this fell to 6% of free responses, perhaps suggesting that this is not what most people naturally think about). Others identified traffic noise and pollution, issues not normally associated with ASB, but can be grouped under wider neighbourhood 'quality of life' concerns. It seems the public's view of ASB can be just as vague as the government's. However, for the majority the government's focus is on youth issues.

Table 1.1 What do you think the government means by anti-social behaviour?

Free responses (n = 831)*	%	Responses to checklist (n = 847)**	%
Vandalism/graffiti/hooligans	17	Rowdy teenagers on the street/youths hanging around	71
Youths hanging around/people being a nuisance	16	Drug dealing	63
Drinking, drunk and disorderly	15	Noisy neighbours	44
Unacceptable/bad behaviour; rowdyism; bad language	13	Mugging	44
Crime: muggings; burglary; criminal damage	12	Burglary	42
Noisy neighbours	10	Graffiti	34
Noise; traffic noise; pollution	8	Speeding	34
Violence; fighting	7	Traffic noise and pollution	22
Intimidation; offensive/threatening/aggressive behaviour; harassment	7	None of these	2
Drug use; drug dealing	6	Don't know	8
Yobbish behaviour/yob culture	4		
Disruptive/disturbance to community	2		
Litter; fly tipping	2		
Speeding	1		
Don't know	5		

Notes:
* Question: 'What do you think the government means by anti-social behaviour?'
** Question: 'Which of the problems on this card do you think the [government's] strategy is aiming to reduce?'

A working definition of ASB

In a focus group with former homeless people in London (see also Millie et al. 2005b), one respondent stated that ASB is simply: 'Stuff that affects you. You know, other people's stuff.' For him ASB was regarded simply as other people's behaviour that he didn't like. His observation may have been near the mark. The sociological notion of 'conduct norms' (e.g. Sellin 1938) is a useful way of viewing what is commonly regarded as anti-social – in effect, ASB becomes something that contravenes certain cultural and societal norms of behaviour. For instance, according to the Chartered Institute of Housing (1995: 3) ASB is '[b]ehaviour that opposes society's norms and accepted standards of behaviour'. Writing about incivilities in America, La Grange et al. (1992: 312) came to a similar conclusion, defining incivilities as 'low-level breaches of community standards that signal an erosion of conventionally accepted norms and values'. However, it is entirely possible that such norms and values vary between different individuals or communities and that *plural* norms of acceptable behaviour are developed, a theme explored in Chapter 3. The danger is that the behavioural expectations of the majority are seen as 'social', while those of minority or marginalized 'outsider' groups are regarded as anti-social (Millie 2006).

With this in mind, there does seem to be a *normative* element to ASB, although which specific behaviours are outside social and cultural norms can be contested. Another element to ASB is that it is *persistent* (e.g. Thorp 1998; Campbell 2002; Millie et al. 2005a; Bottoms 2006). According to Frank Field, MP: 'The distinguishing mark of anti-social behaviour is that each single instance does not by itself warrant a counter legal challenge. It is in its regularity that anti-social behaviour wields its destructive force. It is from the repetitive nature of the nuisance that anti-social behaviour is born' (2003: 45). Thus, one noisy party does not warrant censure as ASB; but holding regular parties in your flat without the cooperation of neighbours can become anti-social.

In formulating a working definition of ASB lessons can be learnt from discussion over what constitutes 'bullying'. This has been another 'slippery' concept; however, within psychological literature some general characteristics have been identified (taken from Olweus 1999; Smith et al. 2002; and Coyne et al. forthcoming):

- It is aggressive behaviour or intentional 'harm doing'
- Is carried out repeatedly and over time
- It occurs in an interpersonal relationship characterized by a power imbalance
- It often occurs without apparent provocation
- Is negative actions carried out by contact (physical or otherwise such as with cyber-bullying).

Much can be learnt from this, especially the criteria of intentionality and repetition. In our work for the London ASB Strategy (Millie et al. 2005b: 9) the following working definition was offered (see also Millie et al. 2005a):

ASB is behaviour that
- Causes harassment, alarm or distress
- To individuals not of the same household as the perpetrator, such that
- It requires interventions from the relevant authorities; *but*
- Criminal prosecution and punishment may be inappropriate

- Because the individual components of the behaviour:
  1   are not prohibited by the criminal law or
  2   in isolation constitute relatively minor offences.

For pragmatic reasons, the basic structure of the 1998 Crime and Disorder Act definition is kept, although the *or was likely to cause* element was removed. It was agreed that ASB ought to be limited to actual behaviour, rather than including perceived threat. The definition is further limited as serious criminality is excluded (as this is adequately covered by criminal law). The role of authorities in intervening is recognized along with the cumulative impact, or persistence, of behaviour that makes it anti-social (Flint 2006a: 5). However, unlike the bullying definition, intentionality was not included. This is something that, legally, is very difficult to determine.

As stated, this was a working definition, but it does at least limit the range of behaviours that are anti-social. What I hope to demonstrate through this book is that an absolute precise definition is not possible. Instead it is the contested nature of what constitutes ASB that has the biggest impact on how 'unwanted' behaviours ought to be tackled, if at all.

The scope and structure of this book

Use of the term 'anti-social behaviour' in a public order enforcement context is primarily a British phenomenon. As a consequence, must of the discussion that follows is focused on a British context. More specifically, when legislation is referred to, for simplicity, this is usually for England and Wales unless otherwise stated. Scotland has its own separate legal system although it too has followed a policy of tackling ASB. Consequently, much of the discussion in this book will be similarly relevant to Scotland. It is also relevant to developments in Ireland (north and south) (e.g. Brown, 2007) and in Australia where ASB is starting to gain capital among politicians and policy makers (e.g. Arthurson and Jacobs 2006). For instance, a conference was held in 2007 at the University of Tasmania in Hobart considered the prospects of applying British policy on ASB to Australia. In North America – and in the United States in particular – there is a long history of work to tackle incivilities, minor disorders and 'quality of life' crimes. This book feeds into these wider debates. It also draws on such literature and experiences from outside Britain where appropriate. Hopefully the book is of use to scholars, practitioners and students interested in the control of low level 'unacceptable' behaviours, wherever they are.

In the next chapter, the extent and nature of ASB in Britain is considered. It is frequently claimed that ASB is a menace wherever you live. Evidence is presented that puts this idea in doubt. In Chapter 3, a theoretical context to discussions of ASB is presented. According to Mooney and Young (2006: 399) the current focus on ASB may be viewed as a simple 'rediscovery of the sociology of deviance circa 1960'. To an extent they have a point and, in this chapter, literature on, for example, normative behaviour, deviancy, 'otherness' and social control, is related to contemporary debates on ASB. Chapters 4 and 5 consider some fundamental questions for those wishing to tackle ASB: first, what causes ASB? and, second, what can be gained by tackling ASB? Criminologists have been arguing about the causes of crime for decades. The causes of ASB are going to be similarly contested. Rationales for tackling ASB are similarly not straightforward, including because ASB itself is a bad thing, that tackling ASB can lead to reductions in crime, or perhaps that it aids regeneration. These and other perspectives are considered.

The next three chapters focus on measures to control or prevent ASB. In Britain, most attention has been on the Anti-Social Behaviour Order or ASBO. Consequently, the ASBO gets its own chapter in Chapter 6. Chapter 7 looks at alternative enforcement options, while Chapter 8 considers how ASB can be prevented. Of course, the type of prevention that is promoted will be strongly influenced by what is thought to cause ASB in the first place; and so these discussions relate back to earlier consideration of causality.

In the concluding chapter the discussion is brought together by looking at a possible future for ASB in Britain. The idea that people can interpret the same behaviour differently is explored further, that people have contested uses and expectations for public shared spaces. The consequences for governing and negotiating behavioural expectations are considered.

Selected reading

The contested nature of what constitutes ASB is something that has been a concern for a number of writers. For the Home Office perspective the best place to look is still:

- Harradine, S., Kodz, J., Lernetti, F. and Jones, B. (2004) Defining and measuring anti-social behaviour. Home Office Development and Practice Report No. 26. London: Home Office.

Academic work that has looked at definitions includes the following:

- Flint, J. (2006a) *Housing, Urban Governance and Anti-social Behaviour: Perspectives, Policy and Practice.* Bristol: Policy Press.
- Macdonald, S. (2006) A suicidal woman, roaming pigs and a noisy trampolinist: refining the ASBO's definition of 'anti-social behaviour', *The Modern Law Review*, 69(2): 183–213.
- Millie, A., Jacobson, J., McDonald, E. and Hough, M. (2005a) *Anti-social Behaviour Strategies: Finding a Balance.* Bristol: Policy Press.
- Ramsay, P. (2004) What is anti-social behaviour?, *The Criminal Law Review*, Nov.: 908–25.

Notes

1 From 2003–07 the 'Together' campaign and the 'Respect' agenda (Home Office 2003a; Respect Task Force 2006).
2 See *Economist* (2005).
3 Fixed penalty notices (see Chapter 7).
4 Under the 2003 Anti-Social Behaviour Act (s.153A) these became known as Anti-Social Behaviour Injunctions or ASBIs – amended with the 2006 Police and Justice Act (s.26).
5 Now the 'Scottish Government'.

2   The extent and nature of anti-social behaviour in Britain

> [ASB] can occur anywhere – in people's homes and gardens, on estates, in town centres or shopping parades and in urban and rural areas. It blights people's lives, undermines the fabric of society and holds back regeneration. (Home Office 2003c: 6)

We have been told that ASB is a problem for all of us in Britain; wherever we live, it 'blights people's lives', it 'undermines the fabric of society'. According to Labour MP, Jack Straw (1996), '[t]he rising tide of disorder is blighting our streets, parks and town centres'. Speaking while Prime Minister, Tony Blair (2004) claimed: 'The scourge of anti-social behaviour affects us all and in our biggest cities, on suburban estates and rural villages. We all know the consequences. People too frightened to go into the city centre at night. Anxious about leaving their homes to go down to the local shops. Terrorised by unruly neighbours.'

These are strong words and, if true, would require a strong policy response. According to Matthews (2003: 5), 'although there is no certainty about what constitutes anti-social behaviour, we are reassured that it can occur everywhere and anywhere'. In Chapter 1, it was noted that problems of ASB may have been over-sold by politicians and by the media. While I believe this to be true, it is a claim that was refuted by the House of Commons Home Affairs Committee in 2005 (para. 19), in stating: 'We do not believe that the problem of anti-social behaviour has been exaggerated by Government or played up by the media. It is a problem that has a day-to-day impact on residents, neighbours and communities.' The extent and nature of ASB in Britain is investigated in this chapter. If ASB is a real problem, then when and where does it occur and in what form?

Counting anti-social behaviour

Over the past decade there has been a growth of an ASB 'industry' in Britain (Brown, 2004; Squires and Stephen 2005b) especially concentrated within housing management, policing and local authority work. For instance, all local Crime and Disorder Reduction Partnerships (CDRPs)[1] are expected to have an 'anti-social behaviour coordinator',[2] many have specialist legal advisors, as well as 'anti-social behaviour teams'. At a national level between 2002 and 2006 work was led initially by the Home Office's 'Together' campaign and then an interdepartmental 'Respect' agenda, both managed by senior civil servant Louise Casey. (Casey was given the title of 'Respect Coordinator' and labelled in the media as the 'Respect Tsar'.[3]) More recently from October 2007 this work has continued as part of a 'Youth Taskforce' established at the Department for Children, Schools and Families, with an *Action Plan* published in March 2008. This is a great deal of policy focus on ASB and, in order to respond, all these people first need to *find* ASB.

The first attempt at establishing the extent and nature of the problem was on 10 September, 2003, when the Home Office conducted a one-day count of ASB. This used the Home Office list of behaviours (as shown in Chapter 1) as its basis. On the day of the count relevant statutory and voluntary agencies were asked to collate all reports from the public about ASB incidents and to submit data to the Home Office. This technique of measurement was methodologically dubious as some agencies would have been quite zealous in collection and classification, while others clearly would have done the minimum. Similarly, many incidents would have been unreported or double-counted having been reported to more than one agency. Also, there was no adjustment for seasonality, with the reason for choosing 10 September seeming to be one of pragmatism. However, having noted the limitations the one-day count was useful in that it, at least, indicated that ASB is a *real* problem with 66,107 reports recorded across England and Wales. The costs of these reports was estimated to be £13.5 million for the one day. The full breakdown is shown in Table 2.1. Significantly, 13,000 reports (20%) came from London (Millie et al. 2005b: 37). Whether this is because ASB is more of an issue in London or because agencies in the capital were better at collating the information is not clear. However, it does hint at a particular urbanity to ASB (of which more is not later).

Table 2.1 Home Office one-day count, 10 September 2003

	Reports Number	Percent-age	Estimated cost to agencies per day	Estimated costs to agencies per year
Litter/rubbish	10,686	16	£1,866,000	£466m
Criminal damage/vandalism	7855	12	£2,667,000	£667m
Vehicle-related nuisance	7782	12	£1,361,000	£340m
Nuisance behaviour	7660	12	£1,420,000	£355m
Intimidation/harassment	5415	8	£1,983,000	£496m
Noise	5374	8	£994,000	£249m
Rowdy behaviour	5339	8	£995,000	£249m
Abandoned vehicles	4994	8	£360,000	£90m
Street drinking and begging	3239	5	£504,000	£126m
Drug/substance misuse and drug dealing	2920	4	£527,000	£132m
Animal-related problems	2546	4	£458,000	£114m
Hoax calls	1286	2	£198,000	£49m
Prostitution, kerb crawling, sexual acts	1011	2	£167,000	£42m
Total	66,107	100	£13,500,000	£3.375bn

Source: Home Office 2003b.

Public perceptions about anti-social behaviour

As ASB is such a subjective concept it is important to consider public perception of incidence. The first place to look is the British Crime Survey (BCS)[4] which has for a number of years included questions on perceived levels of ASB or disorder. For instance, for the past six sweeps of the BCS respondents have been asked to indicate how much of a problem seven different forms of ASB are where they live (within 15 minutes of home). The results are shown in Table 2.2. What is immediately apparent is that the majority *do not* perceive ASB to be a huge problem, contrary to what we have been led to believe. Of the seven categories, six refer to actual behaviours (e.g. noisy neighbours or vandalism) while one refers to simple presence (teenagers hanging around on the streets). Whether presence should be regarded as anti-social is a moot point; but of the seven categories it is the presence of teenagers hanging around that is perceived to be most prevalent, with between 27 and 33 percent of respondents claiming 'high levels' in their area. Rubbish or litter comes a close second, followed by vandalism/graffiti and drug use and dealing.

The general figure for 'high level of perceived ASB' (which is derived from the seven types) is much lower. In 2002/03 this peaked at 21 percent; however, for all other years this was between 16 and 19 percent. Although ASB can be vary serious, for the majority it is clearly not at 'high levels' where they live.

Table 2.2 BCS evidence: percentage perceiving high levels of ASB in their area

	2001/ 02	2002/ 03	2003/ 04	2004/ 05	2005/ 06	2006/ 07
Abandoned or burnt-out cars	20	25	15*	12*	10*	9*
Noisy neighbours or loud parties	10	10	9*	9	10*	11*
People being drunk or rowdy in public places	22	23*	19*	22*	24*	26*
People using or dealing drugs	31	32	25*	26	27	28
Teenagers hanging around on the streets	32	33*	27*	31*	32*	33
Rubbish or litter lying around	32	33*	29*	30	30	31
Vandalism, graffiti and other deliberate damage to property	34	35	28*	28	29	28
High level of perceived anti-social behaviour	19	21*	16*	17	17	18
Unweighted base	*32,824*	*36,450*	*37,891*	*45,069*	*47,670*	*47,138*

Note: * Statistically significant change from the previous year at 5%. The total is derived from the seven individual strands of ASB.
Source: NAO 2006: 15; and Lovbakke 2007: 103.

In 2005 the company Ipsos Mori conducted a survey across England and Wales (n = 1857) that included a question concerning the size of the ASB problem 'in your area'. Examples of ASB were offered, 'such as vandalism and graffiti, nuisance neighbours, people dropping litter and rubbish in the street, drunken behaviour and drug dealing'. The results were similar to the BCS findings. In this instance 16 percent said ASB was a very big problem and 28 percent a fairly big problem – but ASB was not a very big problem, or not a problem at all for 55 percent.

The impact of ASB

In terms of the impact of ASB, 66 percent of respondents to the 2004/05 BCS claimed not to suffer any bad effects from ASB (Upson 2006). This was an increase from 61 percent the previous year (Wood 2004). For those that did suffer, the effects on 'quality of life' were not always seen as serious. Again, drawing from the 2004/05 BCS, while 49 percent of those suffering from noisy neighbours stated there was a high impact on quality of life, this was down to 21 percent for young people hanging around and 18 percent for drunk or rowdy behaviour (Upson 2006: 21). Some ASB appears to be more anti-social than others.

In another national survey (n = 1682) – this time drawing from England, Wales and Scotland – respondents were similarly asked how their quality of life was affected by ASB (Millie et al. 2005a). The results support the BCS findings that most people are not affected by ASB in a major way, as shown in Table 2.3. Across seven categories, only between 6 percent (for begging) and 19 percent (for rowdy teenagers) claimed the ASB had a fairly or big effect on their quality of life. For all categories, the majority claimed the behaviour was not a problem where they lived or, if it did occur, it had no effect or a minor effect on quality of life. Such findings clearly do not fit with Blair's (2004) claim that a 'scourge of anti-social behaviour affects us all'. It seems that, while ASB can be a real and very serious problem for some, it has been over-sold and does not affect everybody.

Table 2.3 Effects of ASB issues on quality of life (%)

n = 1,682	**This is not a prob-lem in my area**	**It occurs but...** ... **has no effect at all**	... **has a minor effect**	... **has a fairly big effect**	... **has a very big effect**	**Don't know**
Abandoned/burnt-out vehicles	58	14	19	6	4	1
Noisy neighbours	63	13	15	5	4	<1
Drug use/dealing	38	22	17	10	7	5
Rowdy teenagers in the street	34	14	32	12	7	1
Litter/rubbish	26	15	41	12	5	1
Vandalism/graffiti	32	13	38	11	6	1
Begging	77	10	7	4	2	1

Note: Percentages may not add to 100 due to rounding.
Source: Millie et al. 2005a, 2007a.

Respondents to the same national survey (Millie et al. 2005a: 10) were asked to identify the worst form of ASB where they lived (again, within 15 minutes' walk of home). No prompt was given and 17 percent said there was no ASB. People's main concern was with rowdy teenagers at 27 percent.

Other worries came a long way behind like vandalism, litter, drug use and public drunkenness (6 to 8% each) and driving offences (4%).

The geography of perceived levels of anti-social behaviour

If ASB is not a problem for the majority, then the next question concerns those who do suffer. And if victims of ASB are spatially concentrated then these concerns could be accentuated. This is something that has been picked up in political and policy rhetoric. For example, in the foreword to the government's Policy Action Team report into ASB (SEU 2000a), Charles Clarke MP stated that ASB, 'is a widespread problem but its effects are often most damaging in communities that are already fragile'. These 'fragile' communities would tend to be poorer, urban and, probably, social housing areas.

The possibility of ASB being an urban concern is supported by other survey evidence (Millie 2007a). Using London as an example, according to the 2003/04 BCS (Moore and Yeo 2004: 4), 32 percent of inner-city Londoners perceived high levels of 'local disorder', compared to 22 percent for outer London and 17 percent across the whole of England and Wales. For the more recent 2006/07 BCS (Lovbakke 2007: 110) 20 percent of people living in urban areas perceived there to be high levels of ASB where they live, compared to just 8 percent of those living in rural areas. This is not to say that ASB does not occur in more rural or out-of-town locations. Fly tipping in particular can be a significant problem in some country areas, and bored young people can get up to mischief in rural communities just like anywhere else. However, there could be something in the urban experience that makes ASB more likely.

Further evidence is provided by analysis of the 2006/07 BVPI General Users Surveys[5] in England, conducted by a team from Ipsos Mori (Ames et al. 2007). They rightly observed that 'variations in perceptions of anti-social behaviour across England are vast' (p. 13). Respondents were asked the same seven-strand questions as in the BCS, regarding the level of different ASB concerns in their local area. Like the BCS, a single index score was calculated. A model to predict perceived high levels of ASB was constructed based on this index score (see pp. 13–17), and 58 percent of results could be explained by this model – based on local deprivation, population increase (net inflow), population density, percentage of the population aged under 45, and recorded levels of violence against the person. These factors broadly pointed to urban and/or poorer areas. The five local authority areas with the highest index scores for perceived ASB were Newham, Tower Hamlets and Hackney (all London Boroughs), Blyth Valley (Northumberland) and Pendle (Lancashire) – scoring between 44 and 53 percent. All, except Pendle, are urban and/or poorer areas. Why Pendle should score so badly is not immediately apparent, although according to the Ipsos Mori analysis, both Pendle and Blyth Valley scored worse than would be expected (Ames et al. 2007: 19). The five local authority areas with the lowest scores were City of London, Broadland (Norfolk), East Dorset, Mid-Suffolk and Derbyshire Dales – scoring between 5 and 9 percent each. City of London is obviously an urban area, but has a unique character as it is dominated by the financial industry and very few people actually live there (unlike all other London boroughs). The other four low scoring areas are all better off, rural or semi-rural districts.

In the national survey by Millie et al. (2005a) key predictors of different ASB issues having a fairly/big effect on respondents' quality of life were determined using logistic regression analysis. All the key predictors were broadly associated with urban and/or poorer areas. For instance, for the variable 'drug use or dealing', the key predictors were: being of black and minority ethnic/mixed origin; living in social housing; and having no qualifications. There was a negative relationship with being of retirement age and with having a university degree or equivalent. For the variable 'rowdy teenagers on the street' the predictors were: living in London; living in social housing; being aged 18–30; having no qualifications; and being of black and minority ethnic/mixed origin. Again, there was a negative relationship with being of retirement age (perhaps indicating that ASB is not as simple as 'yob' teenagers praying on older people).

Anti-social behaviour in areas of social housing

If ASB is a particularly urban concern, then it is sometimes also claimed to be accentuated in poorer areas. For some, this is because the 'ASB industry' is focused within poorer areas and it will therefore find ASB there. For instance, according to Brown (2004: 204):

> [A]nti-social behaviour is deemed to occur principally in social housing areas. This is partly for instrumental reasons – an attempt to solve the problem of low demand social housing by excluding undesirable applicants. But it is also part of broader social control of marginalised populations who can be 'managed' in social housing.

It is certainly true that agencies attempting to control ASB have focused, perhaps disproportionately, on areas of social housing. The history of ASB enforcement is closely tied to housing provision with registered social landlords having a key role to play, for instance via restrictive tenancy arrangements, injunctions and eviction proceedings (e.g. Brown 1999; Flint 2004, 2006a; Hunter 2006; Pawson and McKenzie 2006). Having said this, the relationship between perceived high levels of ASB and living in poorer districts *is* supported by survey evidence. Again drawing from the 2006/07 BCS (Lovbakke 2007: 110), 31 percent of social renters perceived high levels of ASB where they live, compared to 18 percent of private renters and 15 percent of owner–occupiers. Similarly, for the earlier 2002/03 BCS (Thorpe and Wood 2004: 60), 39 percent of those from council estates and low income areas perceived high levels of ASB, compared to 26 percent in affluent urban areas, 15 percent of affluent family areas and 9 percent in affluent suburbs and rural areas.[6]

Of course, there is the danger of falling into an 'ecological fallacy' (cf. Robinson 1950) by suggesting that individuals are more likely to be anti-social if they live in poorer districts. There is the similar concern that all social housing tenants can be labelled as anti-social by association. In work going back to Sutherland (1940), the notion that the poor are more criminal has been questioned as this leaves out a great deal of white-collar criminality. The same can be said about ASB as poorer people certainly do not have the monopoly on such behaviour. But, social housing estates are regularly labelled as dangerous or problem places (see e.g. Box 2.1.), and social renters as problem people (Campbell 1993; Card 2006; Johnston and Mooney 2007).

Box 2.1   Social housing at Elephant and Castle, South London

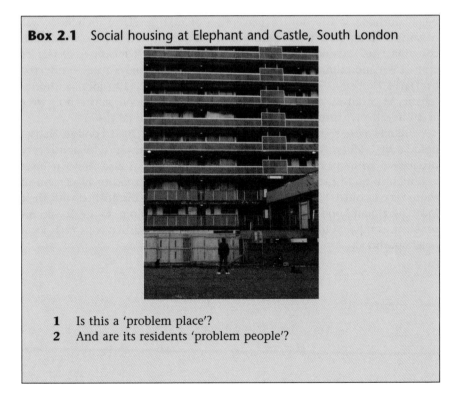

1   Is this a 'problem place'?
2   And are its residents 'problem people'?

Nonetheless, there could be something in the proposition that certain poorer neighbourhoods have concentrations of ASB prone people, or more accurately, those prone to being *accused* of ASB. Important factors behind ASB in areas of social housing will include the unintended consequences of housing and planning policies (Hancock 2001) that have led to concentrations of socially excluded and young families. Also, according to Burney (2000a: 271) problems can be accentuated as 'difficult tenants still have to live somewhere' and this can be the same socially excluded estates. These, and other, causal factors behind ASB are explored in Chapter 4. Although there can be serious problems of ASB in deprived neighbourhoods, it is worth noting that some of this misbehaviour can clearly be misidentified or over-estimated (Millie 2007a, 2008a) simply because it occurs in an area of heightened agency attention.

ASB and neighbourhood dissatisfaction

There is longstanding evidence of a correlation between perceived levels of ASB or incivility and neighbourhood dissatisfaction in Britain. For instance, using data from the 1984 BCS, Hope and Hough (1988: 36) analysed the relationships between incivilities, criminal victimization, fear of crime and neighbourhood satisfaction. A perception of high levels of incivilities was negatively correlated with neighbourhood satisfaction (–.90) and social cohesion (–.62), while being positively correlated with measures of fear of crime (.90) and criminal victimization (.81). Similar analysis was conducted by David Herbert (1993) based on a 1989 survey of 1130 local authority tenants in Swansea. Here incivilities and neighbourhood satisfaction were again negatively correlated (–.32 for analysis by individual cases).

Much more recent evidence is derived from the 2002 London Household Survey (Millie et al. 2005b) (see Table 2.4). For instance, of those very dissatisfied with their local neighbourhood, 59 percent also thought litter and rubbish on the street was a serious problem, compared to 17 percent of those very satisfied. Similarly, 52 percent of those very dissatisfied with their local neighbourhood considered drug use and dealing to be a serious problem, compared to just 8 percent who were very satisfied with their local neighbourhood.

Table 2.4 London Household Survey 2002: householder satisfaction with local neighbourhood and thought ASB issues were a 'serious problem'

	Issue a 'serious problem'						
	Litter and rubbish in the streets	**Vandalism and hooliganism**	**Graffiti**	**Presence of drug dealers/ users**	**Problems with dogs/ dog mess**	**Troublesome teenagers/ children**	**Problems with neighbours**
Very dissatisfied	59	64	40	52	35	41	27
Dissatisfied	51	50	33	34	25	28	9
Neither satisfied nor dissatisfied	37	33	23	23	21	16	2
Satisfied	27	22	17	14	16	10	3
Very satisfied	17	13	11	8	11	4	1
No opinion	*21*	*13*	*6*	*9*	*33*	*8*	*7*

Note: See also Millie et al. 2005b: 16.

In a similar Mori survey for the 'New Deal for Communities' evaluation (Christmann and Rogerson 2004: 5); neighbourhood satisfaction was found to be negatively correlated with 'minor crime and social disorder', 'crime in general' and 'physical disorder/lack of facilities in the area'.

For the 2004/05 Survey of English Housing, conducted by the Department of Communities and Local Government (DCLG), 25 percent believed their local area had got worse, compared to 10 percent thinking it had got better. Of those thinking their area was worse, the main reason was crime and vandalism (see Palmer et al. 2006: 92). For a range of issues – including many anti-social behaviours – respondents were more likely to perceive serious problems if living in deprived areas, compared to non-deprived areas (2006: 94).

Anti-social behaviour as an urban issue

Urban decay may have been always integral to city life. However, since the British economic recession and urban unrest of the early 1980s there has been a particular policy focus on the regeneration and marketing of urban areas in an attempt to reverse this decay. For instance, Lord Scarman's (1981) report that followed the Brixton rioting of April 1981 called for an 'effective co-ordinated approach to tackling inner city problems' (see Scarman 1984: 260). This idea was picked up by the Conservative government, under the steerage of Michael Heseltine, MP (1983), who put in place a range of measures aimed at 'reviving the inner city'. A decade later this had become a push for 'vital and viable' urban living (URBED and DoE 1994). Under Labour this evolved into calls for 'urban renaissance' (Urban Task Force 1999) and, more recently, 'cleaner, safer, greener' town centres (ODPM 2005a). The serious urban unrest in Brixton – and elsewhere – that sparked this focus was clearly more severe than some of the anti-social behaviours currently regarded as problematic. But what is important to current debates is that throughout this period improvements in people's behaviour were regarded as essential for urban regeneration (Millie 2007b). If the above evidence on neighbourhood satisfaction is anything to go by, then there could have been something in this, although it is possibly as much to do with *perceptions* of behaviour as it is with actual behaviour.

Regeneration as a rationale for tackling ASB is explored further in Chapter 5. For now it is worth noting that there are longstanding doubts over the social justice of some regenerative initiatives that have resulted in the 'reclaiming' of urban spaces for the exclusive use of certain populations at the expense of others, both in Britain and in America (e.g. Davis 1991; Loukaitou-Sideris 1993; Bannister et al. 2006; Millie 2008a). In terms of ASB in Britain, these become anti-social 'others' or 'outsiders' (cf. Becker 1963). The perspective is summed up by Bannister et al. (2006: 924) in claiming that:

> [T]he respect agenda [on ASB] taps into longstanding economic and political concerns about the vitality of city centres. There is a zero tolerance of those who are perceived as inhibiting the process of revitalisation, of deterring the consuming majority ... The streets are being reclaimed through the exclusion of those who do not conform to this mode of conduct, but at what cost?

'Respect' may in fact be *more* likely if cities are not 'cleansed of difference' (2006: 924). The apparent unacceptability of teenagers hanging around is a case in point. For instance, a survey of people using Plymouth city centre (Mawby and Simmonds 2004: 78) revealed specific concerns about 'teenagers hanging around on the streets', with 61 percent thinking this is a fairly or very big problem in the city centre, compared to 42 percent in their area of residence. Although teenagers, by definition, 'hang out', perceptions about what they might do have led to the banning of certain youthful activities – such as skateboarding or congregating – from some public and semi-public spaces, leading to spatial exclusion (Rogers and Coaffee 2005; Woolley 2006). The 2003 Anti-Social Behaviour Act (s.30), for instance, introduced dispersal order powers, if an officer has 'reasonable grounds' for believing that:

(a) any members of the public have been intimidated, harassed, alarmed or distressed as a result of the presence or behaviour of groups of two or more persons in public places in any locality in his police area (the 'relevant locality'), and

(b) anti-social behaviour is a significant and persistent problem in the relevant locality.

Crawford and Lister (2007) have expressed concern about the lack of distinction between 'presence' and 'behaviour'. In effect, within a dispersal order area anyone can be dispersed or 'moved on' just for being there; and invariably this will be young people. This is not a new idea. For instance, in 1992 Chicago City Council introduced comparable powers under a 'Gang Loitering Ordinance' (Levi 2008). Concerns in Chicago were more seriously related to drug dealing; but loiterers thought to be drug dealers were also deemed to be an issue, with loitering vaguely defined as 'to remain in any one place with no apparent purpose'. This definition by itself had little to do with suspected drug dealing or gang-related activity. And like the British dispersal order, the emphasis was on *presence*, rather than behaviour. Unlike in Britain, the ordinance was later found unconstitutional by the US Supreme Court (although aspects of the Dispersal Order powers involving returning juveniles to their home have had legal challenge[7].)

Concluding comments

Due to the fluid nature of its definition, ASB is a difficult thing to count. Nonetheless, the evidence presented in this chapter has shown that real problems of ASB certainly do exist and can cause misery for victims of this persistent misbehaviour. Whilst not being a concern for the majority of people in Britain, concerns are concentrated in certain deprived and/or urban areas, as well as in town or city centres. This disproportional impact can have serious consequences for 'quality of life' in some of the poorer areas of Britain. That said, within these areas ASB can be misidentified or over-estimated, leading to problems of labelling social housing estates as 'problem places' populated by 'problem people'. I shall return to the issue of labelling in the next chapter.

It is also worth noting that ASB is *not* solely a British issue – although the policy responses to the problem have been peculiarly British. In addition to the Chicago gang loitering ordinance outlined above, there is a huge American literature on incivility and low level disorders (Wilson and Kelling 1982; Skogan 1990; Sampson and Raudenbusch 1999; Taylor 2001; Beckett and Herbert 2008). Like the evidence of ASB in Britain presented in this chapter, incivility in America has been found in urban and/or deprived neighbourhoods. Much of this literature is considered in Chapter 5 that explores various rationales for tackling ASB. There is also evidence of concern about ASB from mainland Europe (e.g. Burney 2005; ADT Europe 2006).

Selected reading

A good place to start for official statistics on ASB is the Research Development and Statistics website of the Home Office (www.homeoffice.gov.uk/rds). British Crime Survey data can be found in the annual publication *Crime in England and Wales*. A selection of policy and academic work that has considered the extent or nature of ASB in Britain is as follows:

- ADT Europe (2006) *Anti-social Behaviour Across Europe: An Overview of Research Commissioned by ADT Europe*. Sunbury: ADT Europe.
- Card, P. (2006) Governing tenants: from dreadful enclosures to dangerous places, in J. Flint (ed.), *Housing, Urban Governance and Anti-social Behaviour: Perspectives, Policy and Practice*. Bristol: Policy Press.
- Johnston, C. and Mooney, G. (2007) 'Problem' people, 'problem' places? New Labour and council estates, in R. Atkinson and G. Helms (eds), *Securing an Urban Renaissance: Crime, Community and British Urban Policy*. Bristol: Policy Press.
- Lovbakke, J. (2007) Public perceptions, in S. Nicholas, C. Kershaw and A. Walker (eds), *Crime in England and Wales 2006/07*, 4th edn. Home Office Statistical Bulletin. London: Home Office.
- Millie, A. (2007a) Looking for anti-social behaviour, *Policy & Politics*, 35(4): 611–27.
- Rogers, P. and Coaffee, J. (2005) Moral panics and urban renaissance: policy, tactics and youth in public space, *City*, 9(3): 321–40.

Notes

1 CDRPs are locally based partnerships introduced under s.5 of the 1998 Crime and Disorder Act. They typically consist of the local authority, police service, police authority, fire and rescue service and, since 2004, the local primary care trust. Other relevant agencies are also frequently involved (see e.g. Hughes 2001).

2   A label that Jock Young (2007: 12) has described as 'an anarchist's dream'!

3   See, for instance, Johnston (2005) in the *Daily Telegraph*, about the appointment of Louise Casey as 'Respect Tsar'.

4   Despite its name, the British Crime Survey draws from England and Wales only.

5   Sometimes referred to as the Local Government User Satisfaction Survey (LGUSS). The survey is conducted every three years and has a minimum response of 1100 per local authority area (n = 387). BVPI = Best Value Performance Indicators.

6   Categories from ACORN – 'A Classification of Residential Neighbourhoods'.

7   In *R(W)* v. (1) Commissioner of Police for the Metropolis, (2) *London Borough of Richmond-upon-Thames*, (3) *Secretary of State for the Home Department* [2006] EWCA Civ 458. For an explanation of the decision, see Dobson (2006).

3 A theoretical framework for anti-social behaviour

> [A] thing exists only when it is given a name; any phenomenon is real to us only when we can imagine it. Without imagination there would be nothing to experience. So it is with crime [*and anti-social behaviour?*]. (Quinney 1970: v; *my addition*)

As discussed in Chapter 1, ASB, as understood in a public order enforcement context, is a comparatively recent addition to public, policy and academic consciousness. However, in line with Quinney (1970: v), it is entirely possible that ASB exists simply because it has been given the name 'ASB' – in the same way that the labels 'deviancy' or 'delinquency' exist; or for that matter the label 'crime' (Hulsman 1986). Yet, despite its recent prominence, the behaviour commonly encapsulated by ASB is hardly new (Pearson 1983, 1989, 2006; Burney 2005). It consequently does not appear in a theoretical vacuum. For instance, much can be drawn from sociological theory concerning normative and non-normative behaviour that has direct relevance to what is regarded as anti-social. Similarly, work on deviancy and delinquency, labelling theory or moral panics will have resonance to discussions of contemporary ASB.

There is not room in this chapter to go into a full and detailed exploration of *all* criminological, sociological and other theory that may have a bearing on ASB. However, a theoretical framework is provided, consisting of key perspectives that I believe have an influence on understandings of ASB. I have taken a largely sociological perspective; however, criminology as a discipline is such a broad church that other factors – for instance, psychosocial or genetic influences – could be explored. For these, I point the reader to people far more qualified to discuss these subjects than myself (e.g. Farrington 2000; Vold et al. 2002; Tremblay et al. 2004). This chapter explores ideas of labelling, deviance and delinquency and how they relate to contemporary concerns of ASB. The relevance of 'moral panics' and social control is examined and how ASB fits in with contemporary culture. The chapter concludes by considering a differential interpretation perspective, that each of us can have quite different ideas of behaviour worthy of the label 'anti-social'. But first, I want to look at the notion of conduct norms, and the extent to which ASB can be regarded simply as non-normative behaviour.

ASB as non-normative behaviour

The idea that behaviour can be normative or non-normative has been an important strand to elements of sociological and criminological enquiry for a long time and dates back to the work of Emile Durkheim at the end of the nineteenth century (see e.g. 1984, 2003). For fear of over-simplifying his position, Durkheim's view was that, rather than being pathological, crime is normal in society; for instance: 'To classify crime among the phenomena of normal sociology is not to say merely that it is an inevitable, although regrettable phenomenon ... it is to affirm that it is a factor in public health, an integral part of all healthy societies' (2003: 65–6).

Crime's function in society is seen as forming a boundary of acceptability and this boundary is never static. Durkheim famously used the example of a 'society of saints'. In such a society, behaviour that we commonly regard as crime would be absent. However, saints would still find fault in other saints; according to Durkheim: 'If, then, this society has the power to judge and punish, it will define these acts as criminal and will treat them as such' (2003: 66). Thus, although crime is therefore *normal*, it is also behaviour that breaches the acceptable *norms* of a given society. For the saints such breaches could be minor infringements of etiquette or taste. For the rest of us, this could be behaviour that is obviously criminal, such as theft or assault; it could also include behaviours currently regarded as anti-social.

From this position, it can be argued that the recent expansion of criminal justice in Britain to include minor-criminal or non-criminal actions deemed to be anti-social demonstrates the inherent flexibility of the boundary of acceptable – or normative – behaviour (although, by suggesting the boundary has shifted, I'm certainly not saying we live in a society of saints!). And, of course, the boundary will develop; according to Elizabeth Burney (2005: 46), 'social norms develop over the centuries: what counts as good or bad behaviour varies over time as it does over place' (see also Elias 1978; Pearson 1983). This is a point picked by Jock Young (2007) in reference to a statement made by the former Home Secretary, Charles Clarke, MP (2005). Clarke had claimed that his aim by the next general election was to have 'eliminated the anti-social behaviour and disrespect which still blights the lives of so many'. Young responded by calling this, 'a statement of Canute-like munificence – goodness knows what he would make of Durkheim's society of saints' (2007: 12). To claim that ASB can be eliminated is clearly nonsense. What is included as ASB will be ever changing, with the boundary defined by what Durkheim termed the 'collective conscience':

> Thus, since there cannot be a society in which the individuals do not differ more or less from the collective type, it is also inevitable that, among these divergences, there are some with a criminal character. What confers this character upon them is not the intrinsic quality of a given act but the definition which the collective conscience lends them. (Durkheim 2003: 67)

This quotation has significance for developments in labelling theory and social control (of more later). When norms of behavioural acceptability are confused, unclear, or absent, Durkheim described this as a state of 'anomie'. For Durkheim this would be at a time of social and economic change, when there is a lack of regulation and where the boundaries of acceptable behaviour within the new situation have not yet been fully determined. This 'anomie' – literally meaning a deregulation of appetites – becomes the fuel for greater criminality.

The question is: who decides on norms of acceptable behaviour? Are norms decided by society as a whole (the Durkheimian view), by groups within society, or is there such a thing as individualistic norms? Going with the view of the majority runs to risk of labelling certain minority or marginalized groups as 'outsiders' (Becker 1963). Having individualistic norms of behavioural acceptability may please the anarchist (e.g. Ferrell 1998), but could lead to great confusion. For instance, in Chapter 1, a former homeless person is quoted as describing ASB as 'other people's stuff'. For him ASB equated to others' behaviours that he personally did not like. If this is what ASB amounts to, then we'd all be guilty (including Durkheim's saints); after all, we are all capable of doing things that annoy at least someone.

The idea of societal norms – and of anomie – was later taken up by Robert Merton (1938). His perspective differed to Durkheim's in that he viewed anomie as being created by a mismatch between cultural aspirations and the means available to achieve these aspirations. In criminological texts (e.g. Downes and Rock 2007; Newburn 2007), much is made of the context within which Merton was writing, being very much informed by the US economic depression of the 1930s and the failings of the 'American dream'. For Merton, cultural aspirations in the US are thought to be the same across the classes, emphasizing ambition, consumption and wealth; however, the institutional means for achieving these goals are not available to all:

> [US] egalitarian ideology denies by implication the existence of non-competing individuals and groups in the pursuit of pecuniary success. Instead, the same body of success-symbols is held to apply for all. Goals are held to transcend class lines, not to be bounded by them, yet the actual social organization is such that there exist class

differentials in accessibility of the goals. In this setting, a cardinal American virtue, 'ambition,' promotes a cardinal American vice, 'deviant behaviour'. (Merton 1996: 143)

To apply this perspective to ASB may be stretching things, and especially to ASB in a British context. Furthermore, the assumption that all people have the same desires and dreams is simplistic. Yet, there is much in the 'American dream' that translates to contemporary consumerist/ individualist culture, wherever it may be. For Merton, the majority still conformed to the norm by accepting both cultural goals and the institutional means for achieving these goals; yet the 'strain' between goals and means (his perspective has become known as 'strain theory') led to four types of deviant:

- The innovator: accepts cultural goals; rejects institutional means
- The ritualist: rejects cultural goals; accepts institutional means
- The retreatist: rejects both cultural goals and institutional means
- The rebel: replaces both cultural goals and institutional means with something new.

To keep things simple, all four deviate from the norm. In terms of ASB, all four could also describe different types of perceived or actual perpetrator. For instance, a habitual graffiti writer may find status, pleasure and identity in creating a new work (Halsey and Young 2006). Depending on personality, the 'artist' may fit any one of the four categories of deviancy; however, the graffiti writer may not accept the deviant label. The danger is that while innovation, ritualism, retreatism and rebellion may deviate from the norm, this deviation does not always equate to criminal or anti-social activity, or may not be perceived as wrongful action by the perpetrator. By identifying groups as deviant, certain outsider sub-cultures may be singled out for attention (Tannenbaum 1938; Becker 1963; Hebdige 1979; and others). For Merton it was the lower social classes that were more likely to give in to the 'strain to anomie'. Others have questioned this assertion, with Stinchcombe (1964), for example, finding strong rebellious tendencies among middle class high school boys. In terms of graffiti writing, this form of deviancy, or ASB, is certainly not restricted to the poor.

Sellin (1938) famously applied the idea of 'norms' to the study of American sub-cultures. His assertion was that local areas, or particular groups, can develop their own normative values and behaviours that come into conflict with wider societal norms; they may also breach accepted legal rules. This was similar to Thrasher's (1927) findings about Chicago's gangs. The result is behaviour that is perfectly acceptable to one group – the sub-culture or gang – but is differently interpreted as unacceptable to the majority. While Sellin's argument can be applied to some examples of serious criminality, it is relevant to ASB. For instance, continuing with the graffiti writing example, most forms of graffiti are deemed to be unacceptable to the majority; yet for many graffiti writers, and others who identify themselves with certain urban street cultures, this is entirely acceptable activity. For some graffiti writers knowledge that the act is unacceptable to others is itself an incentive to 'tag' more and more locations.

ASB labelled as deviant behaviour

Mooney and Young (2006: 399) have claimed that the current rise to prominence of ASB may be a simple 'rediscovery of the sociology of deviance circa 1960'. Much debate about ASB, especially concerning the subjectivity of definition, would certainly seem familiar to 1960s' sociologists. To support their argument Mooney and Young cite the work of Erikson (1966: 6) who claimed that: 'Deviance is not a property *inherent* in any particular behaviour, it is a property *conferred upon* that behaviour by the people who come into direct or indirect contact with it.' Howard Becker (1963: 9) held a similar view:

> [S]ocial groups create deviance by making the rules whose infraction
> constitutes deviance, and by applying those rules to particular people
> and labelling them as outsiders. From this point of view, deviance is
> *not* a quality of the act the person commits, but rather a conse-
> quence of the application by others of rules and sanctions to an
> 'offender'. The deviant is one to whom that label has been success-
> fully applied; deviance is behaviour that people so label. (emphasis
> in the original)

Downes (1979: 3) described Becker's claim that 'deviance is behaviour that people so label' as, 'superficially a banal and even trivial assertion'. And writing about youthful ASB, Squires and Stephen (2005a: 185) have more recently claimed, 'the concept of deviance may not hold much currency nowadays'. Yet they add: 'in failing to incorporate this notion into our explanatory frameworks for the contemporary governance of youth we throw the baby out with the bathwater because "anti-social behaviour" is such a highly problematic, value-laden, subjective and politically-loaded construct' (Squires and Stephen 2005a: 185).

Deviance is still a helpful concept to use. In terms of the focus of this book, Becker's deviant 'outsiders' become those labelled as 'anti-social'. The work of Becker and others (e.g. Tannenbaum 1938; Erikson 1964; Lemert 1967; and Schur 1971) emphasized behaviour labelled as unacceptable, or deviant, rather than crime as legally defined; an important distinction. I suggest rereading the earlier quotation from Becker, but this time replacing 'deviant' or 'deviance' with 'anti-social' or 'anti-social behaviour'. It still makes a lot of sense. Similarly, consider how ASB might figure in the following observation by Erikson (1964: 11–12):

> Some men who drink too much are called alcoholics and others are not, some men who act oddly are committed to hospitals and others are not ... the difference between those who earn a deviant label and those who go their own way in peace depends almost entirely on the way in which the community sifts out and codes the many details of behavior to which it is witness.

Clearly, some people will be labelled as anti-social, while others behaving in the same way will not. We can all be anti-social, but only behaviour by certain 'outsider' groups gets labelled as anti-social and thereby gets caught up in the ASB enforcement process.

Other arguments over what constitutes 'deviancy' will be familiar to those interested in ASB. For instance, according to Downes and Rock (1982: 4):

> [I]t is clear that there is some basic, if unwritten, agreement that deviance is banned or controlled behaviour which is likely to attract punishment or disapproval. It little matters who issues the ban or how many people support it. Those who deviate tend to make their lives rather more hazardous and problematic.

In this view, in effect, deviancy becomes *anything* that does not fit in with *anybody's* view of how the world could or should be. To illustrate this point, if I break the speed limit on the road then I am clearly behaving in a deviant manner, breaching a ban issued by the state that is generally – if not unanimously – supported. However, if I am a member of that select group of 'petrol heads', and believe cars are meant to driven fast, then the slower driver becomes the deviant, making my life more 'hazardous and problematic'. Philosophically, this makes for an interesting discussion of behavioural acceptability; but for real world application this particular definition is too inclusive. In the same text, Downes and Rock (1982: 26–7) considered the problematic nature of deviancy definition, stating that: 'Ambiguity does seem to be a crucial facet of rule-breaking', something certainly familiar to those studying ASB. They go on to state that, '[p]eople are frequently undecided whether a particular episode *is* truly deviant or what true deviance is: their judgement depends on context, biography, and purpose' (emphasis in the original). Again, this statement could be describing contemporary conceptions of ASB. This is, of course, entirely logical as behaviour deemed to be anti-social also deviates from certain social and cultural norms of acceptability. However, to borrow from Downes and Rock, these norms will depend on 'context, biography and purpose'. Such ambiguity was also identified by

Taylor (1971: 41) who noted: 'A major objection to adopting the concept of deviance is that while codified law is readily accessible, the accepted standards of the group or community are not.' In essence, what constitutes 'normal' behaviour, or what deviates from this norm is going to be a contested concept. In terms of ASB, Whitehead et al. (2003: 4–5) recently stated that, 'virtually any activity can be anti-social' and that ASB is dependent on 'the context in which it occurs, the location, people's tolerance levels and expectations about the quality of life in the area'. ASB clearly has a lot in common with deviancy and can be regarded as a sub-set of deviant behaviour. Like deviancy, there cannot be an agreed list of behaviours that are anti-social in *all* circumstances.

ASB as a form of delinquency

Some writers prefer to talk about 'delinquency' – a term usually allied to juveniles and, as such, only relevant to certain aspects of ASB. It is a term that gained particular popularity from the 1940s to 1960s (e.g. Shaw and McKay 1942; Mannheim 1948; Mays 1954; Cohen 1955; Downes 1966), although it has maintained capital among some criminological investigators. As outlined, 'deviancy' is a problematic concept open to great interpretation. 'Delinquency', at first, appears to have a stronger focus being, according to Albert Cohen (1955: 25), 'malicious, negativistic and non-utilitarian'. Put another way, someone is delinquent if their behaviour has a deliberately negative impact on others or does not take into account the wishes of others. To use the language of contemporary ASB enforcement, someone is delinquent if their behaviour shows a lack of *respect* for others. Where this definition differs from ASB is that the behaviour has to be 'malicious' to be delinquent, whereas ASB seems to include unintentional action, or even presence (as discussed previously). To give an example, someone skateboarding on a busy pavement may not take other users' views into account; however, she or he only becomes delinquent if the action is malicious. Yet, if others *perceive* the skateboarding as anti-social then the intent or maliciousness of the behaviour may not be relevant. According to Taylor and Walton (1973: 92): 'What appears to Albert Cohen to be activity of a "malicious, negativistic and non-utilitarian" nature may, however, be perfectly sensible, constructive and instrumentally creative to the kids themselves.' In short, intent is something that is also open to debate. Again, it is a question of: who decides? As with discussions of deviancy, if it is the majority, then there will always be certain groups – in this case groups of young people – that will attract the label of 'deviant' or 'delinquent' (or 'anti-social'), simply by who they are and the fact that their behaviour, or presence, does not fit in with the norms of the majority.

In Chapter 2, the possibility was explored that certain deprived areas have higher perceived levels of ASB. Of relevance here is the work on 'delinquency areas' in Chicago by Shaw and MacKay (1942), and in Liverpool by John Barron Mays (1954). Both studies considered neighbourhood characteristics that make youthful delinquency more likely; and both concluded that poorer neighbourhoods are those more likely to produce delinquents. According to Mays (1954: 147):

> [J]uvenile delinquency is merely one aspect of the behaviour pattern of underprivileged neighbourhoods ... characterised by a long history of poverty, casual employment and bad housing ... Delinquency has become almost a social tradition and it is only a very few youngsters who are able to grow up in these areas without at some time or other committing illegal acts.

In this view, delinquency becomes something that is learnt by living in certain communities. And rather than being rebellious, a delinquent is conforming to the 'sub-cultural' norms of the area (Downes 1966). Again, there is the inherent danger of labelling. Not only do individuals attract the 'delinquent', 'deviant' or 'anti-social' label, but whole communities or neighbourhoods can be regarded as factories for producing delinquency, deviancy and anti-social behaviour.

ASB as 'otherness'

While ASB is more of a concern in poorer neighbourhoods, it also tends to be an urban problem. And, by definition, the urban context will consist of people with differing expectations and contested understandings of acceptable activity. In the words of Becker (1963) the perpetrators of unacceptable activity are the 'outsiders'; according to Elias and Scotston (1965), it is a question of 'the established' versus the 'outsiders'. This discourse of 'us' and 'them' is apparent in much contemporary debate (Girling et al. 2000; Young 2007). For instance, according to Conservative Party leader David Cameron (2006): 'If the consequence of stepping over the line should be painful, then staying within the bounds of good behaviour should be pleasant. And I believe that inside those boundaries we have to show a lot more love.'

The basic message from the Prime Minister, Gordon Brown, has been the same: 'And we are right to be tough with the small minority of young people whose anti social behaviour undermines our community. But we should also do more to encourage and recognise the vast majority of young people who abide by the values of our community' (2006).

It's a simple message, that we will be nice to you if you stay within accepted 'boundaries' or 'values', but we will come down hard if you don't.

Politicians, of all persuasions, seem keen to perpetuate a discourse of a law-abiding majority verses a criminal (or anti-social) 'other' (Hill and Wright 2003; Millie 2008b). For instance, in the Labour Party Manifesto for the 2005 general election it is clearly stated that: 'People want communities where the decent law-abiding majority are in charge' (p. 44). Politically, this may be entirely sensible, although the majority are hardly law abiding; as stated elsewhere, 'just think of the daily round of motorway speeding, undeclared work, or minor fraud to get a child into a preferable school' (Millie 2008b: 105). But to think that the problems in society are someone else's fault, rather than one's own is, to a certain extent, reassuring.

In Britain the young, almost by definition, have for a long time been thought to transgress such accepted 'boundaries' or 'values' and become a threat to community life. According to Pearson (1994: 1168), 'youth cultures and youth crime assume the appearance of ever-increasing outrage and perpetual novelty'. Each generation seems to find fault with their youth, with the 'demonisation of children' providing 'a new enemy within' (Goldson 1997: 134). For Hill and Wright (2003: 294) this has also been true for contemporary ASB agendas: 'Local child curfew orders, child safety orders and anti-social behaviour orders, supported by increased custodial provisions available to youth courts, indicate an identification of young people as the true threat to community safety.'

ASB as moral panic

Of relevance is the concept of 'moral panic', and its relationship with the cause of such panic, the 'folk devils' (cf. Cohen 1972, 2002). Stanley Cohen famously looked at the youth cultures of mods and rockers in 1960s' Britain, and how their alleged deviancy had been 'amplified' to the extent that such groups were regarded as a threat to the 'civilized' majority. In relation to contemporary discourses on ASB, Pearson (2006: 7) has claimed: 'Clearly we are in the midst of a "moral panic" concerning hoodies, knife attacks, gangsta rap,[1] gun culture, ASBOs, chavs[2] and bling[3] and the rest of it. But that is not to say that nothing is going on.' Of course, calling something a moral panic does not mean the concern doesn't exist. ASB clearly does occur and it can have a serious impact on the victims. However, the extent and significance of the ASB problem has been exaggerated and distorted into a moral panic. As demonstrated in Chapter 2, the extent of ASB in Britain is certainly not as large as we have been led to believe; instead concerns tend to be concentrated in certain neighbourhoods. Yet, according to Tony Blair (2004): 'The scourge of anti-social behaviour affects us all and in our biggest cities, on suburban estates and rural villages.' Blair has not been alone in making such claims. In effect, the contemporary focus on ASB can be seen as a politician-led moral panic – although the media have not been far behind; for instance:

- Life ban for teen thug brothers, *Daily Mail*, 27 Nov. 2002
- We name and shame thugs, *Sun*, 15 Oct. 2003
- Reclaim our streets: hoodies and baddies, *Daily Mirror*, 5 May 2005
- From little angel to ASBO queen, *Daily Mirror*, 7 May 2005
- ASBO yob let off by JPs 8 times, *Sun*, 25 Oct. 2006
- Yobs making town centres 'no-go' zones, *Guardian*, 24 July 2007
- Britons fear rise of the yob, *Observer*, 19 Aug. 2007.

The extent to which some aspects of the press have embraced the ASB agenda is exemplified by a poem by Felix Dennis published in the *Daily Telegraph* in November 2006. To the tune of 'Twinkle, Twinkle Little Star' it went as follows:

> Asbo, Asbo, little law,
> How we wonder what you're for.
> Chavs and yobs who love to fight
> Terrorise us every night,
> Toothless, useless, little law,
> How we wonder what you're for.
>
> On the streets with hoods and knives,
> How they terrorise our lives,
> Though they all should be in bed,
> All you do is boost their cred.
> Asbo, Asbo, can't you see
> You are an accessory ...

The poem is full of derogatory labelling (chav, yob, terror) for hooded young people who 'should be in bed'; it continued in a similar vein. Popular culture has been keen to embrace the ASB agenda, and the 'othering' of outsider groups, particularly the young. Nonetheless, it didn't take the press too long – no doubt to politicians' dismay – to be critical of policies that were introduced to tackle ASB. Some of the apparent absurdities of ASB enforcement became popular targets; for instance, on 15 December 2004 the *Daily Mirror* ran a headline 'Pigs are in breach of ASBO'. A similarly bizarre headline appeared in the *Sun* on 8 March 2006, 'Man's ASBO for tall trees'. However, the media have continued their love of a good yob or thug story. And these stories mainly relate to the young.

Anti-social 'other' as underclass

From a political point of view, it is easier to understand a firm divide between 'us' and a misbehaving, or anti-social, 'them'. And as noted, politicians are fond of telling us they are on the side of the 'law-abiding majority', against the threats that come from young 'yobs'. Such a view owes a lot to the notion of an underclass, an idea that goes back to Victorian times, but gained popularity among the political Right in the 1990s following the work of Charles Murray (1990) and others (e.g. Smith 1992; Morris 1994). For instance, recalling the small US town where he grew up, Murray (1990: 1) recounted the following:

> I was taught by my middle-class parents that there were two kinds of poor people. One class ... simply lived on low incomes ... There was another set of people, just a handful of them. These poor people didn't just lack money. They were defined by their behaviour. Their homes were littered and unkempt. The men in the family were unable to hold a job for more than a few weeks at a time. Drunkenness was common. The children grew up ill-schooled and ill-behaved and contributed a disproportionate share of the local juvenile delinquents.

Simply there were, according to Murray, the deserving and undeserving poor – a classic piece of labelling, or 'othering' – and a view that could conceivably contribute to moral panic (see also Lister 1996). According to MacDonald (1997: 19): '[T]he key figures in the landscape of modern, conservative accounts of the underclass are ... the irresponsible, welfare-draining single mothers and the feckless young man.' It is a view that continues to influence Conservative Party rhetoric and policy (see Social Justice Policy Group 2006). However, it also influenced some within the Labour Party, in particular Frank Field with his talk of 'neighbours from hell' (1989, 2002). And more recently, the underclass label has re-emerged in a pamphlet published by former Home Secretary, and Labour MP, David Blunkett (2008). According to Conservative MP, George Osbourne:

> He probably won't thank me for saying it, but David Blunkett is right. The pamphlet he published this week on social mobility correctly identifies one of the great long-term challenges facing our country: how do we stop what he describes as the 'serious danger of a small but significant underclass developing in Britain'? (2008)

According to an underclass perspective, the underclass are: 'Anti-work, anti-social, and welfare dependent ... [a] "dangerous class", and "dangerous youth" ' (MacDonald 1997: i). Such overt labelling runs the risk of identifying *all* poor or working class people as a dangerous other, and where they live as dangerous places (Campbell 1993; Johnston and Mooney 2007). For instance, Cook (2006) observed the target for New Labour during its successful 1997 election campaign was traditionally Tory voting, middle income, 'Middle Englanders'. As a consequence, it made sense to focus on crimes (and

ASB) seen to be committed by 'others', rather than by 'Middle England'. The poor hardly has the monopoly on illegality; however, it is the misbehaviour of the poor that becomes the more intolerable.

ASB and social control

> How does a community decide what forms of conduct should be singled out for this kind of attention? The conventional answer to this question, of course, is that society sets up the machinery of control in order to protect itself against the 'harmful' effects of deviation ... Yet ... as Durkheim and Mead[4] pointed out some years ago, it is by no means clear that all acts considered deviant in a culture are in fact (or even in principle) harmful to group life. In the second place ... deviant behavior can play an important part in keeping the social order intact. (Erikson 1964: 12)

Determining the precise 'harmful' acts that constitute deviance (or crime, or ASB) is, as outlined in the above quotation from Erikson, a difficult process (see also Feinberg 1984). However, despite these complexities, society will always 'set up the machinery of control to protect itself'. Putting things more simply, Erikson (1964: 10–11) claimed that, 'deviance can be defined as conduct which is generally thought to require the attention of social control agencies – that is, conduct about which "something should be done" '. How social control agencies help to define and interact with behaviour deemed to be anti-social is a theme picked up in other writing on ASB (e.g. Ashworth 2004; Brown 2004; Squires and Stephen 2005a).

There are two key writers that have had the biggest influence on criminological study of social control – these being Michael Foucault (orig. 1977, see 2003) and Stanley Cohen (1985). Cohen (1985: 1) has put forward a simple definition of social control; that it refers to, 'the organized ways in which society responds to behaviour and people it regards as deviant, problematic, worrying, threatening, troublesome or undesirable in some way or another'. This definition accounts for what is often seen as *formal* social control, obvious examples being prison, the police and other agents of criminal justice. At the other end of the spectrum, social control can be less organized and *informal*, including the influence of family, community and cultural expectations and norms. For both Foucault and Cohen, the ultimate form of (formal) social control is incarceration, where one's daily existence is almost totally controlled by the state. Although Foucault rarely used the term 'social control', it is apparent in much that he wrote. For instance – and at the risk of over-simplification – Foucault talked in terms of state discipline, panoptic surveillance and the creation of a carceral society, where 'control' of the population is paramount – as exemplified by incarceration. For Foucault, there exists an expanding carceral network (or control system). Those who hold 'power' determine who are the targets of this carceral network; however, it is not simply the state that holds such power, it has as much to do with knowledge. The effect over time is an increased tolerance of penalty: 'But perhaps the most important effect of the carceral system and of its extension well beyond legal imprisonment is that it succeeds in making the power to punish natural and legitimate, in lowering at least the threshold of tolerance to penalty' (Foucault 2003: 419).

This is an idea that is directly relevant to discussion of ASB. By targeting behaviour that is of either a minor criminal or non-criminal nature – but cumulatively has a detrimental impact – enforcement action against ASB demonstrates an expanding 'carceral network', or greater social control. In such instances, those that hold the 'knowledge' include the state, but also other less obvious agents of control. Other interested parties include schools, care agencies, social landlords and community groups (see e.g. Respect Task Force 2006).

The expansion of social control has alternatively been explained by Cohen (1985) in relation to the notion of net widening and mesh thinning (see also Chapter 1). Cohen describes the criminal justice system as a fisherman's net designed to 'catch' those who breach the criminal law. Yet, Cohen recognized a process of mesh thinning, whereby existing nets are made more able to *keep* the fish that are caught; and net widening, whereby unwanted behaviour previously outside the reach of criminal law is *included* within an ever expanding net (see also Garland 2001; Innes 2003). Criminal justice processes involve a 'dispersal of discipline' – and the expansion of control into areas of ASB is a clear example. Cohen also talked in terms of a resultant blurring of boundaries between deviant and non-deviant behaviour, an idea similarly not unfamiliar to those studying ASB.

To return to earlier discussions of labelling and 'otherness', it is a question of where the nets are cast. If the agents of control only focus on certain populations or areas, then only certain people's unwanted behaviour will be identified as ASB, and will be caught within the ASB/criminal justice net. As noted in Chapter 2, it has been suggested that ASB is found in poorer areas because that is where people look for it (Brown 2004). For instance, the fact that social landlords have a role in tackling ASB means that more ASB is likely to be identified in areas of social housing (Millie 2007a). There is evidence that residents in poorer neighbourhoods do have greater concerns about ASB; however, they are also more likely to be accused of behaving anti-socially. As Burney (2005: 45) has observed, 'those that are more impoverished and marginalised are most likely to experience, and at the same time be blamed for, some of the more obviously unacceptable behaviour'. However, the focus on poorer neighbourhoods by agents of control means the ASB committed by other middle class – or Middle Englander – groups may be missed.

ASB and contemporary culture

According to Jock Young (1999: 98), when writing about the formation of an 'exclusive society': 'To know that there are indeed other ways of doing things which in their own world are considered just as everyday as one's own takes away security.' Accordingly, it is the contested nature of other people's 'everyday' activities that can lead to other people being labelled as anti-social. For instance, certain everyday youthful activities can be interpreted as dangerous or threatening. A case in point is groups of young people congregating; but so too the activities of certain youthful sub-cultures, such as skateboarding, graffiti writing or the new arrival on the urban scene, parcour or free running.[5] These alternative uses of urban spaces can cause clear conflict with other users, leading to the creation of contested spaces (e.g. Aitken 2001; Hadfield 2006). But are these activities anti-social? Box 3.1. shows such activities occurring at London's South Bank in April 2008. This location has attracted skateboarders for over 30 years (see e.g. Ward 1978), with the relevant authorities initially tolerating but more recently encouraging the use of this particular space for youthful expression. In effect the area has become an informal tolerance zone; however, if these everyday 'other' activities are transferred elsewhere, do they become anti-social?

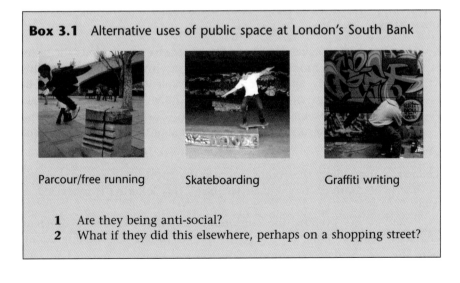

Box 3.1 Alternative uses of public space at London's South Bank

Parcour/free running   Skateboarding   Graffiti writing

1 Are they being anti-social?
2 What if they did this elsewhere, perhaps on a shopping street?

According to Thrift (2005: 134), a level of mistrust or dislike of others is as inescapable part of urban living: '[A] certain amount of dislike of one's fellow citizens is, given the social-cum-biological-cum-technological make-up of human beings, inescapable; the ubiquity of aggression is an inescapable by-product of living in cities.'

Of relevance is a (mis)interpretation of rights that appears to be part of contemporary Britain. In essence, if ASB is the stuff that 'others' do, then 'it is my right to behave how I like, and for others to behave how I would expect them' (Millie 2006). Clearly, this is an unsustainable point of view, making the task of determining what is ASB almost an impossibility. In line with Durkheim, the boundary of acceptable behaviour becomes permanently in flux.

Like many other market-led consumer cultures, life in Britain has become increasingly individualistic and consumerist, which has fuelled demands for the unacceptable behaviour of others to be controlled. The boundary of acceptability seems to be dictated by a 'consuming majority' (cf. Bannister et al. 2006). For instance, in a shopping centre, if you're not there to spend money then your presence is questioned. The exclusion of young people wearing hoodies from Bluewater Shopping Centre in Kent is a clear example (a case that received huge media attention in 2005). But so too the exclusion of some youthful activities such as skateboarding (see Box 3.1). The official reasoning in the Bluewater case was the ability of CCTV operators to identify 'potential' troublemakers. Young people may not be causing any trouble and just want a place to 'hang out'; after all, the mall has always had this appeal for the young (e.g. Matthews et al. 2000; Manzo 2004). Yet, if they choose to wear a hoodie, then they are removed. Writing from an American point of view, Goss (1993: 35) made the following pertinent observation:

> [The mall user] cannot escape the imperative to consume: she or he cannot loiter in the mall unless implicitly invited to do so, and this generally only applies to the respectable elderly; those without shopping bags and other suspicious individuals (teenagers, single men, the unkempt, and social science researchers) will draw the attention of security, who use the charge of loitering as grounds for eviction.

Loiterers – particularly the young, but also the street homeless – are classic outsiders. In contemporary British language, this loitering is relabelled as ASB.

Yet, in the evening the consuming majority takes on a different character, being dominated by large numbers of people out drinking. Along with this comes some very unwelcome ASB and violent conduct. I am not suggesting all this behaviour is tolerated because these people are spending money; however, there is a lot of rowdy behaviour at a level below this that would be deemed as anti-social during the day, but is more acceptable at night – so long as the perpetrators keep spending.

The shifting of the boundaries of acceptable or anti-social behaviour, and of the categories of 'us' and the 'other', are symptomatic of what Zygmunt Bauman (2000, 2007) has famously called, 'liquid modernity'; what Jock Young (2007: 1) describes as 'this fluidity of norm, institution, and social category'. In describing his latest book *The Vertigo of Late Modernity* (2007: 1) Young says it is about 'borders whose normative bases seem at first glance firm, and yet are riven with contradictions and incoherence ... all that is solid melts into air'. If applied to ASB, this seems to be a very good description.

A differential interpretation perspective of ASB

Building on the discussion thus far, in this final section I suggest that what is regarded as anti-social is essentially interpretative; that what in one situation is entirely acceptable, or even celebrated, may be deemed so unacceptable in another that it can lead to anti-social or criminal censure (Millie 2008a). To give an example, Burney (2006) has observed that spitting can be acceptable or tolerable when a footballer is clearing his throat. However, on occasions this is also clearly unacceptable; for instance: 'El Hadji Diouf was fined £58,000 by his club for spitting at Celtic supporters ... when photography recorded the spray of spittle directed at rival fans by Wayne Rooney, the 17-year-old Everton player was given a police warning' (2006: 196). In these instances the persons being spat at and those who witnessed the spitting would have been *offended* by the action (see Feinberg 1985; Duff and Marshell 2006; von Hirsch and Simester 2006). As I have suggested elsewhere (Millie 2008a: 2), 'the behaviour was beyond conventional norms of acceptability and it was beyond people's behavioural expectations for that particular environment'. A further example concerns young people skateboarding. This is perfectly acceptable activity if conducted at an urban skate park or similar specialist space (see Box 3.1), but for the majority of people it becomes problematic if occurring for instance on a shopping street.

Interpretation of behaviour as acceptable or anti-social can also be temporally specific. An obvious example here concerns the loud and boisterous behaviour that can accompany late night drinking – behaviour that is more tolerated and expected in a city centre on Friday night, but is likely to be differently interpreted as anti-social at noon the next day.

Similarly, forms of behaviour can be differently interpreted as acceptable or anti-social by different groups or individuals. Referring to work by Lemert (1951) and Becker (1963), Stanley Cohen recognized that deviancy is a transactional process, 'the result of interaction between the person who commits an act and those who respond to it' (1971: 226). ASB is similarly transactional in that what one person regards as anti-social may be differently interpreted by another and tolerated. It may even be celebrated as a worthwhile contribution to contemporary life. In effect, there are shifting standards of acceptable or anti-social behaviour, dependent on context and interpretation of the action. To take a post-modernist view on the subject (e.g. Bouteillier 2002), there are *plural* norms of acceptability. Of course, the idea of pluralism is not new; and referring to the earlier work of Matza (1969), Downes and Rock (1982: 4) observed: 'If "pluralism" and "shifting standards" work on deviant behaviour to render it ambiguous and fluid, no coherent and definitive argument can ever completely capture it.' However, with official views being that 'you know it when you see it', this seems to be a fair description of behaviour deemed to be anti-social. The extent that the same action can be differently interpreted is illustrated by a discussion during a focus group with former homeless people, as shown in Box 3.2. The participants all had mental health and/or drugs issues and represented a group that is frequently seen as an anti-social 'other'.

Box 3.2 Discussion taken from a focus group with former homeless people in London

Male 2   People stereotype crime, I don't think it is the teenagers.
Female 1 I think the teenagers in gangs ... I get more intimidated by a group of black guys, not just black guys, and white guys ... all of them. On the train there was a gang ... about six of them, they were about 15 [years old]. I felt more intimidated by them than I would by a bunch of addicts.

          ...

Male 1   I think the thing is that large groups of people are very intimidating, but it's a stereotype as well, do you know what I mean? If you're, like, a person who hasn't come into contact with a certain section of society and see a big group of, say, homeless people walking down the street.
Male 3   Yeah it's intimidation
Male 1   But when was the last time you saw a big group of homeless people attack anyone, do you know what I mean? When was the last time you saw a big group of black kids or Asian kids attack someone in the middle of Oxford Street?
Female 1 Oh I don't know, there was that footage in Leicester Square of that bunch of kids, and that was scary.
Male 1   Yeah, but that wasn't the norm.

| Male 2 | People stereotype crime, I don't think it is the teenagers. |
| Female 1 | The only people who scare me in the West End are packs of young lads. |

If people have differing opinions and perspectives as to what behaviour is anti-social, then it is also likely that there can be quite different interpretation of what causes ASB. Such causal issues are explored in the following chapter.

Selected reading

When considering the various theoretical perspectives relevant to discussions of ASB, a good place to start will be a general criminology text. Tim Newburn has recently produced an excellent overview of criminology, while Downes and Rock's 'understanding deviance' will always be useful. These and other further reading are listed below:

- Becker, H. (1963) *Outsiders: Studies in the Sociology of Deviance.* New York: The Free Press.
- Burney, E. (2005) *Making People Behave: Anti-social Behaviour, Politics and Policy.* Cullompton: Willan.
- Cohen, S. (1985) *Visions of Social Control: Crime, Punishment, and Classification.* Cambridge: Polity Press.
- Cohen, S. (2002) *Folk Devils and Moral Panics*, 3rd edn. London: Routledge.
- Downes, D. and Rock, P. (2007) *Understanding Deviance*, 5th edn. Oxford: Oxford University Press.
- Millie, A. (2008a) Anti-social behaviour, behavioural expectations and an urban aesthetic, *British Journal of Criminology*, 48(3): 379–94.
- Newburn, T. (2007) *Criminology.* Cullompton: Willan.
- Von Hirsch, A. and Simester, A. P. (2006) *Incivilities: Regulating Offensive Behaviour.* Oxford: Hart Publishing.

Notes

1 A style of rap music, originating in Los Angeles and celebrating black gang culture.

2   The origin of the term 'chav' is uncertain. Two leading theories are that (1) it originated with the Romany for an unmarried Romany male (chavvy); or (2) it is slang for a boy or girl from Chatham in Kent (dictionary.oed.com). Whatever its origin, it has become a derogatory term for 'a young working class person who dresses in casual sports clothing' (BBC 2005).

3   Ostentatious, flashy jewellery (dictionary.oed.com).

4   See Mead (1918) and Durkheim (1984).

5   Parcour or free running started in the suburbs of Paris and essentially uses the urban fabric as a playground, with buildings and street furniture used for a variety of jumps and outdoor gymnastics.

4 What causes anti-social behaviour?

> Family problems, poor educational attainment, unemployment, and alcohol and drug misuse can all contribute to anti-social behaviour. But none of these problems can be used as an excuse for ruining other people's lives. Fundamentally, anti-social behaviour is caused by a lack of respect for other people. (Home Office 2003c: 7)

In the above quotation from the white paper on anti-social behaviour, the government's perspective was made clear: there may be multiple causal factors behind someone's ASB, but these can be honed down to a simple 'lack of respect for other people'. The suggested response was similarly simple, that people ought to take greater 'responsibility'. The view is that, if people want to live in a particular community, they have to take responsibility for the impact of their behaviour on the rest of that community. Such a suggestion fitted into New Labour's wider communitarian or 'third way' discourses linking rights to responsibilities (e.g. Lund 1999; White 1999; Rose 2000) – an idea that draws heavily from earlier American writing on community (e.g. Mead 1986; Etzioni 1993a). The relevance here is that ASB was regarded as a simple consequence of individuals *not* taking their responsibility to others seriously. In a word, they lacked 'respect' for the community. The notion of 'respect' became the central plank of British government policy on ASB from the launch of the 'Respect Action Plan' in January 2006. It remains key to its replacement from October 2007, the 'Youth Taskforce'. If only it was that simple, a point picked up by Paul Roberts (2006: 37): '[I]t remains unclear, however, why lack of respect for others should be singled out as *the fundamental cause*. Might lack of respect not be a symptom of defective moral education in the home, in school, and in the wider community?' (Emphasis in original.)

In the preceding chapter, it was contended that the same behaviour committed by different people can be differently interpreted as acceptable, tolerable, anti-social or even criminal, depending on context and expectations. Relatedly, ASB may only exist if the behaviour is labelled as 'ASB'. But while the label 'ASB' is a created concept, some of the behaviour commonly deemed to be anti-social is not the figment of someone's imagination. Some very serious and persistent ASB does exist and can have a hugely detrimental impact on individuals and neighbourhoods that are also frequently otherwise disadvantaged. With this in mind, it is important to examine possible causal factors behind behaviour considered anti-social – and these factors are likely to involve more than a simple 'lack of respect'. But after decades of research, criminologists have not come to agreement on definitive causes of crime (see e.g. Muncie 2001; Garland 2002; Newburn 2007). Determining the causes of anti-social behaviour is going to be at least as difficult.

Causes of crime, deviance or ASB will include, for instance, individual or pathological, environmental, through to structural or societal explanations. The main focus for this chapter is possible causal factors identified by the public and whether these are supported by the literature. The idea that most people appear to equate ASB with young people is discussed – and thus the causes of youthful ASB – although, this is within the context that young people are certainly not the only perpetrators.

Popular explanations for what causes ASB

In a recent national survey (Millie et al. 2005a: 10) respondents were asked to identify the worst forms of ASB in their local area. The results are shown in Figure 4.1 and clearly demonstrate the dominance of youth – or 'rowdy teenagers' – as the primary ASB concern.

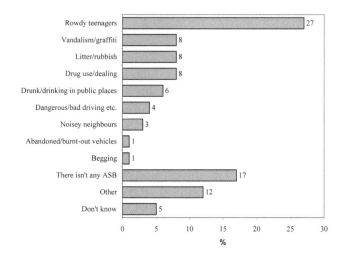

Note: n = 1682.
Source: Millie et al. 2005a.
Figure 4.1 The worst forms of ASB in your local area

According to research by the Institute for Public Policy Research (IPPR) (Margo et al. 2006) people in Britain are more likely than other Europeans to claim that young people are responsible for ASB. But what do people think are the causes of this youthful ASB? The IPPR poll showed that Britons are most likely to claim the root cause is a lack of discipline (79% of British respondents compared to, for instance, 69% of Spanish and 58% of French respondents). The same question was asked in the Millie et al. (2005a) national survey, with the results shown in Table 4.1. This table gives comparative results from another poll, this time conducted by Ipsos Mori (2006). The Mori survey was not specifically about *youthful* ASB; however, youthfulness was implicit in the options given to respondents.

Table 4.1 Perceived causes of ASB: results from two surveys

Which of these do you think are the three main causes of youth ASB?*

	%
Poor parenting	68
Boredom/not enough to do	58
Alcohol and drugs	52
Low respect for others	51
Poor discipline at school	25
Poverty and deprivation	14
Ineffective policing	14
A lack of jobs	9
None of these	1
Don't know	1

Source: Millie et al. 2005a, n = 1,682.

Which one or two of these do you think are the main causes of anti-social behaviour today?**

	%
Parents not bringing up their children appropriately	53
Drug and alcohol abuse	49
Lack of discipline in schools	28
Not enough for teenagers to do	27
Peer pressure	16
The break-up of marriages	14
Other	1
Don't know	1

Source: Ipsos Mori, 2006, n = 2048.

Notes: * England, Wales and Scotland survey of perceptions and experiences of ASB, part of an Office of National Statistics Omnibus Survey, conducted April 2004.

** Great Britain survey of public attitudes to parenting, commissioned by the government's 'Respect Task Force', conducted October 2006.

For both surveys, the number one cause of ASB was thought to be poor parenting (between 53 and 68%). The other main causal factors concerned teenage boredom, drugs and alcohol, a lack of respect and poor discipline in schools. A recent survey of young people aged 16–19 (DCSF 2008) similarly identified parents as those who could do more to help with anti-social young people (68% of respondents). Of course, these results do not mean these particular factors are necessarily the *true* causes of ASB. Other factors are clearly at play, including wider structural or societal changes – or perceived changes – as well as direct and unintended consequences of national and local policy. However, this list is as good a place to start as any. That said, it is certainly worth noting that many of these concerns are far from new. Geoffrey Pearson (1989: 10) in a study of juvenile crime in Victorian Britain recounted that:

> Family life was widely believed to be breaking down. The excessive leniency of the law was indicated frequently enough ... Music Hall entertainers and 'penny dreadful' comics were said to be encouraging immorality and imitative 'copy-cat' crime among the young. The failure of the elementary system of Board Schools ... to exercise effective controls upon the young was also subject to widespread condemnation ... children and youths [were] allegedly running riot outside school hours.

Does this sound familiar? If the music hall and 'penny dreadfuls' were replaced by computer games and the internet, then this would be a good description of contemporary worries about youth and ASB in Britain. A social policy focus on education and the family is similarly not new – although the language has changed to an actuarial focus (e.g. Smith 2006) on 'risk' and 'protective' factors for onset of anti-social or criminal behaviour (France and Utting 2005; Prior and Paris 2005; France 2008). This approach was originally popular in the US leading to developments such as the High/Scope Perry Pre-School programme (Schweinhart et al. 1993; Greenwood et al. 1996). Like many policy initiatives (Jones and Newburn 2007), the idea transferred across the Atlantic to Britain. It draws on psychosocial literature relating to broader conceptions of anti-social attitudes and behaviour (e.g. Farrington

1995a, b). However, it would also apply to programmes seeking to reduce ASB, as understood more narrowly in a public order enforcement context. The aim is to 'get upstream' of the problem. In simple terms, if factors associated with later development of youth ASB and crime are dealt with at an early stage, and pro-social development encouraged, then the young person is less likely to follow a path to deviancy. It is this thinking that has led to developments such as the British SureStart initiative (DfES 2006; Belsky et al. 2007) and other early intervention work (a theme that is explored further in Chapter 8). This approach is relevant to the current discussion as there is a distinct overlap between identified 'risk' factors and the issues thought by the public to cause ASB. For instance, Beinart et al. (2002) conducted a survey of school children aged 7–11 to assess involvement in crime and ASB, and to identify risk and protective factors in a British context. The resulting risk factors that were identified related to family, schooling, community and individual/friendship issues (see Box 4.1).

There is not direct causality between any of these factors and a young person becoming anti-social or criminal; after all, many people have difficult family backgrounds and their behaviour does not become problematic. But risk factors are simply those factors where, statistically, someone is more likely to become deviant. Of course, by identifying certain populations or situations where ASB and crime are more likely to develop involves an implicit danger of labelling. How such early intervention work is packaged consequently becomes hugely significant (see also Chapter 8). These risk factors are further explored below. In line with the issues identified in the public surveys, these are grouped by parental responsibility, the role of teenage boredom, drugs and alcohol, a lack of respect and poor discipline in schools.

Box 4.1 Risk and protective factors for youth 'problem behaviour'

Risk factors

Family

- Poor parental supervision and discipline
- Family conflict
- Family history of problem behaviour
- Parental involvement/ attitudes condoning problem behaviour
- *Low income and poor housing*

School

- *Low achievement, beginning at primary school*
- Aggressive behaviour, including bullying
- Lack of commitment, including truancy
- School disorganization

Community

- Community disorganization and neglect
- Availability of drugs
- *Disadvantaged neighbourhood*
- *High turnover and lack of neighbourhood attachment*

Individuals, friends and peers

- Alienation and lack of social commitment
- Attitudes that condone problem behaviour
- Early involvement in problem behaviour
- Friends involved in problem behaviour

Protective factors

- Strong bonds with family, friends and teachers
- Healthy standards set by parents, teachers and community leaders
- Opportunities for involvement in families, schools and the community*
- Social and learning skills to enable participation*
- Recognition and praise for positive behaviour*

Notes: Italics indicate factors not measured by the 'Communities that Care' Youth Survey, but identified using other data.
* Factors that operate together as a 'protective process'.
Source: Beinart et al. 2002; JRF 2002.

Blame the parents

Like public concerns, much of the policy debate around ASB – and crime and deviance more broadly – regards parents as responsible for their children's misbehaviour (Burney 1999; Gelsthorpe 1999; Arthur 2005). For instance, the following statements are taken from the government's Respect Action Plan published in 2006:

> Parents have a critical role in helping their children develop good values and behaviour. Conversely, poor parenting increases the risks of involvement in anti-social behaviour. (p. 3)

> Where parents' behaviour becomes problematic, children can be placed at serious risk. Worse, poor behaviour and a lack of respect can be transmitted between generations and can result in children and young people getting involved in crime or anti-social behaviour. (p. 6)

To claim that poor parenting can result in poorly behaved children is something of a truism; but there is also clear support from the literature. For instance, there is sizable evidence from the psychosocial literature that bad behaviour or aggression more broadly can be transmitted from parent to child (e.g. Farrington 1995b; Johnson et al. 2004). But it is also true that good parents can have badly behaved children – and vice-versa. Of course, what constitutes 'good' or 'bad' parenting is not always clear (see e.g. Holt 2008). And with the decline of 'traditional' nuclear families, who should take parental responsibility is similarly not straightforward. For instance, according to Loraine Gelsthorpe (1999) there will be difficulty in determining the 'parent' in some Parenting Order cases – as introduced with the 1998 Crime and Disorder Act:

> Is the Parenting Order to be imposed on the legal parent or guardian? The parent with whom the child resides? What if mum lives with her boyfriend – is the parenting order to be imposed on him too? Or on the 'distant' parent who sees the child once a month? Also, is the parent who is denied contact under the Children Act 1989 to be held responsible under the Crime and Disorder Act 1998? It is conceivable that the child or young person might be engaging in criminal behaviour because of a lack of contact with a parent. (Gelsthorpe (1999: 232)

To just 'blame the parents' may be simplistic; and according to the government's Respect Action Plan (2006: 17) 'not all children who experience poor parenting will develop problems [although] the case for supporting parents of vulnerable children and teenagers earlier is strong ...' There is sense in providing support and guidance for parents; but this does not have to come with the threat of censure – the approach preferred by government as demonstrated by its range of parenting orders and contracts (see e.g. Ministry of Justice 2007; Walters and Woodward 2007). According to Burney (2005: 71): 'Censuring parents for failing a moral standard does not sit easily with the idea that they need a helping hand.' Burney has also noted the limits to parental influence as children get older:

> By the time children reach adolescence, the peer group rather than parents is the main influence on conduct outside the home. Bad behaviour is often stimulated by companions, especially in settings which create opportunities … For this age group imposing parenting orders when offspring get into trouble makes limited sense. (2005: 71)[1]

According to Lewis (2007), media and advertising may have as strong an impact on youth behaviour: 'In effect, media and advertising have taken power away from parents in determining the leisure activities, communication norms and behavioural norms influencing young people' (p. 11). It seems that, while parents – however defined – do have a clear responsibility in influencing the behaviour of their children, they are certainly not the sole influence, and this ought to be reflected in government policy, emphasizing parental support rather than censure. Some of these issues are clearly displayed in a transcript shown in Box 4.2, taken from a focus group conducted with parents on a social housing estate.

Research by Hunter and Nixon (2001) has revealed that it is not a simple case of parents being blamed for their children's ASB, but rather, mothers specifically. They looked at the experiences of women headed households involved in ASB, and how landlords and the courts dealt with resultant eviction cases. They made the point that single mothers in general have been targeted and labelled as a 'problem', especially since Murray's (1990) work on the 'underclass' (see also Roseneil and Mann 1996; Gelsthorpe 1999). Hunter and Nixon found that landlords and the judiciary took a punitive approach towards 'women-headed households who fail to control boyfriends' or teenage sons' behaviour' (2001: 408). This gendered aspect to debates on ASB is one that often gets missed. While the women recognized that they had clearly been, 'construed as "other" ' (p. 409), they frequently refused to be labelled as such (see also Phoenix 1996).

Box 4.2 Views on parental responsibility, taken from a focus group with parents living on a social housing estate

Interviewer	*One of the things coming in the last couple of years is the Anti-Social Behaviour Order ... do you know what they are?*
Female	My friend's got one,* I don't think that's fair, because if your child breaks these rules then she's the one that gets kicked out of the house and that, and I don't really think that's fair when it's the kid doing it.
Male	But you've got to keep the kids under control haven't you.
Female	That's it.
Female	But that's alright to say that.
	...
Male	You can control your kid indoors but you can't control them outside.
Male	If you can deal with the situation while you are there, then yes, but while they are outside they are doing what they are doing and you can't help. My kids are a pain in the arse.

Notes: This respondent is more likely describing the conditions attached to an Anti-Social Behaviour Injunction (ASBI; see Chapter 7). For more from this study see Millie et al. 2005a.

Elsewhere, Nixon and Parr (2006: 93) make the pertinent point that: 'Laying the blame on parents is a populist approach that fails to take account of wider social circumstances, such as poverty, that make parenting far harder.' Just because the public are most likely to 'blame the parents' for ASB, this does not mean that mothers, parents or the family more broadly should be the central focus of work to tackle ASB; as Nixon and Parr (2006: 93) also observe: 'By identifying causal primacy with the family the government is absolved of any further responsibility.'

In 2002 Labour MP, Frank Field, tried to take things one step further by introducing to parliament a private member's 'Housing Benefit (Withholding of Payment) Bill'. As he saw it: 'Those who deliberately or constantly break the rules will lose entitlement to the money they receive from taxes paid by decent families whose lives they terrorise' (Field 2002; see also Rodger 2006). According to the Bill (s.1(1)) housing benefit would be withheld from a tenant if: 'in any three year period the anti-social behaviour of a tenant or of any individual living with a tenant has resulted on two or more occasions in an order being made by a magistrates' court against, or in the summary conviction of, the tenant or any individual living with the tenant ...' In this, Frank Field extended parental/tenant responsibility from the family to any individual living in a household. In effect, the tenant is seen as a parent to *all* in the household. The Bill failed to get through parliament; however, Field's ideas survived and were introduced in a revised form in the 2007 Welfare Reform Act (s.31). In certain pilot areas 'housing benefit anti-social behaviour sanctions' are now available for evicted tenants who fail to participate in rehabilitative schemes or do not heed warnings (see DWP 2007). How much a tenant – or parent – can really be held accountable for the actions of others in his/her household is questionable.

Teenage boredom

The second area that the public regards as a cause of youthful ASB is boredom. In Britain, if you were a child in the 1970s, 1980s or even early 1990s, you may remember the BBC TV programme, '*Why Don't You?*', which bravely asked its viewers, '*Why don't you just switch off your television set and go and do something less boring instead?*' The programme came up with creative ways to spend your time, both indoors and out. However, for many young people, the answer to this boredom is just to sit out and chat to their mates. In itself, there is nothing wrong with this and, in fact, it can form an important part of social development. Unfortunately, this is an activity often perceived as being anti-social – just by being present on the street. This situation is demonstrated in the following exchange between 16–18-year-old young men as part of a focus group held in London (Millie et al. 2005b: 21). In policy terms, this group fitted the criteria for being 'NEETs' (not in education, employment or training; see e.g. Rodger 2008):

Male 1   But how can it be irritating? We're not causing [trouble], you know what I'm saying? Have you ever sat in for an afternoon? You can't handle it man.

Male 2   Even sitting outside just on the street corner doing nothing is better than sitting in the house.

Male 3   You have to go out like, you have to just see what's happening around the place.

Of course, for some this boredom and seeing 'what's happening around the place' can lead to vandalism or ASB more broadly, even activity that is clearly criminal such as violence or car theft. According to the government's Social Exclusion Unit (1999: 34): '75 per cent of males aged 16–17 who are charged and appear before the Youth Court are in no formal full-time activity.' There is the possibility that this is such a high figure because this group is visible on the streets and therefore more likely to end up being charged. However, for a minority this 'hanging about' is clearly not enough. This was picked up by a participant in another focus group, this time with 16–18 year old female 'NEETs': 'The kids ... are obviously going to get up to mischief in the area because they're getting bored of doing the same old things' (see Millie 2006).

But boredom has always been a great excuse for deviancy, along with the related influence of peer group pressure. Boredom has been an area of study for cultural criminologists. For instance, Jeff Ferrell (2004: 300) has claimed that the, 'organized boredom of mass obedience' should be confronted by a criminology that is 'hectic, irreverent, transgressive and, above all, fun'.[2] Maybe, but it seems to me that boredom is not a cause of ASB, but rather a *symptom* of other issues in someone's life. This could be something as grand as angst against 'the dehumanizing conditions of modernism' (Ferrell 2004: 287); it could be related to familial problems; or more mundanely, just a simple lack of creativity, '*to do something less boring instead*'. For the young men quoted above, the boredom was, in part, the result of unemployment, but also the paucity of good quality daytime TV. A young person quoted in Millie et al. (2005a: 26) made the observation that, 'like, we're not on the streets out of choice you know, it's cold on the streets'. A police officer in the same study (pp. 25–6) noted the following: 'There's very little for them to do, so there's nothing to take them off the streets. So they're hanging around in the evenings, you know, bored. That's when they start making youth annoyance, criminal damage.' When young people do find something creative to do, if this involves outside 'play' then this itself can also be interpreted as ASB. For instance, a parent in the same study (Millie et al. 2005a: 25) commented that, 'Now you're not even allowed to play football on the street because that's anti-social behaviour and irritates the neighbours,' A lack of open spaces or of areas for teenage play have also been cited as causes of boredom and, relatedly, ASB (e.g. CABE 2004a; Woolley 2006).

The influence of drugs and alcohol

The third causal factor identified in the public surveys was the influence of drugs and alcohol. Returning to the concept of risk assessment, the Home Office's 2003 Crime and Justice Survey (Hayward and Sharp 2005) reveals a strong link between drug and alcohol use and self-reported ASB among young people. For instance, of 10–16-year-olds who said they had committed ASB in the last 12 months, 70 percent had also taken a drug during the last year and 66 percent had felt drunk at least once a month. For 17–25-year-olds the figures were 45 percent taking drugs and 36 percent feeling drunk.

Of course, these figures do not prove causality; as Hayward and Sharp (2005: 3) point out, it may reflect an 'underlying risky lifestyle'. Nonetheless, people's drinking and drug taking habits do impact on others' perceptions of ASB. Within a city centre context, for instance, perceived insecurity has been found to be highly localized, and related to expectations of criminality and ASB (Millie 1997; Bromley et al. 2000). In Britain the night-time city centre in particular is regarded as a problematic location for many, being exclusionary to those who do not fit a younger demographic, or who do not adhere to the drinking – and sometimes drug taking – norms of the consuming majority at this time. For those that 'don't fit in' at this time, this can lead to spatial and temporal avoidance (Bromley et al. 2000; Mawby and Simmonds 2004). Some groups will avoid these city centre 'drinking streets' altogether. However, many that do use the city centre in the evening may avoid specific areas at certain times and can clearly suffer the ASB of others. For instance, as part of a focus group study in London (Mille et al. 2005b; Millie 2006) the following exchanges took place among a group of gay and lesbian residents:

Female 1   They're 17 to 18, onto 20 – even 16 – and when you see them they look kind of thuggish ... I've seen it happen so many times and you think, 'why is this going on?'

Male 1   And they always walk in groups.

Male 2   When coming home from a club we travel in groups ... at the end of the day we have to look after each other.

Male 1   But really, at the end of the day, should we have to live like that?

Concerns about ASB and the night-time economy are not new and can be illustrated by the recent history of labels such as 'lager louts' during the 1980s and 1990s (Ramsey 1989; Comedia 1991) and 'binge drinkers' of the 2000s (Engineer et al. 2003; Roberts 2004). It is possible that the problem has been exaggerated by the media into a typical moral panic. However, there is certainly ASB that is the result of drinking and illicit drug taking. That said, some misbehaviour will be simple 'high spirits', while some will be far more serious than ASB. Where lines of acceptable, anti-social and criminal behaviour are drawn in the night-time economy are not necessarily always clear.

ASB related to alcohol misuse and drugs is not restricted to the city centre, with substance misuse being a factor in many housing disputes and eviction cases (Flint 2002; Nixon and Parr 2006; Pawson and McKenzie 2006). But to continue the city centre focus, during a focus group session with people with mental health and/or drugs problems (Millie et al. 2005b), a former homeless man recalled his experiences of being on the streets in London's Soho: 'The fact of the matter is, if you look at the crime being committed, is that, you know, junkies aren't smashing shop doorways in, it's pissed-up suits who are doing that. And where's the anti-social behaviour orders for those people?'

Drug taking is frequently associated with ASB, although the extent of any link is not known. If this former homeless man is to be believed, drunk city workers are a bigger problem on the streets of London. Examples of differing perspectives relating to drug use and ASB are outlined in Box 4.3, again from London. Here a Kurdish man is quoted saying the visible nature of people dealing and taking drugs is enough to deter him and his family from certain places. A young woman noted the problems associated with drugs paraphernalia being left 'lying around'. The overall impact of this visible evidence of drug use is that such activity seems acceptable in the area. The third quote is from someone who has experience of drug taking. This man's experience hints at the difficulty in using ASB enforcement to tackle drugs problems. Plainly, such problems can be deep rooted and require far cleverer or holistic solutions than simple censure (Papps 1998; Millie et al. 2005a)

Box 4.3   Focus group respondents' views on drugs and ASB

Within this area I've seen people who are freely dealing and taking and they can easily just smoke it in front of people ... but nothing's really done. Because of this you can't really take your children and family for a walk because you don't want them to come across this. (Kurdish man)

Drug users, needles lying around, foil ... I'm obviously not going to touch it, but for a child it's like, 'what's this?' (Young woman, 16–18)

It's all very well and good talking about anti-social behaviour, but if you're in a situation where your life is crap, and your only escape from that crapness is using gear, no amount of ASBOs are going to stop you using gear, you're going to carry on using gear because it's the only fucking thing you've got to cling on to. (Homeless man with mental health and/or drugs problems)

Note: See also Millie et al. 2005b; Millie 2006.

Poor discipline in schools

Poor discipline in schools is another popular reason cited for youthful ASB and for youthful concerns more generally. In both the Millie et al. (2005a) and Ipsos Mori (2006) surveys, poor school discipline was seen as a cause of youthful ASB by around a quarter. What this quarter meant by 'poor discipline' is not clear, although concerns are often expressed about the number of children outside of school when they should be in class. According to research conducted by Beinart et al. (2002; as shown in Box 4.1) school-related risk factors are thought to include low achievement, aggressive behaviour (including bullying), lack of commitment (including truancy), and 'school disorganization'. Again, such concerns are not new; for instance Albert Cohen (1955) thought there to be a link between anti-social attitudes, truancy and school failure. Similarly, Mannheim (1965) thought truants were more likely to get into trouble simply because of greater opportunity (see also Ekblom 1979). Pratt (1983) has talked about a 'truancy crisis' throughout the 1970s making good newspaper copy; however, May (1975: 106, cited in Pratt 1983) puts such debates into context:

> [I]t is only a minority of boys with a record of irregular school attendance who subsequently make a juvenile court appearance ... [and] while a record of irregular school attendance certainly increases the likelihood of a court appearance, the great majority of delinquents have a perfectly good attendance record.

It seems that, while truancy can be a psychosocial risk factor (e.g. Farrington 1995b), a direct causation between truancy and delinquency – and with ASB in particular – is not likely to be clear-cut. Other studies have considered the role of poor academic performance, identifying a link with delinquency (e.g. Maguin and Loeber 1996). Nonetheless, a recent longitudinal study in America by Felson and Staff (2006: 312) only found a 'spurious, not causal' relationship. There is *something* in common between truancy, poor academic performance, delinquency and ASB, but causality cannot be determined with confidence. Despite this muddled picture, the role of school attendance as a preventer of youthful ASB is frequently assumed. For instance – and linked to the earlier discussion of parental blame – Flint and Nixon (2006: 948) recount a case of a 43-year-old mother given a parenting order with the condition that she made her children go to school. She was later, 'jailed for 60 days in 2002 after breaching the terms of her order and failing to ensure that her children attended school'. Following a 'risk' paradigm that equates poor schooling and poor parenting to later ASB and deviancy, such a punishment seems quite sensible. However, the muddled evidential picture makes a jail term an overly harsh penalty.

A lack of respect

In the Millie et al. (2005a) survey, 51 percent of respondents thought that a lack of respect was a causal factor in youthful ASB. This finding would have pleased politicians as it supported their policy focus on 'respect'. Of course, whether governments can make people more respectful is debateable; but according to Thompson (2007: 2) governmental rhetoric 'frequently returns to the need to enforce respect on those who are seen to be lacking it'. Key to this has been the interdepartmental government 'Respect' agenda. But has there really been a decline in respect, thus leading to ASB? For instance, whether respect for elders has declined is questionable; it would certainly be difficult to measure. It seems that adults have always questioned the activities and motives of those younger than themselves, as clearly demonstrated in Stanley Cohen's work on youthful 'folk devils' (1972, 2002). The last few decades have witnessed a decline in deference, but I would argue that this is not necessarily a bad thing. Societal changes have meant that those of higher social standing are not automatically admired and respected – as in the classic 'I look up to him, I know my place' (see also Harris 2006a; McCarthy and Walker 2006). But deference isn't the same as respect (Sennett 2003). It is a point identified in the government's Respect Action Plan, that: 'We should build a culture of respect for the modern age, based on values of mutuality and shared responsibility rather than deference and hierarchy' (Respect Task Force 2006: 5).

Richard Sennett's influence on New Labour, and on Tony Blair in particular, is summarized by Julian Baggini writing in the *Guardian* (2006): 'Sennett ... is more than just the greatest single influence on the "respect agenda" – he more or less set it.' Sennett talked of a need for an inclusive mutual respect, where others are treated as equals. This mutuality can be between different social groups, across generations or it can be between government and citizen. His view is not that of an egalitarianist, that respect will be derived from equality; rather Sennett argues that 'in social life as in art, mutuality requires expressive work. It must be enacted, performed' (2003: 59). Drawing on his musical background, Sennett suggests that this will involve all parts of society working together with an implicit understanding of others' needs in the 'performance'. As an ideal this sounds wonderful, but, as Sennett concedes, 'an enormous gap exists between wanting to act well toward others and doing so' (2003: 59).

For instance, according to Waiton (2001) there is an increasing separation between young people and adults. And this could be exacerbated by local authorities employing specialist youth workers rather than having local parents volunteering to help run a local youth club; it could be by the police being relied upon for providing behavioural control, rather than an extended family of neighbours. It could also be by providing facilities for young people that are physically away from adult spaces. According to Moore and Stratham (2006: 472): '[I]ntergenerational relationships suffer because adults are increasingly relying on police and other agents to control the action of the young, rather than, as in the past, playing an active role themselves in teaching the young what is socially acceptable.' The reasons for this may be tied to notions of declining social capital (cf. Putnam, 2000) or a lack of collective efficacy (Sampson et al. 1997) – ideas that I shall return to. There are related concerns of powerlessness to do anything about ASB. But first I want to consider further how people in Britain explain ASB.

Three narratives to explain causality

Drawing on evidence from focus groups with residents in three areas with problems of ASB and interviews with practitioners (Millie et al. 2005a: viii), three narratives that are frequently used to explain ASB have been found. These are:

1 *Social and moral decline*: Problems of ASB are seen as symptoms of wider social and cultural change – more specifically, a decline in moral standards and family values and a decline in respect.

2 *Disengagement*: ASB is thought to be rooted in the increasing disengagement from wider society of a significant minority of children, young people and adults.

3 *'Kids will be kids'*: ASB is seen as a reflection of the age-old tendency for young people to get into trouble, challenge boundaries and antagonize their elders.

The three narratives are not mutually exclusive with people quite happy to flit between one and another. However, the social and moral decline and disengagement narratives assume that problems of ASB are getting worse. The third narrative, that 'kids will be kids', does not assume problems are any worse than before, but have always been part of growing up. It is the contexts within which these 'kids' find themselves that are changing. The narratives are demonstrated by the quotes included in Box 4.4 that are taken from the same study.

Box 4.4 Respondents' narratives to explain ASB

Social and moral decline narrative:

Things like respect and discipline all seem to have gone out the window. I know people say it's all old fashioned, but I don't think so because I think it's the very essence of being able to live with others and integrate with others. (Youth project coordinator)

Disengagement narrative:

There are a number of youths who are definitely disillusioned, disaffected with society as a whole; some of them have low educational attainment; some of them have disengaged themselves from everything. (Head teacher)

Kids will be kids narrative:

You can't blame the kids, no one is an angel at fourteen, fifteen, sixteen, they are all mischievous. We've all done it. (Local parent)

Note: See also Millie et al. 2005a.

The first of these narratives emphasizing social and moral decline has certainly been a popular theme in political comment on ASB and provided the context for the 'Respect' agenda. There is an assumed loss of respect and an assumed golden age of innocence; as a respondent in a focus group with retired people put it, 'I think the worst thing I ever did [as a child] was pinch apples. And we thought we were really doing something wicked' (Millie et al. 2005a: 22). There is evidence to suggest that such a time was either not as innocent as remembered or never existed in the first place (Pearson, 1983). The 'decline' narrative is evident in the writing of Frank Field, MP (2003: 9), who has stated that, '[t]he moment I realised society was unquestionably changing for the worse is still indelibly etched on my memory.' According to Field (2003: 126), there is a 'plague of disorder which now marks the lives of so many ... the likes of which Britain has not seen for well over a century'. Such a stance has a lot in common with underclass theory (see Chapter 3), and assumes ASB is on the increase. The logical solution will emphasize tougher discipline and individual responsibility, as demonstrated in the government's call for 'respect and responsibility'.

The second narrative relates to social exclusion and was particularly popular among local practitioners. The emphasis is on social, cultural and economic disadvantage as causes of ASB, particularly related to familial and community problems including low aspirations and poor parenting. Like the 'decline' narrative it also assumes ASB is increasing; but it will lead to an emphasis on inclusionary solutions.

The third narrative, that 'kids will be kids', does not assume things are getting worse but reflects the ever present pressures on growing up. Following this perspective, solutions to ASB will be associated with diversionary activities aimed at alleviating youthful boredom. There will also be a need for patience and tolerance for youthful misadventure.

As noted, whether there has been a decline in respect is difficult to measure; similarly for a decline in social and moral values more broadly. The individualistic consumerism promoted during the Thatcher years and beyond may have led to conflict over boundaries of acceptable behaviour and less tolerance for behaviour outside our individualistic notion of social and cultural norms. The result will have been less tolerance of difference. As stated elsewhere (Millie et al. 2005a: 34):

> The balance of probability is that at the start of the 21st century our tolerance for violence is now very much lower than it was 50 or 100

years ago ... On the other hand, only the most myopic of social historians could ignore the decline over several decades of youthful deference, coupled with the emergence of forms of consumerist hedonism, especially those concerned with alcohol and drug use. We may not live in more violent times than our parents or grandparents, but for better or worse, we probably do lead less regulated and less orderly lives, in an age of increasing mobility and family breakdown.

The effect is less about social *decline* than it is about social *change*. Consequently, of the three narratives, some combination between 'disengagement' and 'kids will be kids' explanations seems to make more sense. However, with its emphasis on enforcing standards of behaviour, and on enforcing 'respect', the government's approach to ASB has been closely allied to a fight to reverse social decline and create a civil society (e.g. Blunkett 2003a). Politically, this may have been an astute position to take, but it ran the risk of measuring success against a past that never existed.

A sense of powerlessness

Research by IPPR (Margo et al. 2006) has demonstrated an unwillingness among British people to intervene in instances of ASB. Respondents were given a hypothetical situation where a group of 14-year-old boys were vandalizing a bus shelter. According to their findings, among British respondents one in three (34%) would intervene. This may not seem too bad, but compares unfavourably to 50 percent of Italians, 52 percent of Spanish and 65 percent of German respondents who would intervene.

As well as being unwilling to intervene, British people also exhibit a sense of powerlessness to do anything about ASB, especially within the worst affected neighbourhoods. This powerlessness is evidenced in a fear of retaliation, and a sense that statutory agencies are also powerless to do anything about the problem (see Box 4.5).

Box 4.5 A sense of powerlessness

Today you can't tell them not to do certain things: it's a case of, 'who are you?'. And half the time they just look at you daft and just carry on. (Community activist)

Youngsters today are almost prepared to take you on. They know their rights far more than we did. (Local councillor)

> You daren't say anything to them; you tell the police but the police say it's not a priority. (Retired person)
>
> *Source*: Millie et al. 2005a: 18–19.

This assumed powerlessness is not a cause of ASB, but would certainly be a factor in ASB remaining unchecked. For many this will reflect a demise in social and moral standards; however, like so many things, a sense that we can't do anything about the problem is also not new. Returning to the work of Geoffrey Pearson (1989: 13), he has described youthful street games at the start of the twentieth century. Some of these games were hardly innocent and, if played today, would come under the ASB umbrella: '[S]ome London magistrates appear to have been reluctant to prosecute on police evidence alone, unless local people came forward to offer proof of annoyance by street games. The police view, on the other hand, was that neighbours were often afraid to give evidence because of possible reprisals.'

In relation to current intergenerational work, Moore and Statham (2006: 472) have noted the following:

> [W]hether increased interaction [between generations] can happen without some kind of initial third party mediation is questionable. Fear of retaliation, victimisation, or confrontation with teenagers' parents may deter community members from taking direct action to stop perceived anti-social behaviour by young people.

There is a fear that intervention will lead to abuse – or worse – from the perpetrator, or even from the parent of an anti-social young person (see also Barnes 2006). Together with little faith that the authorities will do anything about the problem, this is a somewhat pessimistic position, but it reflects a disconnection and lack of commonality felt between different groups and across generations.

ASB and informal social control mechanisms

People's reluctance to intervene can be viewed as a reflection of a lack of informal social control. The earlier quote from Pearson (1989) hints that such control mechanisms may not have been part of neighbourhood life at the start of the twentieth century, let alone at the start of the twenty-first. Contemporary concerns can be demonstrated using evidence from a 2002 MORI survey (see Home Office 2004a). Respondents were asked to identify the main problems in their area. The results when shown by perceptions that neighbours do or do not look out for each other are telling (see Table 4.2). For five ASB issues, respondents were more likely to perceive there to be a problem if they also thought that neighbours do not look out for each other.

Table 4.2 ASB problems in your area (by 'neighbours look out for each other')

% Issue	Neighbours do look out for each other	Neighbours don't look out for each other
Teenagers hanging around	36	52
Drug dealing and use	28	43
Vandalism	33	46
Litter	34	46
Disturbance from crowds and groups or hooligans	16	28

Source: MORI 2003 (base: 19,574) (see Home Office 2004a).

Sampson et al. (1997: 918) use the term 'collective efficacy' to describe the situation where there is, 'social cohesion among neighbors combined with their willingness to intervene on behalf of the common good'. It is in effect the opposite of 'social disorganization' (cf. Shaw and McKay 1942). Areas suffering 'social disorganization' are, according to Sampson and Grove (1989: 799), those with high crime and delinquency; they are also characterized by, 'sparse friendship networks, unsupervised teenage peer groups, and low organisational participation'. The concept of collective efficacy has a lot of overlap with 'social capital' (Putnam 2000; Halpern 2005), as demonstrated by social ties, contacts, social networks, groups, civic participation, readiness to help others, etc. According to Putnam (2000: 307): 'Neighborhoods with high levels of social capital tend to be good places to raise children. In high-social-capital areas public spaces are cleaner, people are friendlier, and the streets are safer.' This is an attractively simple perspective. However, there are variations across neighbourhoods. For instance, Walklate and Evans (1999) note that social cohesion is not necessarily absent from high crime areas. Halpern (2005) has similarly found that some poorer neighbourhoods experiencing higher levels of incivility can demonstrate higher levels of 'social capital' than more affluent areas (see also Hancock 2001). Nonetheless, neighbours' unwillingness to 'look out for each other' is still an important element in creating an environment where ASB can flourish.

Like so many things, this is not a new proposition. For instance, according to Pullen writing in 1973 (p. 266) housing provision needs to offer, 'a stable, self-regulating community where such anti-social acts of vandalism do not go un-noticed'. It is the existence of such 'stable, self-regulating' communities that is thought to be in decline. Particularly in urban areas, neighbourhoods are increasingly characterized by a high turnover of residents with the result being less knowledge of who your neighbours actually are; as Burney (1999: 15) has observed: 'As social and economic structures diversify, so it is often claimed, individuals are less dependent on their immediate neighbourhood and other people within it. Traditions and loyalties which formerly played a greater role in social relations are eroded and with them ... the sense of whom to trust.'

Such societal processes were also observed across the Atlantic, with Oscar Newman (1995: 155) claiming, 'the terrible byproduct of a diverse, highly mobile society unfettered by past moral constraints may be a devastating loss of civility and commonality among neighbors' (see also Jacobs 1961; Newman 1972). If this is the case, then work to better the social capital or 'collective efficacy' of an area may improve local ties and improve informal mechanisms of control, thus reducing incidence of ASB (see also Sampson and Raudenbush 1999).

In terms of New Labour's ASB and respect agendas, the idea of actively involving communities had a ready audience. By the time of the Respect Action Plan (Respect Task Force 2006: 27) the government was calling for 'Respect Standards' where social landlords and partners, 'involve the community in setting and enforcing [local standards]'. Whether such an approach will be successful is open to debate. For instance, according to Walklate and Evans (1999) some poorer neighbourhoods – precisely those areas where ASB is thought to be highest – have a culture of non-cooperation with the police. This is illustrated in Box 4.6, which gives part of a transcript of a focus group conducted with parents living on a social housing estate (see also Millie 2007b). Rather than involving the authorities, some within this group preferred to deal with the issues themselves, although it was acknowledged that this could also escalate the problem. And while many of the participants had a lot in common, a lack of community, or 'collective efficacy' was evident. For instance, instead of intervening 'on behalf of the common good' (Sampson et al. 1997: 918), motivations were more individualistic; as one male participant put it, 'none of the community gets together anymore, people just get on with what they are doing themselves, and then if it comes your way it comes your way, we'll deal with it when it comes to up'.

Box 4.6 An excerpt from a focus group with parents on a social housing estate

Interviewer *Is there anything the community can do to try and sort it out?*

Male You can't, none of the community gets together anymore, people just get on with what they are doing themselves, and then if it comes your way it comes your way, we'll deal with it when it comes to up.

Female I think we'd all end up arguing anyway.

Male	On scruffy estates like these you just deal with it when it comes to it.
Male	A lot of people around here have been brought up to not phone the police and just deal with it yourself.
Female	It's a no-win situation.
Female	It's like protecting your kids, if somebody's going to whack my kid then I'm sorry but I will whack them, because I am there to protect my kids. If my kids are fighting one-on-one I will stand there and say, 'yes, you fight one-on-one' because that's the way I was brought up. I wasn't allowed to go home and say, 'I've just been battered' because I was battered myself and just told to get out there and deal with it.
Interviewer	*Do the rest of you think like that?*
Female	I would say that you should just walk away, but when you get picked on, it takes a bigger man to walk away.
Female	I can't see my son running in and saying, 'he just battered me', but then he would have them at school saying, 'you pussy, you ran off', I was brought up like that you see, if my son came running in I would send him back out there to deal with it.
Female	My kids haven't been brought up to fight; we've always told them that it takes a bigger man to walk away.
Female	I've only got young ones, they come home and say, 'such and such has just smacked me', and all we do is go and see their mum and get it sorted out that way.
Female	But there are some parents you can't approach.
Female	I know.
Male	I've tried all that but I just end up fighting with the mums and the dads, and it's just caused one big row because then my brothers have got involved.

There is strong evidence to suggest that governments and local authorities have had a part in declining neighbourhood 'collective efficacy' and consequent informal social control. Such developments may have been accidental, but follow a law of unintended consequences. For example, housing allocation policies have for a long time been recognized as important determinants in creating less popular estates, which become more marginalized and the home for those with fewer choices to look elsewhere – often including many young families (e.g. Baldwin et al. 1976; Gill 1977; Hancock 2001). For instance, according to Owen Gill (1977: 5): 'Through the processes of allocation this leads to a situation in which those whose economic resources are low and whose power is therefore minimal are allocated accommodation in areas that become increasingly disadvantaged'. Those who can afford to, move out, thus contributing to housing market decline and abandonment (Urban Task Force 1999; Cole and Nevin 2004; Millie 2007b). This process has been exacerbated by the local authority housing 'right to buy' policy introduced in 1980 (Jones and Murie 1998). According to Cole and Nevin (2004: 10) certain estates become unpopular because: '[A] range of factors, such as unpopular property design, stigma and high levels of perceived crime and anti-social behaviour, [which] interact to reduce external demand and result in a high proportion of existing residents wanting to leave.'

As previously noted, according to Burney (2000) 'difficult' tenants still need to be housed somewhere, and is often the same low demand estates. Writing in 1973, David Pullen observed similar processes at work in low demand blocks of flats: 'The ... consequence of the property being seen as second class is that the bureaucracy is liable to treat the tenants as just that. The temptation to use already down-graded areas as dumping grounds for bad risk tenants must be considerable' (p. 266).

During the 1980s and 1990s local authorities in Britain were also experiencing significant cuts in other non-housing budgets. For instance, according to the Urban Parks Forum (2002), £1.3 billion in revenue expenditure had been lost to public parks over the previous 20 years. The way local authority services were managed and delivered changed radically with the introduction of Compulsory Competitive Tendering (CCT) following the 1980 Local Government Planning and Land Act. Rather than providing all services inhouse, local authorities had to put many contracts up for tender, often going for the cheapest option. The impact on informal social control was that local authority personnel became less visible in public places, and thereby less able to deter or intervene in ASB. For instance, the 1980 Act was extended with the 1988 Local Government Act to include leisure and sports facilities. According to Greenhalgh and Worpole (1995: 58) this resulted in, 'cheaper grounds maintenance contracts, but the savings are often lost to parks department budgets, and public concerns for safety and supervision as a result remain largely unmet'. In public parks this proved particularly problematic with some gaining reputations as places to avoid: 'The "keeper-less park" has joined the driver-less train, the unstaffed railway station, the unsupervised playground or underground car park, as one of the ghostly sites of public Britain' (Greenhalgh and Worpole 1995: 59).

There have been positive developments since mid-1990s, for instance with increased funding for parks from the National Lottery from 1997 onwards, and the introduction of 'Green Flag' awards in 1996, currently run by the Civic Trust (the awards include criteria for public safety). However, according to the Green Flag Manual (CABE 2004b):

> When the Green Flag Award scheme was first developed negative media coverage of public parks was commonplace. Local and national newspaper reports reflected stories of crime, neglect and dereliction. Against this miserable backdrop of bad news the future for Britain's rich and diverse asset of public parks looked bleak. Of course there was, and still is, a serious problem of under investment ... it is evident that many of Britain's parks are now significantly less well maintained.

The report gives examples of positive developments in park provision and quality. Nonetheless, it is possible that, had local authorities not cut back on spending on parks, concerns about ASB and crime in these shared public spaces may not have become so significant in the first place (see also CABE 2005a).

It is perhaps no coincidence that the rise to prominence of ASB in public debates accompanied the retreat of many agents of informal social control. But according to Jones and Newburn (2002) this is part of a much longer historical process. By analysing changes in people's occupations using census results, Jones and Newburn traced the demise of many informal (what they termed 'secondary') social control occupations, at a time when more formal (or 'primary') social control occupations, such as the police and private security, saw huge increases. Their results are shown in Table 4.3.

Table 4.3 Primary and secondary social control occupations in Britain: changes from 1951

	1951	1971	1991
Police officers	84,585	115,170	149,964
		+36%	+77%
Security guards and related	66,950	129,670	159,704
		+94%	+139%
'Roundsmen/roundswomen'	98,143	43,360	49,182
		−56%	−50%
Bus (and tram) conductors	96,558	57,550	2471
		−40%	−97%
Rail ticket inspectors/guards	35,715	46,800	15,642
		+31%	−56%

Source: 1951, 1971, 1991 Census (based on Jones and Newburn 2002: 141).

The demise of informal – or secondary – control occupations is likely to have adversely impacted on constraints on misbehaviour. However, the rise in numbers for formal social control occupations does not necessarily equate to the state stepping in to fill the gap. For instance, during the 1990s there was an increased managerial focus for policing, leading to greater emphasis on volume crime, perhaps shifting focus from more minor disorders or anti-social behaviours. More recent developments in 'reassurance' and 'neighbourhood policing' have attempted to remedy this situation (e.g. Innes 2005; Millie and Herrington 2005).

The responsibility for informal social control is not restricted to those whose job it is to be working in public places. As Jane Jacobs (1961: 35) famously promoted, there needs to be 'eyes upon the street, eyes belonging to those we might call the natural proprietors of the street'. These could be police officers or park keepers; but also simply the local residents. In reference to the aims of community policing, Connolly (2006: 80) has observed the following: 'Community policing doesn't just require the police being visible; it also requires the community to show up too and on foot. Sadly many residents choose not to. Instead of walking even less than a mile, one in five opt for their cars instead'[3].

While most town and city centres remain busy with pedestrians, especially during the day, some residential neighbourhood pavements in Britain are rarely full of activity. It is possible that this retreat from our streets has left others to claim ownership – including gangs of youths in certain deprived or urban neighbourhoods.

Other unintended consequences of policy

Along with more obvious developments relating to a demise in informal social control, there have been other government policies that will have led to a rise in ASB – or at least in behaviour perceived to be anti-social. A case in point is the introduction of 'care in the community' for people with psychiatric disorders; as Burney (2000: 271) has noted:

> One of the more obvious failures of 'care in the community' has been the frequency with which people discharged from psychiatric care are dumped in 'sink estates' … Nobody wants to live next door to someone who cannot deal with rubbish, plays loud music to drown out 'voices', and exhibits paranoid reactions.

A completely different development has been the expansion of policy to address environmental issues. One such example is the introduction of charging for the deposit of commercial waste. The result for some businesses has been the anti-social practice of fly tipping – illegally dumping rubbish by the side of the road, in car parks or other open spaces.

A further development in government policy has been the adoption of the European Convention of Human Rights with the 1998 Human Rights Act. In many ways this has been an excellent development; however, again following the rule of unintended consequences, how this has been interpreted by individuals may not be the same as intended. Building on the individualistic consumerism typical of late modernity, a focus on rights has for some been misinterpreted as a right to behave 'however I like'. This is in sharp contrast to the mutuality of respect promoted by Sennett (2003) and advocated by the 'Respect' agenda (see also Chapter 8).

Concluding comments

As expected, determining the precise causes of ASB is not an easy task. As with determining causes of crime, there is not just one contributing factor, but a whole range of societal, individual and policy factors that have made ASB such a concern in contemporary Britain. And government agencies have to take some of the blame, although impact is often unintentional. What this chapter has demonstrated is that ASB is not simply due to 'a lack of respect for other people' (Home Office 2003c: 7). Of course, what you think causes ASB will influence the choices made in determining possible solutions. For instance, if poor parenting is seen as the primary reason why young people become anti-social, then parenting programmes and early intervention will be possible solutions. Similarly, if ASB is thought to be due to teenage boredom, then diversionary activities could be the answer. A range of enforcement and preventative options are explored in Chapters 6 to 8. But first, the next chapter focuses on rationales for tackling ASB.

Selected reading

As there is a wide range of suggested causes of ASB, the relevant literature is equally varied. Those listed below give a flavour of the range of issues:

- Ferrell, J. (2004) Boredom, crime and criminology, *Theoretical Criminology*, 8(3): 287–302.
- Gelsthorpe, L. (1999) Parents and criminal children, in A. Bainham, S. Day Sclater and M. Richards (eds), *What is a Parent? A Socio-legal Analysis*. Oxford: Hart Publishing.
- Jacobs, J. (1961) *The Death and Life of Great American Cities*. New York: Vintage Books.
- Pearson, G. (1983) *Hooligan: A History of Respectable Fears*. Basingstoke: Macmillan.
- Putnam, R. D. (2000) *Bowling Alone: The Collapse and Revival of American Community*. New York: Simon & Schuster.
- Prior, D. and Paris, A. (2005) *Preventing children's involvement in crime and anti-social behaviour: a literature review*. Research Report No. 623. Nottingham: Department for Education and Skills.
- Sampson, R. J. and Raudenbush, S. W. (1999) Systematic social observation of public spaces: a new look at disorder in urban neighbourhoods, *American Journal of Sociology*, 105(3): 603–51.
- Sennett, R. (2003) *Respect: The Formation of Character in an Age of Inequality*. London: Penguin Books.
- Squires, P. and Stephen, D. E. (2005a) *Rougher Justice: Anti-social Behaviour and Young People*. Cullompton: Willan.

Notes

1   See also Wikström (2003).
2   A phrase Jock Young (2002) had previously used to describe the British 'National Deviancy Conference' of the late 1960s and early 1970s.
3   See DfT (2004).

5 What can be gained by tackling anti-social behaviour?

If ASB is to be tackled then it is helpful to know why. From a governmental perspective this may seem a ridiculous question; after all, if people are suffering then something clearly needs to be done. Nonetheless, many perspectives have been put forward as to what can be gained by tackling ASB, most straightforwardly because ASB is a menace that needs to be dealt with, but also because there may be an impact on wider criminological and societal concerns (Jacobson et al. 2005, 2008). For instance, according to the government's 'Respect' website:

> Anti-social behaviour ruins lives. It doesn't just make life unpleasant; it prevents the renewal of disadvantaged areas and creates an environment where more serious crime can take hold. Anti-social behaviour is a major issue in some of the UK's more deprived or disadvantaged communities. Anti-social behaviour is also expensive. It is estimated to cost the British taxpayer £3.4bn a year. (www.respect.gov.uk, accessed Feb. 2008)

Within this one statement a whole range of rationales are put forward that can be summarized as follows:

1 ASB itself is a bad thing: '*Anti-social behaviour ruins lives.*'
2 A regeneration rationale: '*It prevents renewal of disadvantaged areas.*'
3 A crime fighting rationale: '*creates an environment where more serious crime can take hold.*'
4 An equality rationale: '*a major issue in some of the UK's more deprived and disadvantaged communities.*'
5 To benefit the agencies involved: '*Anti-social behaviour is also expensive.*'

This is an impressive list; and if tackling ASB truly has this impact then there is no question that it should be dealt with. However, just as ASB is a contested concept, then determining what can be gained by tackling ASB is going to be similarly disputed. In this chapter, these various rationales are considered in terms of their theoretical origins and practical implications. Other rationales that are considered are a community building rationale and as a way of by-passing the criminal justice system.

Because ASB is a bad thing

The most straightforward reason for tackling ASB is that, in itself, it has a negative impact on victims and communities. Famously in New York during the 1990s Commissioner Bill Bratton introduced a style of policing that focused on minor disorders and misdemeanours in an effort to improve New Yorker's quality of life. In fact, these low level issues (including much anti-social behaviour) became known as 'quality of life crimes' (Bratton 1997; Harcourt 1998, 2001; Innes 1999; Vitale 2008). The phrase 'quality of life crimes' itself may be fairly meaningless; after all, most forms of crime or ASB will negatively impact on quality of life. However, 'quality of life' now appears elsewhere as a justification for tackling ASB, incivilities and minor misdemeanours – for instance in Britain (Tuffin et al. 2006) and in Australia (Dixon and Maher 2005). The New York strategy more broadly became known as 'zero tolerance' policing and drew heavily from Wilson and Kelling's (1982) 'broken windows' perspective, of which more later.

What I wish to emphasize here is that by focusing on quality of life, the view is that such issues *in themselves* ought to be tackled because they are making people's lives miserable. In Britain this has been a major focus for politicians with the former Labour Home Secretary David Blunkett claiming in 2004 that the government's campaign was a direct response to public frustrations at having to live with ASB. According to Blunkett, '[m]ore and more, people around the country are saying "we don't have to tolerate this", and are no longer putting up with graffiti or vandalism'.

There are also related concerns of 'fear of crime'. For instance, in the government white paper on ASB (Home Office 2003c: 13) fear was cited as a clear factor in tackling ASB: '[I]t is fear of crime – rather than actually being a victim – that can so often limit people's lives, making them feel afraid of going out or even afraid in their own homes.' 'Fear of crime' is a hotly debated concept (e.g. Irving 2002; Farrall 2004; Hough 2004; Millie 2008c; Walklate and Mythen 2008). As an emotional response to victimization – or danger of victimization – criminologists have found it difficult to determine what it is exactly they are measuring with 'fear of crime' surveys. For instance, do 'fear of crime' measures relate to frequency or intensity of emotional reaction? As Mike Hough (2004: 173) has observed: 'Discussion slips from "fear" to "worry" to "concern" about crime as if they were synonyms. They are not.'

However, despite the limitations of the terminology, a link between incivility and fear is a long held view. At its simplest, according to Wilson (1975) and Garofalo and Laub (1978), experiencing minor disorders and incivilities can cause people to fear crime. This view was developed by Hunter (1978, cited in Taylor 1999a), whose view was that there existed a link between local disorder and fear because residents and local agencies are unable or unwilling to intervene. A sense of powerlessness to intervene in ASB was explored in Chapter 4 and was related to intergenerational concerns and intimidation (and fear of reprisals from perpetrators, and sometimes from the parents of perpetrators). As a local councillor interviewed in a recent study put it (Jacobson et al. 2005): 'I've done it myself – you see a group of youths standing about ... and they're laughing and talking, and they're being loud the way young people are, and you immediately see them as threatening.'

According to Ralph Taylor (1999a: 67), '[I]t is not just the presence of the signs of incivilities that is threatening to [residents], but the meaning attached to them.' It is how we interpret these signs that will dictate whether we take them to mean anti-social behaviour – or otherwise – and whether this get translated into fear (or worry, or concern). However, the assumed causal relationship between disorder/incivility/ASB and 'fear of crime' is not straightforward. According to Taub et al. (1984) some neighbourhoods with high levels of disorder simply do not have high levels of fear. Similarly, in a longitudinal study of incivility conducted by Taylor (1999b, 2001) in the US city of Baltimore, Maryland, worsening physical conditions did not lead to greater fear of crime. It was explained in Chapter 3 that a lot will depend on our behavioural expectations for a particular place and time. How these expectations interact with 'signs of incivility' will be important; as the local councillor cited above noted about groups of youths, 'you immediately see them as threatening'. Such cues or 'signs of incivility' can be highly subjective.

Martin Innes and colleagues have focused on relationships between disorder and fear of crime in their work on a 'signal crimes' perspective (e.g. Innes and Fielding 2002; Innes 2004a). Their view is that, rather than disorder leading to crime, they are functionally equivalent (a view shared by Sampson and Raudenbush 1999). Innes and colleagues claim that certain incidents act as 'signals' that are 'disproportionately influential in terms of causing a person or persons to perceive themselves to be at risk in some sense' (Innes and Fielding 2002: 17). These 'signals' may be serious crimes, but are as likely to be minor incivility or ASB, 'less serious events which are nonetheless significant due to them being experienced directly' (Innes et al.

2002: 19). However, there is a danger that they may also be entirely legitimate behaviours, such as groups of young people congregating. The 'signal crime' perspective was influential in the British experiment with 'reassurance policing' (Innes 2004b; Millie and Herrington 2005; Tuffin et al. 2006), where police officers were to focus on priorities identified by local residents – whatever they may be – in order to maximize impact on local fears and to improve public confidence in policing decisions. Difficulties naturally arose when these local priorities differed from centrally dictated police performance indicators and targets (Herrington and Millie 2006). Despite this, a focus on 'the local' has continued in Britain under the 'neighbourhood policing' banner (Home Office 2005a; Innes 2005; Quinton and Morris 2008).

A crime fighting rationale

While ASB can be tackled because it is a 'bad thing' that may negatively impact on 'fear of crime', what is also often suggested is a crime fighting rationale. There are two versions of this viewpoint. The first is an order maintenance perspective that, if left unchecked, ASB within a neighbour-hood becomes the norm and is causally linked to more serious criminality taking hold (e.g. Wilson and Kelling 1982). The second perspective is in terms of criminal careers (e.g. Farrington 1992) that if the anti-social activities of a young person are not dealt with, then this young person may move onto more serious criminal activity. These two perspectives are considered in turn.

An order maintenance perspective

Of greatest influence here has been a magazine article written over 25 years ago by James Q. Wilson and George Kelling. This is their famous 'broken windows' perspective (1982). Rather than being functionally equivalent, they saw disorder and crime as causally linked. They saw incivilities acting as signals of dereliction that, if left unrepaired, can cause people to think crime is on the rise and also act as attractors for further incivility and crime. They were not the first to focus on incivility in this way and in their article Wilson and Kelling cite an earlier experiment by Philip Zimbardo (1973). Zimbardo described how a car abandoned on a city street became a source of spare parts and then, once stripped, a target for vandalism and a dumping ground for rubbish. His experiment was to buy two old cars, leave them outside the Bronx campus of New York University and in Palo Alto, on a street near Stanford University in California, and film what happened. To indicate the cars were abandoned: 'The licence plates of both cars were removed and the hoods opened to provide the necessary "releaser" signals' (1973: 86). In New York, the stripping started within 10 minutes: 'In less than three days [in the Bronx], what remained was a battered, useless hulk of metal ... In startling contrast, the Palo Alto car not only emerged untouched, but when it began to rain, one passer-by lowered the hood so that the motor would not get wet!' (p. 88). Zimbardo's conclusion was that, for the vandalism to occur, there needed to be suitable 'releaser cues' to indicate the car was abandoned, plus feelings of anonymity, as provided by life in the Bronx but less so in Palo Alto. These ideas were taken much further by Wilson and Kelling. Their view was that low level disorders – like the vandalized car – can damage public confidence and increase fear of crime. This can lead to disempowered local communities as fear causes people to withdraw from public space, thus reducing informal social control and contributing to rising crime and urban decay. Like Zimbardo's idea of 'releaser cues', Wilson and Kelling claimed that once incivility is the norm, others will join in; that 'one unrepaired broken window is a signal that no one cares, and so breaking more windows costs nothing'. Versions of this perspective have attracted a lot of political attention on both sides of the Atlantic (e.g. Taylor 2001; Innes 2004a). And in New York it became the motivation behind Bratton's 'zero tolerance' policing. In Britain, the political focus on ASB at a national level has been closely allied to 'broken windows'. For instance, according to a speech made by Tony Blair when Prime Minister:

> In isolation a bit of vandalism here or graffiti there might seem trivial, but their combined effect can seriously undermine local quality of life. Some criminologists talk of the 'broken window' problem. They argue that a failure to tackle small-scale problems can lead to serious crime and environmental blight. Streets that are dirty and threatening deter people from going out. They signal that the community has lost interest. As a result, anti-social behaviour and more serious criminality may take root. (Tony Blair 2001)

As already noted, certain aspects of 'broken windows' were adopted in New York under a programme that became known as zero tolerance policing (Burke 1998; Kelling 1998). This particular strategy took the 'broken windows' perspective further still. While minor disorders were targeted in order to improve 'quality of life', they were also tackled, not so much because they can lead to crime, but because the perpetrators were often also criminals. It is the classic Al Capone argument that 'big fish' can be caught by focusing on their minor infringements. Chicago gangster Al Capone was famously convicted in 1931 for tax evasion, rather than for his much more serious, but difficult to prosecute, criminal activity. In New York under Bratton, one focus was fare evasion on the transit system. According to George Kelling (1998), one of the authors of the 'broken windows' approach:

> It was discovered that in some neighbourhoods large numbers of fare-beating arrestees either were carrying weapons or had outstanding warrants for serious felonies. Bratton [then Transit Police Chief] immediately communicated these ideas back to police as evidence of the importance of their efforts. Morale soared as crime immediately began a steep decline.

Elsewhere Kelling and Coles (1995) report that squeegee merchants in New York – who come up to your car at a red light to clean your windscreen – were often wanted by the police. Similar targets have been suggested in the UK. For instance, a small study by Chenery et al. (1999) found that people who parked illegally in disabled bays were frequently of interest to the police for more serious crimes, and sometimes because the car itself was stolen. The assumption is that, if committing serious crime is acceptable, then an offender will think nothing of committing more minor indiscretions. It is logical from this position that focusing on local disorder and ASB may also have wider crime control benefits.

However, such a perspective has not received universal approval in Britain (see Jacobson et al. 2005). For instance Brian Hayes (1998), a former Deputy Commissioner of the Metropolitan Police, has written: 'I was given very little convincing evidence in New York that their experience of big fish being caught by targeting minnows would be replicated in London.' His view was that those targeted for 'quality of life' offences in New York were often found to be carrying guns and knives and he did not believe this culture translated to London.[1] There is a bigger problem with this perspective in that a focus on orderliness and ASB means the criminal justice net has to be cast much wider (cf. Cohen 1985). Clearly, not all perpetrators of minor disorders or ASB will be criminally active, or for that matter will all people living in disorderly neighbourhoods – yet they will be labelled as such. This view is supported by Bernard Harcourt (1998, 2001), a vocal critic of the 'broken windows' approach. Harcourt's perspective is clearly shown in the two quotations included in Box 5.1.

Box 5.1 A critic's view of 'broken windows'

The disorderly are, after all, the usual suspects under a regime of order-maintenance policing. The squeegee man, the panhandler, the homeless person, the turnstile jumper, the unattached adult, the public drunk – these are apparently the true culprits of serious crime. Wilson and Kelling refer to them as 'disreputable or obstreperous or unpredictable people'. They are the ones, Wilson and Kelling argue, who turn a stable neighborhood into 'an inhospitable and frightening jungle'. (Harcourt 1998: 343)

The order-maintenance approach turns disorderly persons into dangerous and threatening people. Once upon a time, the disorderly were merely the 'losers' of society ... Today, however, the disorderly are the agents of crime and neighborhood decline. The squeegee man, the peddler, the homeless – they are what *causes* serious crime. Loitering, panhandling, soliciting prostitution, graffiti writing – these activities foster serious criminality. As a result, disorder in itself has become a harm that justified the criminal sanction. (Harcourt 2001: 21)

There is a clear risk of labelling the disorderly or anti-social 'other' as criminally deviant (see also Chapter 3). That said, crime reducing gains can be made, although perhaps not as great as originally claimed by Bratton and his supporters. Eck and Maguire (2000), for instance, conducted a review of studies on 'broken windows' styles of policing in America and found little support for the approach having contributed to the 1990s' drop in crime. As Levitt and Dubner (2005) and Harcourt and Ludvig (2006) have pointed out, crime fell across all the USA, 'even in cities that did not adopt innovative policing strategies' (Harcourt and Ludvig 2006: 299). Despite this, an order maintenance perspective may still have value in gathering intelligence and in apprehending *some* more serious criminals, although it will have to be more sophisticated. It is a question of targeting police resources without unduly focusing on minority or marginalized populations – not an easy thing to do.

Harcourt (2001) has also claimed that, rather than greater orderliness leading to less crime, it is more broadly the greater attention paid to neighbourhoods by police engaged in order maintenance styles of policing. This may lead to resentment of the police among some communities. Jeff Ferrell (2006) has a more fundamental objection to Wilson and Kelling's 'broken windows', and the assumption that such 'symbols' will lead people to think crime is on the rise. According to Ferrell (2006: 262):

> [T]he [broken windows] theory constructs a series of abstract, one-dimensional meanings that it arbitrarily assigns to dislocated images

and idealized audiences. In fact, as any city dweller knows, the symbolic texture of the urban landscape is far more complex. To the extent that 'broken windows' do in fact function as symbols, for example, they may symbolize any manner of activities to any number of audiences, depending on situational and historical context.

Ferrell suggests a more subtle reading of signs of disorder/order. He uses graffiti as an example, some styles of which may indicate a particular ethnic history to some members of a neighbourhood, rather than being read as signs of crime. Also, perhaps a change from gang-related graffiti to hip hop styles may be read as symbols that a neighbourhood has become *less* criminal. As is so often the case, despite attempts at simplicity, there are no simple solutions.

A criminal careers perspective

A further crime control argument is that tackling ASB has the potential to stop perpetrators of deviant activity before they graduate to more serious forms of crime. As outlined in Chapter 4, there is a large literature that focuses on risk and protective factors for the development of anti-social and criminal behaviour (e.g. Farrington 1995b; Prior and Paris 2005; France 2008). I do not want to repeat this here; however, from this perspective, tackling juvenile ASB will logically have benefits in halting a criminal career before it gets going. The study of criminal careers gained some popularity during the last few decades of the twentieth century (e.g. Blumstein et al. 1988; Sampson and Laub 1992). In Britain, the most influential has been the continuing Cambridge Study of Delinquent Development, which ran from 1961 (e.g. West and Farrington 1973; Farrington et al. 2006). Despite its name this study was not in Cambridge; instead it traced 411 males from South London from the age of eight in 1961, up to the age of 50 in 2003. The results have supported a view that peak offending occurs during adolescence. However, the overall picture is more complicated, with frauds – for instance involving tax evasion – being common from age 27 up. Evidence from the Cambridge Study is given in Table 5.1, reproduced from Farrington et al. (2006: 33), showing patterns of self-reported offending at different ages.

Table 5.1 Evidence of criminal careers from the Cambridge study of delinquent development

Offence type	Percent at age				All ages***
	10–14 (n = 405)	15–18 (n = 389)	27–32 (n = 378)	42–7 (n = 365)	(n = 402)
'ASB'					
Vandalism	70.1	21.1	1.1	0.8	74.6
Other offences					
Burglary	12.6	10.8	2.4	0.0	20.4
Theft of vehicle	7.4	15.4	2.9	0.0	20.9
Theft from vehicle	8.9	13.4	2.1	0.5	20.4
Shoplifting	39.8	15.4	5.6	2.2	47.5
Theft from machine	14.6	19.0	1.6	0.3	29.6
Theft from work	*	*	24.1	11.8	28.7
Fraud	*	*	52.6	36.4	64.6
Assault	35.6	62.0	37.1	14.5	73.1
Drug use	0.5	31.4	19.4	17.5	40.0
Any offence (8)**	77.8	76.3	47.4	27.9	93.3

Notes: * No comparable data. ** Prevalence for eight types of offence (excluding fraud and theft from work). *** The 'all ages' number is 402 because all men with self-report data at 2 or more were counted.
Source: Adapted from Farrington et al. 2006: 33.

Of relevance to the study of ASB is the inclusion of 'vandalism' (the only offence type that would fit under most classifications of ASB.[2]) Of those interviewed at age 10–14, 70 percent admitted to vandalism. By the time they were 15–18 this fell to 21 percent and was just 1 percent by age 27–32. While these results show that this particular ASB is most common among adolescents it does not, however, demonstrate causality to later development of a criminal career. From the Cambridge Study evidence it seems most other criminal activity is also most prevalent during the teen years. As a consequence, instead of targeting adolescent ASB to prevent later development of criminal careers, one approach could be to target children younger than 10–14 – in terms of identified risk and protective factors – in order to prevent criminal *and* anti-social careers. Such very early intervention has been tried and is examined in Chapter 8.

A regeneration rationale

A further rationale for tackling ASB is that it has wider regeneration benefits. As noted in Chapter 2, social policy in Britain gained a strong urban focus following the riots in Brixton and elsewhere in 1981 (Scarman 1981; Heseltine 1983). More recently, there has been massive investment in disadvantaged neighbourhoods via various 'area-based initiatives' (ABIs), for instance, via the:

- Single Regeneration Budget 1995–2001 (e.g. Rhodes et al. 2002, 2005)
- New Deal for Communities from 1998 (e.g. ODPM 2005b; Beatty et al. 2008)
- National Strategy for Neighbourhood Renewal/Neighbourhood Renewal Fund from 2000 onwards (e.g. SEU 2000a, b, 2001)
- Neighbourhood Management Pathfinder Programme from 2002 (e.g. SEU 2000c; DCLG 2006a).

In the original consultation document for the National Strategy for Neighbourhood Renewal (SEU 2000b: 44), four key principles for 'renewal' were identified: reviving local economies; reviving communities; decent services; and leadership and joint working. In describing the second principle of 'reviving communities', the government clearly associated revival with tackling ASB (see Box 5.2).

Box 5.2 The government's *National Strategy for Neighbourhood Renewal,* principle 2

Reviving communities: the involvement and leadership of local people is vital to turning round deprived neighbourhoods and helping them to thrive. This means staving off threats to local stability like anti-social behaviour, drugs, crime and the downward spiral of neighbourhood abandonment. But it also means encouraging and harnessing the creative side of community life, building up local people's ability to get involved in decisions that affect them, and giving them opportunities to do so.

Source: SEU 2000b: 44.

The emphasis is on the assumed link between ASB, crime and neighbourhood decline (as with a 'broken windows' perspective); and also that empowered communities have a clear role in 'turning around deprived neighbourhoods' (SEU 2000b: 44). The idea of turning neighbourhoods around has a lot to do with making them attractive and viable – both economically and socially. For instance (and as noted in Chapter 4), at their extreme, problems of ASB are thought to have contributed to 'urban flight' and housing market decline and abandonment (Urban Task Force 1999; Cole and Nevin 2004). The logic is that, by tackling ASB and crime, neighbourhood decline may be stopped or reversed. It is a perspective that has some support in the American literature (e.g. Skogan 1986, 1990; Taylor 1999b). And as noted, it has also found support in British policy on ASB and neighbourhood regeneration (SEU 2000a, b; Millie 2007a). This perspective may downplay other factors that influence neighbourhood decline (Hancock 2006, 2007); however, there is a logic to linking ASB and regeneration strategies. For example, the US criminologist Wesley Skogan (1990: 3) has extended the 'broken windows' view to focus on the role of incivility in creating spirals of neighbourhood decline: 'Disorder erodes what control neighbourhood residents can maintain over local events and conditions. It drives out those for whom stable community life is important, and discourages people with similar values, from moving in. It threatens house prices and discourages investment.' As noted above, Ferrell's (2006) criticism of a 'broken windows' perspective was that it lacked sophistication; essentially that it ignored different audiences' subjectivity in what they read as signals of decline. This may be true; however, there is still value in Skogan's assertion that disorder – or a particular *reading* of disorder – can drive people out of a neighbourhood. More broadly, Skogan was concerned with the role of informal mechanisms of social control in being able to counter 'social disorganisation' (cf. Shaw and McKay 1942), as characterized by poor friendship networks, unsupervised teenage peer groups and low organizational participation (Bursik 1988; Sampson and Grove 1989). These are all factors that are thought to precipitate neighbourhood decline. It is logical from this that *good* informal social control will reverse such decline and 'turn' a neighbourhood around.

However, a link between ASB and decline can be expressed in different ways. Alternative perspectives are given in Box 5.3 which gives three quotations from practitioners interviewed in recent studies of ASB (Millie 2007b). The three views are that (1) ASB leads to neighbourhood decline; (2) that ASB reflects neighbourhood decline; and (3) that ASB is something that will affect wider investment in a town or district.

Box 5.3 Three perspectives linking ASB to
neighbourhood decline

ASB leads to neighbourhood decline:

It can stymie any attempts to improve the neighbourhood if you've got
a continuing anti-social behaviour and crime problem, because the
perceptions are, 'well this isn't an area worth investing in'. More
upwardly mobile residents move out. It can cause a decline in the area.
(Local director of education)

ASB reflects neighbourhood decline:

I think in some ways, things like graffiti de-valuing the public space, or
the public realm that people live in, is often a sign of the decline of a
neighbourhood. (Local director of environmental health)

ASB affects wider investment in a town/district:

If you've got visitors it is very off-putting if there's large amounts of
rubble, litter, whatever it may be, which then has an impact on the
wealth of the area. Because we're obviously affecting business visitors
and tourism to the area. (Community safety partnership officer)

Source: Millie 2007b: 118–19.

In practical terms, it may not be so important to determine causality; as
one respondent in the study put it, 'Something will start off the decline and
then it becomes "chicken and egg" and then you have a downward spiral'
(Millie 2007b: 119). Elsewhere in the same study the positive impact of
neighbourhood regeneration on ASB was noted by a local community
activist. This woman lived in a deprived neighbourhood; as she put it: 'Well
of course, if you live in degradation and poverty then it brings you down'
(2007b: 119). The houses on her street were refurbished, and the properties'
front gardens remodelled along 'defensible space' lines, with new walls to
give clear demarcation between private and public spaces (cf. Newman 1972).
Her response was: 'But it [the regeneration] has given you a lift, you know
what I mean? They've got more people out in their gardens ... I think it's a
different outlook when you don't see the windows closed up.'

There are some problems with a regeneration rational for tackling ASB.
Regeneration that actively involves *all* who live or work in an area may be

beneficial; however, as noted in Chapter 2, there are social justice issues of regeneration efforts that 'reclaim' urban spaces for the exclusive use of certain populations at the expense of others. This can be a particular concern for town and city centre regeneration. The usual suspects of young people, street people and other categories of 'them' may be deemed as anti-social and removed from view, simply because they are seen as offensive to the 'consuming majority' (Bannister et al. 2006). For example, Box 5.4 shows local campaigns in Nottingham against the 'anti-social behaviour' of street begging and graffiti. The message for begging is that it funds drug addiction and that anyone who sees people begging in the city should call an 'anti-social behaviour hotline'. Similarly, if anyone sees graffiti then they should call the city's 'clean up team'. Both examples demonstrate the importance that issues of ASB are thought to have and that, by tackling them, the appeal of Nottingham's city centre will be maintained for the 'consuming majority'.

Box 5.4   Campaigns against ASB in Nottingham city centre

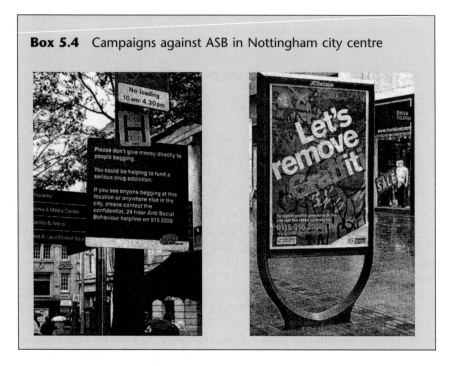

In the evening and night-time city centre, the 'consuming majority' is the group most likely to be accused of ASB. In studies of Swansea and Cardiff (Millie 1997; Bromley et al. 2000), people's perceived insecurity was found to affect whether they would visit the city centre at all in the evening and night. Similarly, those who visit the pubs and clubs that dominate many urban centres may be deterred from certain streets or bars. If the aim of regeneration is to create an economically viable urban centre then, so long as the pubs and clubs are busy there is no concern. However, if the aim is to create inclusive urban living then this can clearly be problematical.

An equality rationale

According to the Home Office's online (2008) *Crime Reduction Toolkit* for ASB, the aim of the toolkit is: 'identifying problems, developing responses and monitoring progress at local neighbourhood level with the aim of making communities safer and creating sustainable areas, in which people wish to live, work and stay'. The aim of 'making communities safer' is fairly uncontroversial. However, linking this to issues of sustainability takes the ASB agenda into a different policy direction. While it is related to a regeneration rationale – with an emphasis on creating places where people wish to 'live, work and stay' – sustainability is a much broader concept. Ever since becoming a major policy objective for New Labour in the early 2000s (see e.g. Johnstone and MacLeod 2007; Raco 2007) the creation of sustainable communities has been closely allied to policy on reducing ASB and crime and making places safer (Defra 2005; ODPM 2005c, d). It also linked to Tony Blair's 'liveability' agenda put forward in a speech in June 2000. According to Blair:

> The one public service we all use all the time is the streets where we live. And in too many place, streets and public spaces have become dirty, ugly and dangerous ... We need to make it safer for children to walk or cycle to school in safety. We need local parks which are well looked after and easily reached by pushchair. We need streets to be free of litter, dog mess and mindless vandalism. (Cited in House of Commons 2003: 7)

This was another government agenda clearly influenced by the 'broken windows' perspective. Of relevance is the concept of 'environmental equality', which simply refers to people's differing access to good quality environments (Eames and Adebowale 2002; Lucus et al. 2004). In literature on environmental equality issues range from access to healthy food and clean air, through to anti-social behaviours such as litter, fly tipping, graffiti and vandalism. The logic is that, neighbourhoods where such ASB is highest become poorer quality environments in which to live or work. As these are also frequently some of the more deprived social housing estates – as shown in Chapter 2 – then there is a compounded disadvantage to living in such neighbourhoods. The view is that *all* neighbourhoods should be attractive and absent of ASB, and it is ASB that contributes to their assumed lack of sustainability. Of course, what *is* a quality environment is open to subjective interpretation. As noted above with regard to the 'broken windows' perspective, the sensibilities of one group may be offended by visible cues of degradation and disorder, such as graffiti or poor neighbourhood repair; yet this might be viewed differently and be acceptable to at least some of those who actually live there. According to Johnstone and MacLeod (2007: 75):

> In the endeavour to create such 'sustainable communities', the government … is actively targeting visible signs of 'disorder' within England's 'broken' neighbourhoods, ranging from void housing and a degraded urban environment to forms of anti-social behaviour (ASB) that are likely to unsettle the sensibilities of 'respectable' citizens.

This brings us back to the discussion in Chapter 3 regarding the labelling or 'othering' of anti-social people or neighbourhoods. With regard the creation of sustainable communities, there is a clear danger of imposing the sensibilities of the 'respectable' on people and places deemed to be 'disrespectable' – or as Blair saw it, places that are 'dirty, ugly and dangerous'. If the reason for tackling ASB is to include an element of 'equality', then this ought to be without imposing views of respectability from on high.

A community building rationale

In Chapter 4, it was suggested that people's reluctance to intervene in cases of ASB can be viewed as reflecting a lack of informal social control. It could be argued that, while *improved* informal social control can be regarded as a mechanism for tackling ASB, the reverse may also be true. Tackling ASB may itself lead to greater collective efficacy, or 'social cohesion among neighbors combined with their willingness to intervene on behalf of the common good' (Sampson et al. 1997: 918), thus improving mechanisms of informal social control – a process ultimately leading to the building of 'community'.

New Labour in particular, with its communitarian leanings (e.g. Hughes 1996), has been keen to encourage 'community'. In terms of crime control, ever since the Morgan Report (Home Office 1991) recommended the delivery of crime prevention through local partnership working,[3] community has been regarded central to the governance of crime in Britain. However, 'community' has remained a moving target and is, simply, not easy to define. It can refer to a particular geographical location, there can be communities of common interest, there are religious communities, virtual online communities or even the global community. However, in policy on ASB community is usually equated to neighbourhood, although within any neighbourhood there may be any number of 'plural communities' (see e.g. Crawford 1997; Jones and Newburn 2001). Despite this muddle, the government has been keen to encourage 'community involvement' and to nurture collective efficacy or 'social capital'.

In Britain, communities (or more accurately neighbourhoods) have been canvassed for their policing priorities – an idea tried in Chicago with the Chicago Alternative Policing Strategy (Skogan and Hartnett 1997) and, as noted, translated into a British context via 'reassurance policing' and more recently 'neighbourhood policing'. In terms of ASB, there is scope in exploring these ideas and developing a shared governance of ASB strategies at a local level between residents or users of public spaces and agencies (Millie et al. 2005a). It is an approach that was picked up as part of the Respect Action Plan (Respect Task Force 2006). However, there will be questions of whether those canvassed are representative of *all* local views, including those of marginalized populations. Similarly, so-called 'community leaders' are often self-appointed and may only represent the views of particular interest groups (e.g. Jones and Newburn 2001). There is also a risk that community governance of crime can be interpreted at the neighbourhood level as vigilantism (Johnston 1996; Edwards and Hughes 2002). Robert Putnam (2000: 21–2) in his work on American community life and social capital gives the following warning:

> Sometimes 'social capital', like its conceptual cousin 'community', sounds warm and cuddly ... Networks and the associated norms of reciprocity are generally good for those inside the network, but the external effects of social capital are by no means always positive ... urban gangs, NIMBY ('not in my backyard') movements, and power elites often exploit social capital to achieve ends that are antisocial from a wider perspective. Indeed, it is rhetorically useful for such groups to obscure the difference between the pro-social and antisocial consequences of community organizations ... Social capital, in short, can be directed toward malevolent, antisocial purposes, just like any other form of capital.

Putnam went on to suggest that, 'it is important to ask how the positive consequences of social capital – mutual support, cooperation, trust, institutional effectiveness – can be maximized, and the negative manifestations – sectarianism, ethnocentrism, corruption – minimized' (2000: 22). He usefully divides the concept of social capital into bonding and bridging social capital. Bonding social capital is exclusive and inward looking and can be exemplified by involvement in certain sports or social clubs, ethnocentric organizations or some faith organizations. Bridging social capital by contrast is more outward looking and inclusive with examples being civil rights movements, certain youth groups and interfaith organizations. It is not as simple as one being always better than then other; as Putnam observes (2000: 22): 'Bonding social capital is good for undergirding reciprocity and mobilizing solidarity.' But the encouragement of bridging social capital will be more useful if the aim is to involve all within a neighbourhood in the local governance of ASB. Similarly, the reverse may be true that a focus on local ASB may act as a catalyst for promoting more inclusive or bridging social capital.

But this does not have to be a formally constituted arrangement; as Misztal has noted (2000: 238). 'The fine-tuning of informality and formality is central to the creation of social trust'. According to Harris (2006b: 122): 'Formal systems are characterised by inertia, they need constantly to be refreshed; whereas social relationships in neighbourhoods are organic, requiring a healthy ecology that reflects informality and also requiring that most of the time formality keeps its distance.'

This is a situation that policy makers in government may find difficult. As Harris also notes (2006b: 122), while, 'government explores ways of encouraging civility within a formal network', it is also often from a confrontational perspective with the, 'announcement of a "Respect Squad" from which "Mission Squads" will be selected and will emerge to do battle with locals behaving anti-socially'. This is an approach that is not likely to lead to improvements in inclusiveness, collective efficacy, social capital or 'community'.

To benefit the agencies involved

The cynical perspective is that ASB will be tackled purely for the benefit of government and the agencies involved. There is the possibility that the government can benefit from an aggressive policy on ASB as the result is greater social control of 'dangerous' populations – a view perhaps having more in common with 'underclass' theory (e.g. Murray 1990). As suggested in Chapter 1, politicians may have created or exaggerated the problem of ASB in order to create a target for public fears. This could then be seen to be tackled by a benevolent state. This is similar to that claimed by Curtis (2004) in his documentary about the war on terror, that much of the threat was a 'phantom menace', with fear being used as a powerful political tool. As Hughes and Follett (2006:161) have noted:

> [T]he problem of 'anti-social behaviour' may also be interpreted as a classic 'moral panic', stoked up by politicians seeking votes and mass media campaigners chasing improved readership figures by trading on the politics of fear, whether it be the *stranger* both without and

within the nation (epitomised by the asylum seeker ...) or, in this case, the 'anti-social' *outcast* from the domestically reared 'under-class'.

It seems unlikely that the government has been quite so calculating as to have created the problem, after all, there are genuine concerns of ASB in some neighbourhoods. However, there is strong evidence that these concerns have been *exaggerated* (as explored in Chapter 2). For the Labour Party, the idea of political benefit from tackling ASB was strongly informed by their exposure to 'broken windows' styles of policing, especially in New York (Millie et al. 2005a; Hughes and Follett 2006). For instance, in 1995 Labour's Jack Straw – then Shadow Home Secretary – met with Commissioner Bill Bratton in New York to discuss the apparent successes in reducing crime. As Ben Bowling (1999: 531–2) observed:

> Straw could hardly have failed to be impressed by the good news stories which had been arriving in the UK from across the Atlantic. Among the headlines were: Crime is Down, Again; the Suddenly Safer City ... as *New York* magazine put it – with 'Biggest Apple' understatement – The End of Crime as We Know it. Mr Straw returned from New York flirting with a new catch phrase – 'zero tolerance' – and pledging that if it won the next general election Labour would 'reclaim the streets for the law abiding majority' from the 'aggressive begging of winos, addicts and squeegee merchants'.

As populist campaigns go (see Garland 2001; Roberts et al. 2002), this must have seemed like a winning ticket. Throughout the 1990s there had been an increased politicization of crime in many Western countries, but particularly in Great Britain (e.g. Tonry 2004; Newman and Jones 2005). And ever since Tony Blair's famous speech in opposition in 1992, claiming to be 'tough on crime', and 'tough on the causes of crime', there has been 'a fight between Labour and the Conservatives for an assumed popular vote, with greater emphasis on populist and punitive policies' (Millie 2008b: 107). There was clear political advantage in devising innovative, yet punitive, crime control strategies. For Labour this translated into a focus on ASB. Since then all three main political parties have adopted policies on ASB.

A less cynical view is that there may be further benefits to the agencies involved because they are tackling issues that are important to the public. This may translate into a growth in support for the agencies involved. For the police, by involving the general population in policing decisions – as with reassurance/neighbourhood policing – then there is possible payback in greater confidence in the police, and legitimacy for policing decisions (FitzGerald et al. 2002; Millie and Herrington 2005). A lot of work to tackle ASB will involve closer working between different interested parties, be they the police, local authority, registered social landlord or perhaps town centre manager. There is a possible further benefit in that such partnership arrangements could be strengthened. And, following a crime fighting perspective (either in terms of 'broken windows' or in terms of criminal careers) there could be longer term financial benefits to tackling ASB; as claimed in the government's white paper on ASB (Home Office 2003c: 14), '[E]ffective action will not only improve people's quality of life by dealing with the problem, it will also free up the time and resources of those who deal with its consequences'. If problems of ASB *do* lead to more serious crime and environmental decline, then tackling issues before they get too serious is logically going to be cheaper. Of course, the evidence is ASB leading to crime is less certain.

As a way of by-passing the criminal justice system

In this final section it is suggested that the concept of 'ASB' was introduced by politicians because, by using civil law or 'summary justice' for 'minor crimes', this could by-pass a slow and expensive criminal justice system. Tony Blair, in particular, seemed to have lost faith in the criminal justice system (Blair 2003), for instance claiming that, 'it is next to impossible for the police to prosecute without protracted court process, bureaucracy and hassle, when conviction will only result in a minor sentence' (see also Chapter 1). According to the 2003/04 BCS this view seems at first to have public support, in that three-quarters thought courts are too lenient (Allen et al. 2005). However, when the public is asked how confident it is in the criminal justice system (CJS) it tends to be more supportive. Results from the 2003/04 BCS showed that three-quarters of respondents were fairly or very confidence in the CJS (Allen et al. 2005). And according to a 2003 MORI survey (see Roberts and Hough 2005: 36) 56 percent of people are satisfied with the way crime is dealt with in their local area. A lot depends on what specific question is asked. For the MORI survey, only 34 percent were satisfied with the way crime is dealt with nationally. But whilst acknowledging public frustrations with the courts, a push to by-pass the CJS seems to have come more from politicians. By using civil measures associated with ASB legislation, this is a way of restricting the behaviour of people who are otherwise criminal, but where there is not the evidence for a criminal prosecution. A case in point is the use of ASBO powers to tackle more serious criminality (more of which in Chapter 6).

Concluding comments

In this chapter, a variety of rationales for tackling ASB have been considered, ranging from ASB being a 'bad thing', that it has an impact on fear of crime, or actual criminality, or that it affects regeneration. Similarly, ASB can be tacked as an issue of inequality or as a way of 'community' building. The aim may also be to by-pass the CJS – despite the due process concerns that go with such a perspective. What you think causes ASB will have an impact on strategies put in place to tackle ASB. Similarly, the rationale for tackling ASB will dictate the form of enforcement or prevention. For instance, if the aim of tackling ASB is to catch more serious criminals for minor indiscretions (as in New York), then the method will be focused on high profile police work and enforcement. If the objective is to tackle ASB as an issue of environmental inequality, then strategies will have more balance between enforcement and prevention. In the following three chapters, different enforcement and preventative options are considered, starting with the Anti-Social Behaviour Order. When reading these three chapters, it is worth considering what rationales for tackling ASB are most relevant to these approaches. Also bear in mind the range of causal factors and how these relate to different enforcement and preventative strategies.

Selected reading

Much of this chapter draws on work I did with Mike Hough and Jessica Jacobson at the Institute for Criminal Policy Research at King's College London. A summary of this work can be found in Jacobson et al. (2008). For literature on a crime fighting rationale the best place to start is Wilson and Kelling's (1982) famous magazine article; but also look at counter arguments (e.g. Harcourt 2001). For a regeneration rationale the work of Lynn Hancock is a good place to start. The list below is not exhaustive, but covers some of the main perspectives considered in this chapter:

- Farrington, D. P., Coid, J. W., Hartnett, L. M. et al. (2006) Criminal careers up to age 50 and life success up to age 48: new findings from the Cambridge Study in Delinquent Development. Home Office Research Study No. 299. London: Home Office.
- Hancock, L. (2007) Is urban regeneration criminogenic? in R. Atkinson and G. Helms (eds), *Securing an Urban Renaissance: Crime, Community, and British Urban Policy*. Bristol: Policy Press.
- Harcourt, B. E. (2001) *Illusion of Order: The False Promise of Broken Windows Policing*. Cambridge, MA: Harvard University Press.
- Jacobson, J., Millie, A. and Hough, M. (2008) Why tackle anti-social behaviour? in P. Squires (ed.), *ASBO Nation: The Criminalisation of Nuisance*. Bristol: Policy Press.
- Millie, A. (2007b) Tackling anti-social behaviour and regenerating neighbourhoods, in R. Atkinson and G. Helms (eds), *Securing an Urban Renaissance: Crime, Community and British Urban Policy*. Bristol: Policy Press.
- Wilson, J. Q. and Kelling, G. L. (1982) Broken windows: the police and neighbourhood safety, *The Atlantic Monthly*, Mar., 249(3): 29–38.

Notes

1   Although he may have since changed his mind following more recent crime developments in Britain's capital.
2   Farrington et al. (2006: 60) talk about anti-social behaviour, but from a psychosocial perspective relating to anti-social personality. Here I have focused on ASB as understood from a public order enforcement perspective.

3   Delivered in the form of 'Crime and Disorder Reduction Partnerships' (CDRPs), following the 1998 Crime and Disorder Act.

6 The anti-social behaviour order (ASBO)

> It's official. We are now living in 'ASBO Nation' ... in a week when the word 'ASBO' entered the Collins English Dictionary and a Hull poet researching dog names for a literary festival discovered a Staffordshire bull terrier called ASBO. (Bright et al. 2005)

Any text on ASB in Britain would be incomplete without due consideration of the Anti-Social Behaviour Order, or ASBO. As the above quotation demonstrates, the term 'ASBO', for better or worse, is now firmly embedded in the British consciousness to the extent that we are thought to live in an 'ASBO nation' (see also Squires 2008). As noted previously, the Labour government's strategy and campaigning on ASB has come under a number of banners; however, the assumed merit of tough enforcement has been central throughout. There was the Home Office 'Together' strategy from 2002 to 2006 and then the 'Respect' agenda from 2006 to 2007. Then this was replaced by the Youth Taskforce in October 2007, under the steerage of Ed Balls, MP, at the Department for Children, Schools and Families. With the launch of the Youth Taskforce Action Plan in March 2008 (Youth Taskforce 2008) there was a noticeable shift in rhetoric – a minor shift, but a shift nevertheless. Soon after being appointed as Children's Secretary in Gordon Brown's first cabinet, Ed Balls stated: 'Every Anti-Social Behaviour Order marks a failure ... It's a failure every time a young person gets an ASBO. It's necessary – but it's not right ... I want to live in the kind of society that puts ASBOs behind us' (reported by Blackman in the *Daily Mirror*, 2007). This was signified as a break from Blair's tough line on crime and ASB (e.g. by Branigan in the *Guardian* 2007). However, by the time the Youth Taskforce Action Plan was published (Youth Taskforce 2008: 8) there was still an emphasis on 'making good use of the strong package of measures that the Government has developed', and toughness was still central to the plan. The Action Plan called for a three-track 'deeper' approach to tackling ASB centred on: (1) tough enforcement; (2) non-negotiable support; and (3) better prevention (p. 9). Clearly, despite the softer rhetoric of politicians a hard line on ASB – and the use of ASBOs in particular – is not going to disappear in a hurry.

Ever since their introduction with the 1998 Crime and Disorder Act, ASBOs have gained praise and condemnation, almost in equal measure. In this chapter, the merits and limitations of the order are considered; but, first, it is worth considering their popularity among the public. In a national survey on ASB (Millie et al. 2005a: 13) respondents were asked the following hypothetical question: 'If there was more money to spend in your local area on tackling ASB, should this be spent on tough action against perpetrators, or preventative action to deal with the causes?' This may have been a slightly loaded question; however, the responses were telling. Only 20 percent opted for 'tough action', whereas 66 percent chose 'preventative action'. This would put into question the government's emphasis on toughness in response to ASB, the central pillar of this approach being the use of ASBOs. However, there was support for ASBOs specifically. First, the majority (63%) had heard of the order. They then had ASBOs explained to them and were asked about their likely effectiveness: 60 percent thought they would be effective in dealing with disruptive neighbours and 55 percent effective with youths who disrupt their neighbourhood.

It is worth noting that this particular survey was conducted in April 2004. By May 2005 in a national survey by Ipsos Mori, 92 percent had heard of ASBOs (although this included 55 percent who know just a little about ASBOs or had heard of them, but knew nothing about them). According to the Ipsos Mori survey 39 percent thought ASBOs are effective at 'stopping people from causing anti-social behaviour', whereas 46 percent thought they were either not very effective or not effective at all. There was greater confidence in the use of ASBOs in 'showing the local community that something is being done about anti-social behaviour' (53 percent effective). Respondents were then given some information about the order and asked if they supported the issuing of ASBOs to people responsible for ASB. In this case, a massive 82 percent supported the use of ASBOs (including 42 percent who strongly supported it).

This survey evidence indicates that, while people generally prefer preventative action over tough enforcement, when ASBOs are explained, the orders do have public support and this support is despite a general perception that they will not work (for instance, 46 percent of the Ipsos Mori respondents thought they were ineffective at actually stopping people from committing ASB).

Origins of the ASBO

The ASBO originated in a 1995 Labour Party report, entitled *A Quiet Life: Tough Action on Criminal Neighbours*. At that time the proposal was for a generic 'Community Safety Order' and – as the title of the report suggests – the focus was on criminal acts. However, quoting work on repeat criminal victimization by Farrell and Pease (1993), the report also emphasized persistence; more specifically the *'repeated* acts of nuisance or aggression, each one in itself not enough to attract significant punishment' (Burney 2005: 19). According to *A Quiet Life* (1995: 1), everyone has 'a right to go about their lawful business without harassment, interference or criminal behaviour by their neighbours'. The proposal was for: 'a new composite charge ... as one criminal offence where there has been a series of linked incidents of anti-social behaviour or harassment. This single serious offence should enable the courts to impose an appropriate level of punishment' (Labour Party 1995: 1).

According to Burney (2005: 20) two issues were highlighted: 'insufficient punishment for repeat low-level crimes and witness intimidation'. Together these contributed to what the report called the current 'system failure'. It was a concern that residents in certain neighbourhoods were suffering from the 'dripping tap' of minor crimes and that very little could be done legally about it. To illustrate the argument a case of 'Family X' was given, where a Blackburn family 'terrorized' their neighbourhood, 'despite numerous court appearances for attempted robbery, burglary, damage and public disorder' (Burney 2005: 20). The report also cited the case of *Coventry City Council v. Finnie* (1995).[1] The Finnie brothers were aged 26 and 29 and their criminal activity on a particular estate was enough for the city council to seek their exclusion from this area. The council attempted to use existing injunction powers under the 1972 Local Government Act (s.222 (1)), giving the brothers a one-mile exclusion zone. According to *A Quiet Life* (1995: 3):

> The two brothers were allegedly responsible for a series of crimes on the estate and had served custodial sentences for offences ranging from burglary to assault. Their mother, Janet Finnie, 54, welcomed the decision to ban them. 'My boys have caused havoc around here and I feel extremely sorry for the other families' she said.

According to Macdonald (2006: 196): '[A]t the *ex parte* hearing hearsay evidence had been admissible. So it had not been necessary to identify witnesses in order to obtain the injunction.' However, the Finnies later applied to have the injunction set aside, leading to the council withdrawing, as they could not get any victims or witnesses to come forward.

The theme of a criminal justice 'system failure' was further explored in another Labour Party document by MPs Jack Straw and Alun Michael (1996).

This time the focus was on youth offending more broadly, according to which, 'the youth justice system in England and Wales is in disarray. It simply does not work' (p. 1). In line with a criminal careers perspective (see Chapter 5) the emphasis was on tackling unacceptable behaviour before it progressed to more serious crime: 'The public are inadequately safeguarded, victims despair, the agencies involved grow more frustrated and the persistent young offenders too often go unchecked. Too little is done to change youngsters' behaviour early in their offending career' (Straw and Michael 1996: 1).

Criminal justice was clearly going to be a priority for Labour; and one of its pledges in its May 1997 election manifesto was the introduction of the 'Community Safety Order'. By September 1997 it had produced a consultation document on the proposed order; however, the focus had shifted from 'unlawful acts' to anti-social behaviour. By the time of the 1998 Crime and Disorder Bill (and Act) the Community Safety Order had morphed into the ASBO and its focus had shifted even further away from being a criminal sanction. These shifts in focus are demonstrated in the three quotations included in Box 6.1 – the first taken from *A Quiet Life*, the second from the 1997 consultation paper and the third from the 1998 Act. The ASBO became part of British civil law in April 1999.

Box 6.1 Narrowing of focus to ASB with the 1998 Crime and Disorder Bill

Taken from A *Quiet Life* (Labour Party 1995: 9):

'An application for an order could be sought where there was evidence of chronic anti-social behaviour. This could include: a) multiple convictions ... b) evidence of the commission of such multiple offences, even where there had not been a conviction; other evidence of unlawful acts by an individual or members of his or her household likely to interfere with the peace and comfort of a residential occupier. In this connection, 'unlawful acts' would include a criminal offence or civil wrongs such as tort, nuisance, trespass, assault, interference with goods etc ...'

Taken from *Community Safety Order: A consultation paper* (Home Office 1997 paras 1 and 9):

'Anti-social behaviour causes distress and misery to innocent, law-abiding people – and undermines the communities in which they live. Neighbourhood harassment by individuals or groups, often under the influence of alcohol or drugs, has often reached unacceptable levels, and revealed a serious gap in the ability of the authorities to tackle this social menace ... The conduct which would trigger consideration of an application for a Community Safety Order will be set out in statute. It will include conduct which: causes harassment to a community; amounts to anti-social criminal conduct, or is otherwise anti-social; disrupts the peaceful and quiet enjoyment of a neighbourhood by others; intimidates a community or a section of it.'

Taken from the *1998 Crime and Disorder Act* (s.1):

'An application for an order under this section may be made by a relevant authority if it appears to the authority that the following conditions are fulfilled with respect to any person aged 10 or over, namely: (a) that the person has acted, since the commencement date, in an anti-social manner, that is to say, in a manner that caused or was likely to cause harassment, alarm or distress to one or more persons not of the same household as himself; and (b) that such an order is necessary to protect persons in the local government area in which the harassment, alarm or distress was caused or was likely to be caused from further anti-social acts by him ...'

ASBOs as civil law

As introduced, the ASBO has acted as a two-step prohibition (Simester and von Hirsch 2006; see also Chapter 1). It is two step in that it is a civil order in the first instance; however, breach of the order is a criminal offence carrying with it criminal censure. According to Macdonald (2003: 630): 'The structure of a civil injunction with criminal penalties for breach was designed so as to allow the orders to be imposed without the necessity of ... frightened and intimidated people, frequently neighbours, giving evidence'; at least, this was the original intention (Labour Party 1995). Yet when introduced in the 1998 Crime and Disorder Act, it was not that clear whether ASBOs were punishment or preventative or whether they were entirely civil or criminal, or new pseudo-criminal law that fitted somewhere in between; as Gardner et al. (1998) suggested, it seemed to be a 'hybrid law from hell'. Early Home Office guidance (1999) did not help in claiming that ASB is both criminal and sub-criminal behaviour. It is an important point of law with implications for admissibility of evidence and also relates to Article 6 of the European Convention on Human Rights.[2] As Andrew Ashworth (2004: 289) has noted, 'the government intended to sail as close to the wind as possible' in having the benefits of both civil and criminal law, one example being 'sentencing on breach that would take account of earlier conduct not proven or admitted in a criminal court'.

Some *form* of clarity came with the House of Lords' judgement in *Clingham and McCann* (2002)[3] (Bakalis 2003; Macdonald 2003; Burney 2005; Judicial Studies Board 2007). In making judgement, the Law Lords agreed that ASBOs are preventative 'for the purposes of protecting persons from further anti-social conduct' (Lord Hope para. 75). It was also agreed that ASBOs are civil orders; for instance, according to Lord Styne (para. 18):

> There is no doubt that Parliament intended to adopt the model of a civil remedy of an injunction, backed up by criminal penalties ... The view was taken that the proceedings for an anti-social behaviour order would be civil and would not attract the rigour of the inflexible and sometimes absurdly technical hearsay rule which applies in criminal cases.

The explanation given for ASBOs being civil orders was that:

> The Crown Prosecution Service is not involved in the decision; ASBOs do not appear on criminal records; There is no immediate imposition of imprisonment ... The equivalent in Scotland is clearly intended to be civil; [and] ASBOs ... are designed to prevent anti-social behaviour rather than to punish the offender. (Bakalis 2003: 583–4)

How much the prevention imperative of issuing an ASBO can be separated from the criminal punishment for breach is a moot point. But, according to Lord Hutton (para. 113), in the same judgement:

> [T]he striking of a fair balance between the demands of the general interest of the community (... represented by weak and vulnerable people who claim that they are the victims of anti-social behaviour which violates their rights) and the requirements of the protection of the defendants' rights requires the scales to come down in favour of the protection of the community and of permitting the use of hearsay evidence in applications for anti-social behaviour orders.

Thus ASBOs are clearly civil (despite breach being criminal) and hearsay evidence is admissible, including the use of professional witnesses. There has been criticism of this position. For example, Bakalis (2003: 585) questions why ASBOs deserve special treatment: 'would not *all* criminal offences be more effectively and easily prosecuted without the rule against hearsay evidence?' According to the 1995 Civil Evidence Act (s.1(2)a) hearsay evidence is defined as 'a statement made otherwise than by a person while giving oral evidence in the proceedings which is tendered as evidence of the matters stated'. In ASBO cases, there are some caveats attached to its use; for instance:

> Hearsay evidence is admissible under the Civil Evidence Act 1995. However 'the willingness of a civil court to admit hearsay evidence carries with it inherent dangers'. Claimants should state, by convincing direct evidence, why it is not reasonable and practicable to produce the original makers of statements as witnesses. If statements involve multiple hearsay, the route by which the original statement came to the attention of the person attesting to it should be identified as far as practicable. When hearing such applications, it is better for judges to start their judgements with an analysis of the direct oral evidence received, and then to move onto the evidence of the absent named witnesses and anonymous witnesses.[4] (Judicial Studies Board 2007: 43)

The full list of admissible evidence in ASBO cases is given in Box 6.2.

Box 6.2 Evidence on behalf of the applicant in ASBO cases

Evidence can include:

- Evidence of breach of an ABC (Acceptable Behaviour Contract)
- Witness statements of officers who attended incidents
- Witness statements of people affected by the behaviour
- Evidence of complaints recorded by the police, housing providers or other agencies
- Witness statements from professional witnesses, for example council officials, health visitors or truancy officers
- Video or CCTV evidence
- Supporting statements or reports from other agencies, for example probation reports
- Previous relevant civil proceedings, such as an eviction order for similar behaviour
- Previous relevant convictions
- Copies of custody records of previous arrests relevant to the application
- Information from witness diaries

Source: Home Office (2006a: 22); Judicial Studies Board (2007: 22–3).

ASBO characteristics

As introduced, ASBO cases were heard by magistrates sitting as a civil court.[5] As civil orders, the legal test was intended as the civil 'balance of probabilities', rather than the criminal 'beyond reasonable doubt' (Ashworth et al. 1998). However, following the House of Lords ruling in *Clingham and McCann*[6] (e.g. Macdonald 2003; Burney 2006) it was decided that the criminal standard of proof should apply, despite also concluding that the ASBO is *not* a criminal charge. To further muddy the picture, as noted, hearsay evidence was still admissible. In the ruling, Lord Hope (para. 82) focused on the consequences for the recipient, which can be very severe: 'I think that there are good reasons, in the interests of fairness, for applying the higher standard of proof when allegations are made of criminal or quasi-criminal conduct which, if proved, would have serious consequences for the person against whom they are made'.

According to the 1998 Crime and Disorder Act (s.1): 'An application for an order under this section may be made by a relevant authority.' This 'relevant authority' was stipulated as either the local authority or police. This has since expanded to include: local authorities, police, British Transport Police, registered social landlords or housing action trusts, the Environment Agency, Transport for London or 'any person or body of any other description specified in an order made by the Secretary of State' (Judicial Studies Board 2007: 6). ASBOs are for a minimum of two years in duration and can be indefinite in length (there is no mechanism for renewal). There has been concern that two years is unduly long for juveniles, let alone having an ASBO indefinitely. ASBOs can be given to anyone from the age of 10. Developmentally and socially a lot can happen over two years in a child's or young person's life. As a result, the Howard League for Penal Reform (2005) has called for the abolition of ASBOs for children. The director of the charity, Frances Crook, has stated: 'Prevention and welfare should be the only factors when deciding how to respond to children who misbehave and penal sanctions should have no place.' ASBOs also come with powerful restrictions on liberty with the following limitations:

- *Geographical*: Limits on where the recipient can be. These restrictions can be on a particular street or for a local authority area. Following the 2002 Police Reform Act (s.61), restrictions could be for the whole of England and Wales. Those applied for by British Transport Police can be, for instance, from the whole national railway network
- *Temporal*: Restrictions on the time that the recipient may be in certain locations

- *Association*: Restrictions on who the recipient may be seen with
- *Behavioural*: Restrictions on certain behaviours.

According to Ashworth (2005) there is no limit to the number or combination of conditions that can be attached to an order and that 10–15 conditions is not unusual (see also Burney 2002; Campbell 2002). And following the judgement in *McGrath* (2005),[7] '[t]here is no requirement that the acts prohibited should by themselves give rise to harassment, alarm or distress' (Sentencing Advisory Panel 2007: 7). There is concern that some ASBOs are issued with entirely inappropriate conditions. For instance, according to the children's charity Barnardo's (2005: 2):

> The conditions of ASBOs made on children give cause for concern; many of them appear to be very lengthy (almost all banning orders are for two years or more) and some are almost 'undoable', for example three brothers were given lifetime bans from a town centre. Some of the conditions are actually counterproductive ... [for example, a] young man was banned from the area of town in which his drug rehabilitation treatment was located.

Giving evidence to the Home Affairs Committee (House of Commons 2005: 69) Rod Morgan, then chair of the Youth Justice Board, was asked if inappropriate conditions were common. His response was that, while he could not say definitively: 'My suspicion is that it is relatively uncommon.' Common or not, inappropriate cases have been cited and some particularly illuminating examples are given in Box 6.3.

Box 6.3   Examples of inappropriate ASBOs or inappropriate conditions

A young person in Sussex whose ASBO precluded him from entering any motor vehicle. This meant he was unable to accept lifts from YOT [Youth Offending Team] staff to Positive Activities schemes. It also meant he could not go into a probation minibus to take him to do his community service. (House of Commons 2005: 68)*

In one case, a young person's home was in the exclusion zone and had a bail condition to reside at his home address. (House of Commons 2005: 68)**

Kim Sutton, a 23-year-old woman ... [was banned] from jumping into rivers, canals or onto railway lines after she had attempted suicide on four occasions. At her appeal against the order, Sutton's counsel not only argued that her personality disorder meant that she needed help and that legal sanctions could be counter-productive, but also that the effect of the ASBO was to criminalise suicide and attempted suicide, which are not criminal offences. (Macdonald 2006: 199)

In 2004 an 18-year-old youth was made the subject of an ASBO in [Manchester] ... with a condition not to congregate with three or more other youths. He was subsequently arrested for breach of his order when he was entering a local youth club on the grounds that there were more than three youths in the premises. This was a successful club with a good reputation ... and on that particular evening the session scheduled for the youths was how to deal with anti-social behaviour. (Fletcher 2005: 5)

[A] 13 year old autistic boy was served with an ASBO after neighbours complained about the noise the boy was making when jumping on his trampoline – notwithstanding the fact that the local authority were aware he had autism and that trampolining has been found to be therapeutic for people with autism. (Macdonald, 2006: 198–9)

Notes: * Ev 149, HC 80–11 (Youth Justice Board). ** Ev 27, HC 80–11 (Children's Society).

Of course, there may well be other examples of ASBOs that have been entirely appropriate for the recipients' particular circumstances. However, what these examples demonstrate is that more thought is needed when ASBOs – and ASBO restrictions – are considered. Returning to the Home Affairs Committee (House of Commons 2005: 4), its recommendation was that, 'the minimum term of ASBOs (currently two years) be removed in relation to young people and [we] consider that research is necessary to establish the reasons for those few ASBOs which have been issued inappropriately or contain inappropriate conditions.'

Categories of ASBO

Since introduction the scope and range of ASBO sanctions has grown. As noted, following the 1998 Crime and Disorder Act ASBOs were initially only available via the magistrates' court sitting in a civil capacity. Such orders are now referred to as *stand-alone ASBOs* as they are the sole purpose of the hearing. A big change came with the 2002 Police Reform Act (s.65), which saw the introduction of the *interim stand-alone ASBO*. Prior to a full hearing an interim ASBO can be granted '[w]here there is an urgent need to protect the community' (Home Office 2004b).[8] The 2002 Police Reform Act also expanded the scope of ASBOs to include 'orders in county court proceedings' (s.63) and 'orders on conviction in criminal proceedings' (s.64). *County Court*

ASBOs are fairly self-explanatory, in that they were introduced to cover the ASB of someone party to county court proceedings – for instance, a registered social landlord seeking possession. The orders on conviction represented more of a departure as they shifted focus to the anti-social consequences of someone's *criminal* behaviour. These orders have become known as 'criminal ASBOs', or *CrASBOs*.[9] In such instances, the case is heard in a magistrates' criminal court or in a crown court. Following the 2005 Serious Organised Crime and Police Act (s.139) the CrASBO is also available as an *interim order on conviction*.

If the introduction of ASBOs is controversial, then the use of interim ASBOs has the potential to be even more so. An interim order is given in an attempt to immediately address the recipient's alleged misbehaviour. But in the hurry for prevention and prohibition, the order is given only on the evidence of the 'relevant authority'. Squires and Stephen (2005a: 99) have observed that, '[c]ases may be determined without the defendant necessarily being heard – and, in the case of Interim Orders, without the defendant even being notified' (see also Stone 2004). Someone given an interim ASBO may, in theory at least, have it repealed once he or she has a full hearing for a stand-alone ASBO or CrASBO. But the problem is one of presumption of innocence. If someone is already given an interim order, then the presumption is surely one of guilt at the hearing for a full stand-alone order? As the Director of Liberty, Shami Chakrabarti (2006: 18), has argued about ASBOs more broadly:

> [T]alk of prevention and prohibition permits successful argument in our highest courts that run directly counter to political pronouncements. In this parallel universe judges have on occasion been persuaded that the presumption of innocence is not breached by legislation that is preventative rather than punitive in nature. In reality, however, and over time, the new antisocial behaviour justice system delivers swifter, easier and harsher accusation, proof and punishment.

There is further controversy surrounding the use of CrASBOs as they shift the agenda, in a form of mission creep, away from controlling ASB to controlling crime. At court, the sentencer has the option to grant a CrASBO post-criminal conviction. Initially, there was some confusion whether this gave the sentencer a second bite at the cherry, so to speak, that the accused was being punished twice for the same offence. The counter argument – and the one that has been used to justify the use of CrASBOs – is that a sentence upon conviction (a criminal sanction) is designed as punishment of the offence committed; however, the post-conviction ASBO (a civil sanction) is designed to be preventative of similar behaviour occurring in the future. From a policy perspective this may sound ideal as in means the law becomes tailored to an individual's misbehaviour. However, this had further blurred the boundaries between civil and criminal procedure (Chakrabarti 2006).

The breach of an ASBO is a criminal offence and, as such, a criminal level of proof is required at breach hearings. The range of sentencing options for breach is as follows:

- *For adults*: Up to five years in prison; community order; absolute discharge; fine; compensation order; or deferred sentence
- *For those under 18 (in the youth court)*: detention and training order up to two years; all other community sentence options; discharge; or fine.

With a maximum penalty of five years' imprisonment, the penalty for breach can clearly be out of proportion to the original behaviour (Ashworth 2005; Hewitt 2007).

ASBOs and human rights

One of the major criticisms of the ASBO is that it breaches certain basic human rights; as Ashworth et al. noted back in 1998 (p. 10): 'It is quite clear that the government has devised this method of *de facto* criminalising through the civil courts precisely as a device to get round the due process protections of the criminal law.' The result is the kind of net widening discussed previously (cf. Cohen 1985). Behaviours that had previously been annoying, but tolerated for generations, are now criminalized, without the due process of checks and balances or having to go through a criminal trial. In effect, ASBOs can criminalize the trivial.[10] The Council for Europe Commissioner for Human Rights (Gil-Robles 2005: 34) has also been critical, stating that: 'The ease of obtaining such orders, the broad range of prohibited behaviour, the publicity surrounding their imposition and the serious consequences of breach all give rise to concern.' The government clearly would not agree. The government's position is compared to that of the European Commissioner for Human Rights in Box 6.4.

Box 6.4 ASBOs and human rights

The British government's position:

[E]veryone has rights under the European Convention of Human Rights (ECHR), including those individuals who behave in an anti-social manner. There must be a balance between their rights and those of the victims of the anti-social behaviour. However, it should be remembered that an ASBO only requires a person who has behaved anti-socially to stop doing those things which caused or were likely to cause harassment, alarm or distress to others, things which they should not [have] been doing anyway. No one has a right to behave anti-socially and everyone has a right not to be subjected to anti-social behaviour. (Respect website 2007b)

The view of the European Commissioner for Human Rights:

It seems to me that detention following the breach of an ASBO drawn up in such a way as to make its breach almost inevitable (such as not entering a demarcated zone near one's residence) and which was applied on the basis of hearsay evidence in respect of non-criminal behaviour, would almost certainly constitute a violation of article 5* of the ECHR. Such cases would appear to occur and, in so far as they do, the functioning of ASBOs needs to be addressed. (Gil-Robles 2005: 36 para. 116)

Note: *Article 5 (1) of the ECHR states, 'Everyone has the right to liberty and security of person. No one shall be deprived of his liberty save in the following cases and in accordance with a procedure prescribed by law: [Including] (a) the lawful detention of a person after conviction by a competent court; and (b) the lawful arrest or detention of a person for non-compliance with the lawful order of a court or in order to secure the fulfilment of any obligation prescribed by law [etc.].'

The British government clearly does not see any problem, claiming that perpetrators are given ASBOs for things which *they shouldn't be doing anyway*. That ASB is defined so loosely that these 'things' could include almost *anything* is not something considered in its justification. As demonstrated in the examples already given in Box 6.3, these things which they should not be doing could be a young person going to a youth club, a woman who has previously attempted suicide going near bridges or an autistic boy using a trampoline in his own garden. If these are not examples of up tariffing or criminalizing behaviour, then I do not know what is. Other similar examples have been listed by the probation trade union NAPO (Fletcher 2005) and by a website calling itself *State Watch*, under the banner of *ASBO Watch*.[11]

As noted previously, there are related concerns that certain minority or marginalized groups will be over-represented among ASBO cases – including the young, street people and other categories of 'them'. There is particular concern that people with learning or behavioural difficulties whose behaviour may be more unusual or challenging may be caught up in ASBO enforcement (Millie 2007a; Nixon et al. 2008); for instance, people with conduct disorders, hyperkinetic disorders (such as attention deficit hyperactivity disorder), autistic spectrum disorders or personality disorders (e.g. anti-social personality disorder). According to the British Medical Association (2006), alcohol and substance misuse can sometimes be linked to mental health problems, thus increasing the scope for such people being accused of ASB. As children and young people are a particular target for ASB enforcement, it is worth noting that one in ten children under 16 in the UK is thought to have a clinically diagnosed mental health disorder (British Medical Association 2006). How many of these become the target of ASB action is not known; although mental disorders have been found to be most prevalent among children and young people in disadvantaged areas – precisely the areas where concerns about ASB are already heightened (Green et al. 2005). A survey of 51 Youth Offending Teams (YOTs) (BIBIC 2005, 2007) found that over a third of those under 17 given ASBOs were also diagnosed with a mental health disorder or an accepted learning disability. Although the survey gained responses from just 38 percent of all YOTs, the results do hint at a particular problem. This is not to say that people with mental heath or learning difficulties should never be given an ASBO, but that there may be more appropriate responses, especially as some disorders will make it very difficult for the young person to understand the conditions attached to an order. The breakdown of results from this survey is shown in Table 6.1.

Table 6.1 BIBIC survey of ASBOs and young people with learning difficulties and mental health problems (results for 51 Youth Offending Teams)

ASBOs between April 2004 and April 2005	n	%
Number for under-17s	345	100
Of these, number involving children with diagnosed mental disorder or accepted learning difficulty	127	37
Including any one or more of the following:		
Attention Deficit Hyperactivity Disorder	50	15
Autism/Asperger Syndrome	27	8
Dyspraxia/dyslexia	10	3
Global development delay	2	1
Cases where estimated level of understanding was below the expected 10 years of age	2	1
Other (specify) (including emerging personality disorders, severe depression, non-educational attainment, suicide attempts, fixed term exclusions, psychosis, emotional behaviour disorder, special educational needs, self-harming, learning difficulties, attachment disorder, conduct disorder)	70	20

Notes: 1. Source BIBIC (2007). 2. Survey of youth offending teams (response rate 51 out of 135, 38%).

A further human rights issue connected to ASBOs was identified by Gil-Robles (2005: 34, para. 110) who claimed: '[S]uch order look rather like personalised penal codes, where non-criminal behaviour becomes criminal for individuals who have incurred the wrath of the community.' One of the principles of criminal law is its deterrent threat. As a certain form of behaviour is illegal for all citizens, then there is the same deterrent threat for all. ASBOs create a form of personalised deterrent threat – or 'personalized penal code' – tailor made to match an individual's misbehaviour. For instance, going to a youth club is clearly legal activity; however, it becomes criminalized for the young person on an ASBO with the condition not to congregate with groups of other young people. As stated elsewhere (Millie et al. 2005a: 37): 'The principle of universality should be abandoned only under clearly specified circumstances.' There needs to be much more explicit justification for the deployment of ASBOs and agreed limits to their use.

Publicity

Possibly the highest profile human rights concern has been regarding the publicity or 'naming and shaming' of ASBO recipients (e.g. Burney 2005; Cobb 2007); yet according to the Home Office (2005b: 2): 'Publicity is essential if local communities are to support agencies tackling anti-social behaviour.' Publicity is seen to be important in terms of public reassurance that something is being done, it provides local residents with the information to be able to inform on any breaches and it is intended as a deterrent to others. Such publicity has included 'wanted'-style posters containing photos and details of the order, leaflets sent to residents, local newspaper and TV announcements and website information. Despite Article 8 of the ECHR supposedly protecting a right to private and family life, the practice was deemed appropriate in *R(T) v. St. Albans Crown Court* (2002) and in *Stanley v. Metropolitan Police Commissioner* (2004).[12] An illustrative example is given by Phil Scraton (2005: 6):

> In September 2003 ASBOs were obtained against seven young men ... 3,000 copies of a police approved leaflet entitled 'KEEPING CRIME OFF THE STREETS OF BRENT' were distributed, containing photographs of the seven young men, their names, their ages and the details of the orders. The local authority posted details of the proceedings on its web-site, describing the gang as 'animalistic', 'thugs' and 'bully-boys'. It justified the publicity by stating the necessity to keep people in the community fully informed. The behaviour of the young men had been threatening, abusive and violent ... Yet [the publicity] had set a precedent ...

A more recent example is from a local Crime and Disorder Reduction Partnership in Bury, Greater Manchester. The partnership published on its website details of *ASBOs in your neighbourhood* (www.burysafe.org accessed Apr. 2008). Under the heading *Current anti-social behaviour orders*, the website states:

> Much has been said about the effectiveness of ASBOs and we want to ensure that people who have been given them stick to their conditions. There are currently 51 live ASBOs for Bury. Not all of them will appear on this website as some of the subjects have moved out of Bury, some of them have stopped offending, some of them are

in prison, and some ASBOs are particular to a very small area. We will only publicise those that you need to know about to make sure the order is complied with.

The website goes on to list the names and gives photos of nine people given ASBOs in the last six months, the dates of each order, a list of conditions, along with maps for area restrictions. According to the website: 'Because we can't be everywhere we need your help ... Please let us know if you believe breaches are happening so that we can do something about it.' According to Burney (2005: 96) publicity is most controversial in juvenile cases, 'given the traditional anonymity of court proceedings afforded by s.39(1) of the Children and Young Persons Act 1933'. Following the 2005 Serious Organised Crime and Police Act (s.141) there are no automatic reporting restrictions on ASBOs made in any court. Courts have to give reasons for imposing restrictions, although they still have discretion under the 1933 Act to restrict some or all details in juvenile cases. For juveniles, the issue of naming and shaming can be particularly problematical; for instance:

> 'Naming' cannot be separated from 'shaming', and shame by itself, without any reintegrative[13] process, is likely to be counter-productive, resulting in rejection of the ethical standpoint of the accusers ... It enhances the outcast aura which can be very damaging to the personality and prospects of a child. It may increase defiance and bravado, with the ASBO as a macho badge. (Burney 2005: 97)

Thus, publicity is thought to be stigmatizing for some, yet for others acting as a 'badge of honour'.

The use of ASBOs

It would be useful at this point to give some figures for ASBO usage. Despite the ASBO being a flagship policy for Labour, the Home Office did not routinely collect data during the first year of implementation (Campbell 2002). However, better information was gathered from 2000 onwards, although some areas have not been great at keeping records. Also, the Home Office has not been too speedy at presenting ASBO statistics. For instance, at the time of writing in 2008, the most up-to-date available figures obtained from the courts are for 2005 (Home Office 2006b). However, these figures are useful in showing the history of ASBO uptake and are presented as quarterly totals in Figure 6.1. The figures are for 2000 onwards due to earlier recording being more haphazard.

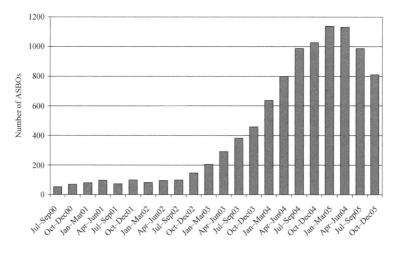

Source: Home Office (2006b).
Figure 6.1 ASBOs in England and Wales, 2000–05 (quarterly totals)

When first introduced there was a slow uptake of the orders; for instance, from April 1999 to May 2000 there were just 104 ASBOs granted nationally (see Burney 2002; Campbell 2002). Lord Warner was given the task, via the formation of an 'Action Group', to determine why so few orders were being sought. According to Charles Clarke MP (2000), then a minister at the Home Office:

> The Anti-social Behaviour Order Action Group concluded that, in order to give increased impetus to the take-up of applications for Anti-Social Behaviour Orders (ASBOs), there was a need to spread the good practice that already existed in certain areas of the country. To achieve this, the Action Group drew up practical guidance on considering and applying for ASBOs, and also set up a series of seminars … providing an opportunity to hear about, and discuss, the experiences of those who had successfully obtained such orders.

The slow uptake was thought to be due to a lack of knowledge, rather than a lack of enthusiasm, and led to the publication of early guidance (Home Office 2000). Despite this, the number of ASBOs remained low through to 2002 (see Figure 6.1). However, what followed in 2003 was a huge expansion (see also Table 6.2).

Table 6.2 ASBOs in England and Wales, 1999–2005 (by age)

	Apr 99 –May 00	Jun 00 –Dec 00	2001	2002	2003	2004	2005
Frequency							
Age 10–17	..	*62*	193	249	620	1318	1555
Age 18+	..	*63*	144	169	698	2057	2416
Age unknown	*104*	*12*	13	8	18	65	89
Total E&W	*104*	*137*	350	426	1336	3440	4060
%							
Age 10–17	..	*45*	55	58	46	38	38
Age 18+	..	*46*	41	40	52	60	60
Age unknown	*100*	*9*	4	2	1	2	2
Total E&W	*100*	*100*	100	100	100	100	100

Source: Home Office 2006b.

A major influence was the introduction of CrASBOs with the 2002 Police Reform Act, meaning that ASBOs could be used in a far wider set of circumstances. The 426 figure for 2002 increased by over 300 percent to 1336 in 2003. In 2005, 4060 ASBOs were granted. One effect of the introduction of CrASBOs was a shift in the age of ASBO recipients. For 2001 and 2002 there were more juveniles than adults being given ASBOs, and from 2003 there are more adults. Matthews et al. (2007: 18) have noted, '[t]he obvious attraction to practitioners of CRASBOs is that they are quicker and less costly than processing stand-alone ASBOs.' Cost has been a major factor and, in the 2002 Home Office review by Campbell, the average ASBO was estimated at £5350. If cost of appeals and breaches was excluded the figure was £4800. By 2004 (Lemetti and Parkinson 2005) the Home Office had estimate the average cost at £2500. However, CrASBOs were often much cheaper as they were tagged onto existing processes. On average, in 2004 a CrASBO cost £900 compared to £3200 for a stand-alone order.

Throughout the period 1999–2005 the courts refused only a tiny fraction of all orders sought. From 1 April 1999 to 31 December 2005, out of 9925, just 72 were refused. Some areas have been more enthusiastic ASBO users, with Manchester City Council being the heaviest using local authority. Over this same period (see Home Office 2006b) there were 458 ASBOs granted in the Manchester City Council area. This compared to 194 in the area of Liverpool City Council. The lowest numbers were logically found where fewest people live, but there is great variety in use across urban areas. Over this period there were 65 ASBOs in Middlesbrough, but just 14 in Hartlepool. Within London, the Borough of Camden had 172 ASBOs, while similarly inner-urban Southwark had 37. It is highly unlikely that Manchester residents are more anti-social than those in Liverpool or that Camden has more ASB than Southwark. The different usage levels were due to local politics, policies and strategies. For instance, for much of this period Bill Pitt led the assault on ASB in Manchester as he was an enthusiastic advocate of ASBOs (he later went on to advise the Respect Taskforce). Camden in London had a high use of ASBOs is the council decided to use them against drug use and dealing, as well as street sex work – both issues for the area. Other areas were clearly less enthusiastic users of ASBOs or saw them as a last resort (more of which later).

Characteristics of ASBO recipients

As noted, ASBOs are now more frequently given to adults than juveniles, although it is worth noting that a lot of these will be CrASBOs for more serious *criminal* behaviour, rather than for ASB. At the time of writing no national data were available comparing stand-alone ASBOs to CrASBOs. That said, there is evidence to support this position. In interviews with 66 ASBO recipients, Matthews et al. (2007: 20) found that those up to age 18 had received 19 stand-alone orders and ten CrASBOs; whereas those aged 19 and over had received 24 CrASBOs compared to 11 stand-alone orders.

There are also no recent official data relating to the gender of ASBO recipients. However, Campbell (2002: 8) found that ASBOs are far more likely to be given to males (84%) than females (16%). As for recipient ethnicity, research conducted by the Runnymede Trust (Isal 2006) found that ethnicity data were simply not collected by the government and, just as worryingly, they are not adequately monitored at a local level. Similarly, there are no publicly available data on the social status of ASBO recipients.

The paucity of data from the Home Office or the Ministry of Justice means other sources of information have to be used. As already noted, there is some evidence that many ASBOs are given to people with mental health or learning difficulties (e.g. BIBIC 2005, 2007; Nixon et al. 2008). As Smith (2007: 75) has observed, '[E]vidence was beginning to build up of ASBOs being used in a simplistic attempt to control behaviour with complex and deep-seated antecedents.' There is also evidence of ASBOs being used to control other categories of 'them', including street people and homeless (Macdonald 2006; Millie 2006; Moore 2008) and street sex workers (e.g. Matthews 2005; Scoular et al. 2007). To give just one example, in March 2004 the *Wandsworth Borough News* gave the headline *Three-year vice ban for Asbo prostitute*. According to the report:

> Issuing the Asbo, magistrates declared themselves satisfied that Garcia had acted in an antisocial manner likely to cause harassment, alarm or distress to others by loitering on residential streets for the

purposes of prostitution. Should she be caught soliciting within the next three years she faces a jail sentence of up to five years, on top of any sentences for additional crime. (Williams 2004: 35)

A particularly useful piece of research is by Young et al. (2006) in the King's Cross area of Camden in London. As noted, Camden – and King's Cross in particular – has a specific history tied to street prostitution and drug use and this is reflected in the analysis by Young et al. of ASBOs issued in this area. Up to the research period (Nov. 2005–Aug. 2006) the borough had successfully applied for 218 ASBOs since they were introduced in April 1999. (As noted, Camden has the highest use of ASBOs in London.) Of these, 54 were for the area of King's Cross. Reflecting the prominence of street sex work in the area, 41 percent were for females and 59 percent for males. The vast majority of ASBOs were for adults. Uniquely, the study also gathered data on ethnicity. The results for the 54 ASBOs in King's Cross are shown in Table 6.3, indicating a disproportionate representation of African/Caribbean recipients.

Table 6.3   Ethnicity of ASBO recipients in King's Cross, 1999–2006

%	2001 Census (whole of Camden)	ASBO recipients in King's Cross (n = 54)
White	73	53
Asian	10	4
Africa/Caribbean	8	37
Duel/mixed heritage	4	6
Chinese or other	4	0
Total	*100*	*100*

Source: Young et al. 2006.

These findings could indicate a particular problem. That said, Young et al. (2006: 84) noted that they may also reflect the particular crime concerns of the area. In King's Cross, nine out of ten ASBOs given for drug crime (as dealers or users) were to African/Caribbean males. The ASBOs in this area were for the following behaviours (2006: 23):

- Prostitution (17)
- Public drug usage (12)
- Drug dealing (6)
- Begging (4)
- Robbery (4)
- Kerb crawling (3)

- Carding (1)[14]
- Touting (1)
- Street drinking (1).

What is immediately apparent from this list is how for from 'anti-social' behaviour the use of ASBOs has gone, including many clearly criminal behaviours (robbery, drug dealing) and other behaviours that are locally deemed unacceptable (prostitution). What is needed is a similarly detailed breakdown of national statistics made available by government to determine the frequency of such cases elsewhere.

But do ASBOs work?

A major problem when writing about ASBOs is that the Home Office has, to date, not properly evaluated their effectiveness; as Squires and Stephen (2005b: 520) have observed: 'Large-scale national evaluation accompanied the rolling out of all the other new youth justice orders after 1998; if the ASBO was such a central component of the overall strategy, it is strange that its evaluation has been overlooked.' As noted, the initial uptake and implementation issues of ASBOs was looked at in the Home Office report by Campbell (2002). However, since then it has been up to other agencies, campaign groups and academics to assess their usefulness – or otherwise. According to Rubin et al. (2006: 9) '[t]here is little reliable data on the effectiveness of ASBOs.' While this is certainly true, it is possible, by bringing different sources together, to build a picture of whether ASBOs may have a *plausible* impact. How you measure effectiveness is entirely dependent on what the aims of the order are. At its crudest, the aim of an ASBO is to stop certain forms of behaviour and to give respite to victims. A straightforward way of assessing effectiveness on these terms is to consider breach rates and to compare these to other enforcement measures. Breaches for ASBOs are particularly important as they can lead to criminal prosecution.

Breach

The evidence of ASBO breach has to be at a criminal standard and will involve breaking the conditions attached to the order or reconviction (as with CrASBOs). However, a breach rate can be a bit of a crude measure of effectiveness. As has been found with probation work (Hearnden and Millie 2004), there are issues around how strictly breach proceedings are followed or whether those on the order should have some flexibility. That said, it is a useful starting point. According to a Home Office press release (2006c), 47 percent of all ASBOs were breached, with 41 percent of adults and 57 percent of juveniles breaching their orders. No time period was given for these data although, following a 'Freedom of Information'[15] request, more detailed information has been made available (Home Office 2007a). The 47 percent breach rate referred to the period June 2000 to December 2005 (4568 ASBOs breached at least once from a total of 9749). The area with the lowest rate was Northamptonshire with 11 percent of 84 ASBOs breached. At the other extreme, Gwent issued 72 ASBOs, of which 64 percent were breached. Similarly, Cleveland had 115 ASBOs and breached 64 percent.

There may be a range of explanations for the differences between areas, including different enforcement practices, approaches to ASBO publicity or perhaps different groups targeted. The headline figure of nearly half of all ASBOs breached seems on the face of it quite high. But the nature of the conditions attached to the order can make some degree of breach highly likely; it is a question of how many breaches warrant formal breach proceedings and a criminal trial. As an Anti-Social Behaviour Coordinator put it in a recent communication to the author during 2008: '100% of both ABCs[16] and ASBOs are breached to some degree. However, usually a warning letter reminding them of their ABC or ASBO will do the trick. Of those who continue to breach, they are prosecuted through the criminal courts in the usual manner.'

In terms of comparison to criminal disposals, up-to-date figures are not available as the Ministry of Justice has stopped publishing breach data.[17] However, for 2004[18] 31 percent of Community Rehabilitation Orders were breached; similarly, 37 percent of Community Punishment Orders; 25 percent of curfew orders, 49 percent of Drug Treatment and Testing Orders; and 60 percent of Community Punishment and Rehabilitation Orders (Home Office 2005c: 90).

According to parliamentary written answers, as recorded in *Hansard* (Coaker 25 June 2007), 'In England and Wales during 2005, there were 7,556 occasions where breach of an ASBO was proven in court. A custodial sentence was given on 3,440 of those occasions.' The 7556 total is higher than the number of ASBOs issued during 2005 because the breach could be for *any active* ASBO. It should also be noted that the decision to imprison would have been influenced by other offences sentenced at the same time or by previous convictions (Sentencing Advisory Council 2007: 17). That said, a 46 percent custody rate is high. For instance, for the same year 2005 the custody rate for all persons sentenced for indictable offences was just 28 percent. In magistrates' courts, the custody rate was 14 percent and in the crown court, which deals with the more serious offences, it was 60 percent (Home Office 2007b: Tables 2.1 to 2.3).

Also, having 3440 people imprisoned for breaching an ASBO at a time of prison over-crowding is a potential concern for the wider criminal justice system (see e.g. Millie et al. 2003; Carter 2007; Phillips 2007). As elsewhere, specific figures are difficult to come by; and there is limited information on juveniles in custody as a result of ASBO breach. For instance, according to research for the Youth Justice Board (Brogan and PA Consulting 2005: 18) between June 2000 and December 2002 170 juveniles breached their ASBOs. Full details was available for 166, of which 71 (43%) ended up in custody. A more specific example is from Hassockfield Secure Training Centre in County Durham. During 2004, 17 percent of boys and 33 percent of girls at this centre were there because they had breached an ASBO (Donovan 2004). According to the Howard League for Penal Reform (2004), 'the current upward trend in the numbers of juveniles held in penal establishments is not wholly unconnected with the use of imprisonment for those breaching ASBOs.'

Impact on ASBO recipients

There are a few studies that have looked at the impact of receiving an ASBO. All have taken slightly different approaches and none has a very large sample size. That said, some common themes have emerged. For instance, Matthews et al. (2007) interviewed 66 ASBO recipients and found their response to gaining an ASBO ranged from anger and to one case of relief. The most common response was that the ASBO was unfair, inappropriate or disproportionate. A study conducted for the Youth Justice Board (Solanki et al. 2006) included 45 recipient interviews. The study found that many young recipients did not understand clearly the conditions attached to their order and often breached these conditions. Some parents and practitioners interviewed saw the orders as a 'badge of honour' among the young people. Most respondents saw the need for strong support to be attached to the order. Similar concerns were found in a smaller study by Wain (2007), which included interviews with 21 ASBO recipients. Some illustrative quotations from these studies are shown in Box 6.5.

Box 6.5   ASBOs: some views from recipients

Issues with ASBO conditions:

I can't see my family. Most don't live around here where I am boxed in. They live across here [points on a map]. I have to breach the ASBO if I want to go and see them. (ASBO recipient, in Matthews et al. 2007: 32)

It's hard to remember [my ASBO conditions], but I know a couple of them. (16-year-old male recipient, in Wain 2007: 79)

It's not like I didn't comply with the conditions, it's just like when I was out, I didn't think oh I've got an ASBO, I'm not allowed to do this so I won't do it. (17-year-old male recipient, in Wain 2007: 80)

ASBOs make criminal and anti-social behaviour more likely:

It certainly turns you into a violent, angry young man and I've never been violent ... [but] I am fucking fuming ... fucking fuming. (Adult recipient, in Matthews et al. 2007: 32)

I want to do certain things, just to be arrested because of this stupid ASBO. It is like a little child, you can't do this, you can't do that, don't touch this, don't touch that. That is what it's like. (37-year-old male recipient, in Matthews et al. 2007: 39)

Benefits of having an ASBO:

I was angry at the time as the ASBO meant I couldn't go round my own town, but looking back it's the best thing that could have happened as it led to me being arrested and so getting treatment in prison. I only heard about rehab in prison ... (Male recipient, in NAO 2006: 23)

It is just that I am paranoid. I don't really want to go to prison. Never been and don't want to go there. So I keep my head down until my ASBO is finished ... (Male recipient, Matthews et al. 2007: 40)

The available evidence gives a mixed picture in terms of the impact of ASBOs. It seems recipients are more sceptical than positive about their order. This is perhaps understandable given the major restrictions that can be placed on their day-to-day lives. That said, a few do see benefits in having an order. And while some recipients may not be happy with their order, others may see it more positively. An example is provided in Box 6.6, which is taken from Bradford's *Telegraph & Argos* newspaper. The article quotes the mother of a juvenile recipient who claims the ASBO had halted a criminal career. Yet others have been less supportive. In a focus group with local parents (Millie et al. 2005a: 28), one respondent commented: 'If you have one of those anti-social behaviour orders on you, nationwide, how is it enforceable?'

Box 6.6   Example of positive press for ASBOs

'Asbo saved my son from crime'

The mother of the youngest boy to get an Asbo in Bradford says the controversial punishment has saved her son from turning into a career criminal and spending life behind bars.

Debbie Williamson said she had feared her tearaway son, Aneeze, would continue to spiral out of control.

But the anti-social behaviour order issued two years ago when he was 11 has helped halt his law-breaking habits which included burglaries, arson and shouting abuse at neighbours and shopkeepers ...

... Miss Williamson, who also has a nine-year-old son and a 19-year-old daughter, said Aneeze's Asbo had only bought him shame and frustration at being shackled.

Under the order he cannot go out without a responsible adult – not even to his grandmother's house just a street away from his own.

Source: Reported by Kathie Griffiths in Bradford's *Telegraph & Argos*, 3 Nov. 2006.

Neighbourhood impacts

The main impact for the victims of ASB is the supposed respite the order can give them. If handled well, then residents have the opportunity to regain control of the situation, thus impacting on levels of social capital or collective efficacy. In a series of focus groups held in three areas suffering from problems of ASB (Millie et al. 2005a), residents were asked about ASB in general and also their views of ASBOs. In one focus group held with local parents, I asked the simple question: whether ASBOs would be useful. The first response was: 'Yes, if the person is in when they are supposed to be in, and at the place they are supposed to be. But you can't have enough police to control the streets, never mind to fund this.' ASBOs were seen as a nice idea, but difficult to implement effectively. In another focus group with parents, a similar concern was expressed: 'To have a nationwide ban you've got to be up to some serious stuff ... you must have done the same thing, whatever it is, an awful amount of times to get one of them ... How is that enforceable?' In a focus group with retired people, one respondent commented: 'It's got to be really extreme before they give them one of them. By that time they have caused a lot of aggravation and pain to people, and even then it's not going to change them.' This resident thought there was a need for immediate, and effective, respite to the problem. For him, ASBOs would not help.

In a separate study in London, a focus group was held with people with mental health and/or substance misuse problems (Millie et al. 2005b; Millie 2006). The emphasis changed, as illustrated in the following exchange:

Female 1   Well in practice [the ASBO] seems to be more about the individual than the actual act itself.

Male 3   One of the problems in the West End is the police, once your face in known it's like, for me for instance, is, I'm known to the police. And I try to stay out of trouble now because I'm on my methadone and all this …

Male 2   It's not about like actually stopping people doing [drugs], it's about driving people out of an area, that's what it is … The whole notion of anti-social behaviour orders, you know, they're social exclusion orders, you know what I mean. They prevent you ever from joining society as you know it. So effectively you're locked out of anything once you've got one of those on you.

Clearly, whether members of the public support the use of ASBOs is very much dependent on their particular experiences and perspective. One point that would concern those trying to implement an enforcement strategy is a lack of faith in ASBO effectiveness among those living in neighbourhoods most affected by anti-social concerns.

Practitioners' views on ASBOs

Practitioners' views on ASBOs are similarly varied and depend very much on who you talk to. A local authority Head of Litigation I interviewed back in 2003 was concerned that ASBOs were a shortcut to a criminal record: 'I'm filled with horror at the idea of a 14 year old acquiring a criminal record for kicking a ball against a wall.' In the same study,[19] a local authority director of environmental health saw the cost of ASBOs as a major disadvantage: 'What nobody seems to recognise is that once you've gone down a certain [ASBO] route how costly it is to society. Whereas that money could be used to much better effect for things like putting on youth activities.' Other practitioners are far more supportive. For instance, a police officer interviewed in Matthews et al. (2007: 12) saw the benefit as: 'Generally it has an impact by helping to take out some of the main players in that group of kids.' A British Transport Police officer in the same study thought ASBOs worked in some circumstances, but not others: 'I don't think that ASBOs work for kids on council estates – they're not geared for that, but drug addicts here – it works' (2007: 13).

In the small study by Wain (2007: 69) a Youth Offending Team manager saw the criminalization of young people as the main problem: 'I feel that ASBOs lead to more criminality – a young person may not have any criminal behaviour until they receive an ASBO and breach it.' A youth worker in the Matthew et al. (2007: 13) study saw a lack of partnership working as a main problem: 'What's happening is that a lot of ASBOs are being made without social services interventions, without YOT [Youth Offending Team] knowledge and so forth. So prohibitions are often sort or like irrelevant or too stringent or basically you are setting the kids up to fail.'

The varied level of YOT involvement in the ASBO process was also identified by Dearling (2006) and in a Youth Justice Board study into the use of ASBOs (Solanki et al. 2006). If ASBOs were being given to juveniles, then the involvement of the YOT seemed an important principle.

In a number of studies, local practitioners regarded ASBOs as a last resort and promoted a tiered approach to tackling ASB, with a number of 'softer' options leading up to ASBO imposition (e.g. Millie et al. 2005a; Solanki et al. 2006; Matthews et al. 2007). There are also calls for greater support for perpetrators of ASB and, according to a National Audit Office Report (2006: 27), specific support in relation to mental health and social services.

ASBOs as last resort

Early Home Office guidance published in 2000 emphasized that ASBOs should not be used as a last resort; yet, from very early on, some local authorities were taking a different position. For example, the head of Liverpool City Council's Anti-Social Behaviour Unit when interviewed in 2000 (Reid 2002: 219) claimed their approach was one of balance: 'The approach taken is not heavy-handed, rather it is characterized by a balanced range of interventions which result in only 10% of cases being dealt with through formal Orders ... they are not Orders of last resort but Orders to be used when appropriate to do so ...'

Some local partnerships have implemented a stepped approach. For instance, Blackburn has run a three-stage scheme involving warning letters. Here only 11 percent of juveniles who received the initial warning letter later came to police attention (Hodgkinson and Tilley 2007). Similarly the Safer Swansea Partnership has a four-step system where the first step is a warning letter with an ASBO very much a last resort. Key to a tiered approach has been the development of an Acceptable Behaviour Contract.

The Acceptable Behaviour Contract (ABC)[20]

According to Bullock and Jones (2004: 14) an ABC is a, 'written, voluntary agreement between a youth, the local housing office and the police'. The ABC has since been extended to include registered social landlords and has also been used for people living in private property. The idea was first developed in London by Paul Dunn of the Metropolitan Police with Alison Blackburn of Islington Borough Council Housing Department, with the first contract signed in November 1999 (Dunn 2004). The ABC is very similar to an ASBO in that it lays out conditions for the recipient to adhere to in an attempt to address ASB. However, the fundamental difference is that the scheme is voluntary and usually involves the young person and their parent/guardian in drafting the agreement. It is a clear example of what Adam Crawford (2003) has termed 'contractual governance'. The young person is not obliged to sign the contract, but there may be consequences if it is signed and then breached. For instance, it may be used in evidence for a possession action (for a tenant in social housing). And since introduction the ABC has also been used in evidence for subsequent ASBO applications. An ABC is usually set for six months and then reviewed. The reason the ABC is included here is that it has become integral to a model of enforcement where an ASBO is the sanction of last resort. Early evaluations of ABC schemes have been promising, although some issues needed to be ironed out. For instance, in a small study in Brighton by Stephen and Squires (2003) ten out of 13 young people given an ABC completed their contracts. However, Stephen and Squires (2003: 4) make the important point that, '[t]he young people need to be empowered to recognise more positive reasons for change than the perverse incentives of possible eviction or "reward".' However, the authors suggest: 'If employed in an anti-oppressive manner ABCs can offer new opportunities for family empowerment' (2003: 4). By giving the young person and his or her parent a voice in the process, it means the usual power relationship between tenant and local authority or police is shifted. According to Stephen and Squires there is also scope for involving the victim more in a restorative justice process. In a larger study by Bullock and Jones (2004), 85 percent of those involved in ABC schemes were happy with them. The main issues identified were the common problems of a lack of resources and time constraints.

An example stepped approach to ASB

The ABC was promoted nationally in Home Office guidance published in 2003, as part of a process that may ultimately lead to an ASBO application:

> It is important that all concerned should understand that ASBOs and ABCs are in no sense competing for business ... Where an ABC is

selected as the best option, it is recommended that it should contain a statement that the continuation of unacceptable behaviour may lead to an application for an ASBO. Where a contract is broken, that should be used as evidence in the application for an ASBO. It may also be possible to use the evidence of anti-social behaviour which was originally collected for the ABC in any subsequent ASBO application. (Home Office 2003d: 7)

An example of a stepped plan is from the Safer Swansea Partnership in South Wales. The Swansea model uses both ABCs and ASBOs and follows a four-step approach. The aim is to address the person's ASB before it gets to the ASBO application stage (step four). The full process is shown in Box 6.7.

Box 6.7   Safer Swansea four-step plan

Step 1: When referrals of anti-social behaviour are made to the team they send out a warning letter to the individual and their parents or guardians. In the majority of cases, this is enough to nip the behaviour in the bud. If the behaviour continues, a second warning letter is sent. Annual figures show that out of 1281 warning letters sent out, only 282 had to be followed up with second warning letters.

Step 2: The next step is to pay a home visit to the individual and his or her family to explain the effect their behaviour is having on people around them and what will happen if they do not stop. The visit also aims to pin-point potential causes of the behaviour [and gives the individual an opportunity to put their side of the story].

Step 3: If there is still no improvement a multi-agency case conference is called where officials from the police, education, housing, Youth Offending Team and more, meet to discuss the best possible action route. This could mean encouraging the person to sign up to an Acceptable Behaviour Contract.

Step 4: In extreme cases where the behaviour is not improving or likely to change, the team approaches the magistrates' court for an ASBO, Individual Support Order, Child Support Order, Parenting Order or other antisocial behaviour sanctions. Safer Swansea believes this process works so well because it reprimands those whose behaviour is ruining the quality of life for others, but helps and supports those who just need to a gentle push back onto the rails.

Source: http://www.saferswansea.org.uk/asb_asbo.asp (accessed April 2008).

According to recent figures (Safer Swansea Partnership 2007) only 22 percent of people got as far as step two in 2005 and 11 percent in 2006. The numbers involved at each stage of the model in Swansea for 2005–06 are shown in Table 6.4.

Table 6.4   Safer Swansea intervention data

Intervention	2005	2006
Step 1: warning letter 1	1281	1387
Step 2: warning letter 2	282	158
Personal warning signed	(34)	29
Personal warning breached	–	12
Step 3: ABC	30	11
ABC failed to attend	7	2
ABC breached	6	3
Step 4: ASBO/CrASBO	8	0
ASBO breached	6	0

Note: (1) Data kindly provided by Nicci Southard-Stuart, Anti-Social Behaviour Reduction Coordinator for the Safer Swansea Partnership. (2) Data re. personal warning signed in 2005 relates to period 01.09.05–31.12.05 only.

This approach is seen as a success because it does not lead to many ASBO applications. In fact, for 2006, despite 1387 initial warning letters being sent, there were no ASBOs that year.

Support for ASBO recipients

Support for juveniles on ASBOs is provided by legislation relating to Parenting Orders and Individual Support Orders. Following the 1998 Crime and Disorder Act (s.8), when an ASBO is given to a child under 16 the court can also make a civil Parenting Order (PO), 'if it is satisfied that it is desirable to do so in the interests of preventing further offending or anti-social behaviour' (see Youth Justice Board 2006). If certain conditions are met, Parenting Orders can also be made when the young person is 16 or 17. With the 2003 Anti-Social Behaviour Act (s.25) 'Parenting Contracts' were introduced, as similar arrangements to ABCs. Fitting in with notions that parents are responsible for their children's behaviour (e.g. Burney 1999; Gelsthorpe 1999; see Chapter 4) working with parents is seen as an important element in dealing with youthful ASB. According to recent guidance (Ministry of Justice 2007: 3): 'Help and support for the parent of young people who become involved in offending or anti-social behaviour should be part of a wider programme of action to support families. Parents are the biggest single influence on a child's life ...' Yet, like the ASBO, this comes with threat of criminal sanction. Although various warnings, reviews and cautions are suggested following breach (Youth Justice Board 2006: 22), ultimately breach of a Parenting Order is a summary offence and carries the maximum sentence of a £1000 fine, a community order or conditional or absolute discharge (it does not carry a criminal record). Parenting measures are discussed in more detail in Chapter 7.

A less punitive approach was with the introduction of the Individual Support Order (ISO) with the 2003 Criminal Justice Act (s. 322 and 323). ISOs were intended to run alongside stand-alone ASBOs for 10–17 year-olds in an attempt to address what is thought to be the underlying causes of the ASB. Drawing on classic New Labour rhetoric, Hazel Blears, MP (2005), has described it thus: 'What it seeks to do is, I suppose, is that the Anti-Social Behaviour Order is tough on the anti-social behaviour and the Individual Support Order is tough on the causes of it.' The order comes with positive requirements for the recipient to attend appropriate courses (up to two sessions per week), such as for anger management or relating to drugs use. Youth Offending Teams can deliver ISOs as part of their wider preventative work, such as through 'Youth Inclusion and Support Panels' (see Chapter 8). The main issue with ISOs is that, so far, they have not been used to any great extent. For instance, from 1 May 2004 (when introduced) through to 31 December 2004 there were only seven ISOs nationally, representing 2 percent of all ASBOs issued to 10–17-year-olds at magistrates' court civil hearings. For the year 2005 there were 42 ISOs; but this still represented only 7 percent of appropriate juvenile ASBOs (McNulty 2007). There have been complaints from agencies about a lack of funding; as a Youth Offending Team manager interviewed in 2005 noted, 'the court is now obliged with young people to consider the attachment of an ISO to an ASBO ... The issue for me is let's just say we get 50 ASBOs ... then I could end up with 50 ISOs. Well that's two case-workers. Who's going to fund it?'[21] Research by the Youth Justice Board (Solanki et al. 2006) has also revealed a lack of knowledge about ISOs amongst sentencers. As Donaghue (2007) has observed, the judiciary has a vital role in determining the scope of ASB and use of ASB remedies. If sentencers are unaware of all the options to them, then they will not be used. The government, via the Youth Justice Board, has made an effort to make them more widely known (Fassenfelt 2006); and recently (March 2008) has called for a greater expansion in the use of ISOs, providing 'challenge and support grants' to 52 areas in England and Wales for this purpose (Respect website 2008; Youth Taskforce 2008).

Another development has been the introduction of Intervention Orders (IOs) with the 2005 Drugs Act (s.20). These are similar in concept to

Selected reading

There is very little published research into the effectiveness of ASBOs, with the government being especially slow at publishing ASB data. Currently, the most up-to-date figures can be found at www.crimere-duction.homeoffice.gov.uk. For further information on the use of ASBOs the reading listed below is a good place to start:

- Brogan, D. and PA Consulting (2005) *Anti-social Behaviour Orders: An Assessment of Current Management Information Systems and the Scale of Anti-social Behaviour Breaches Resulting in Custody.* London: Youth Justice Board.
- Campbell, S. (2002) A review of anti-social behaviour orders. Home Office Research Study No. 236. London: Home Office.
- Fletcher, H. (2005) *ASBOs: An Analysis of the First 6 Years.* 20 July. London: NAPO.
- Gil-Robles, A. (2005) Report by Mr Alvaro Gil-Robles, Commissioner for Human Rights, on his visit to the United Kingdom, 4–12 November 2004, Office of the Commissioner for Human Rights, 8 June 2005, CommDH(2005)6. Strasbourg: Council of Europe.
- Home Office (2006a) *A Guide to Anti-Social Behaviour Orders.* London: Home Office.
- Matthews, R., Easton, H., Briggs, D. and Pease, K. (2007) *Assessing the Use and Impact of Anti-Social Behaviour Orders.* Bristol: Policy Press.
- Solanki, A., Bateman, T., Boswell, G. and Hill, E. (2006) *Anti-Social Behaviour Orders.* London: Youth Justice Board.
- Squires, P. (2008) *ASBO Nation: The Criminalisation of Nuisance.* Bristol: Policy Press.

Notes

1 [1995] QBD 432.
2 As signed up to by Britain with the 1998 Human Rights Act.
3 [2002] UKHL 39.
4 See also *Moat Housing Group South Ltd v. Harris and Hartless* [2005] 3 WLR 691, [2005] 4 All ER 1051.
5 Developments have meant ASBOs can also be heard in county and crown courts – more of which later.
6 [2002] UKHL 39.
7 *McGrath* [2005] 2 Cr App R(S) 85.

8   See also the Magistrates' Courts (Anti-Social Behaviour Orders) Rules 2002 No. 2784 (L. 14).

9   Available from Dec. 2002.

10   The introduction of CrASBOs results in the trivialization of behaviour that is clearly criminal. Cases of CrASBOs given to convicted burglars, for instance, are not uncommon. I would argue that burglary is *more* than just anti-social.

11   See http://www.statewatch.org/asbo/asbowatch-extreme.htm.

12   [2002] EWMC 1129 and [2004] EWHC 2220 (Admin) (see Burney 2005: 96–7).

13   See e.g. Braithwaite (1989); Ahmed et al. (2001) (and Matthews 2006 for a critique).

14   Placing of cards in telephone boxes to advertise sex work (see also Sanders 2005).

15   In line with the 2002 Freedom of Information Act.

16   Acceptable Behaviour Contracts, more of which later.

17   This is officially due to a lack of confidence in the collection of breach records.

18   Following the 2003 Criminal Justice Act (implemented 2005), the range of community disposals was simplified into one generic community order (with a range of options).

19   For more from this study, see Jacobson et al. (2005, 2008).

20   In some local authorities known as an Acceptable Behaviour Agreement (ABA).

21   Taken from a small study of ASB in a Midlands city by the author, unpublished.

7 Other enforcement options

The mood of the meeting having soured somewhat, I asked my son if he had any questions. He asked the man if he shouldn't go out any more. The man assured him that they were not trying to discourage youths from going out, just not to stand in groups of more than two ... my son still goes out, but he is cautious of the police and remains concerned that he may again fall foul of them, despite having broken no law. Small wonder that he and his friends now cover their faces when they go out – the hoodie is the uniform of choice. (Chris Paling, *Times Online* 2006).

Although much political and media attention is on ASBOs, they are only one part of the enforcement 'armoury'. Space does not permit a detailed examination of all available enforcement options; however, some of the more significant options are considered, including: housing legislation; legislation to enforce 'better' parenting; on-the-spot fines; closure and abatement notices; and, finally, various area-based restrictions including Disposal Orders and Designated Public Place Orders. But, first, I want to consider what happened before this contemporary focus on ASB. As stated elsewhere, behaviour deemed to be anti-social is hardly new.

What did we do before all this anti-social behaviour?

With the sheer quantity of legislative powers introduced over the past ten years to tackle ASB, it would be easy to think that such issues had never been dealt with before. This is, of course, a nonsense; as Burney (2005: 46) has put it, '[p]eriodic anxiety about what would now be called anti-social behaviour can be glimpsed anecdotally over the centuries.' There may always have been concerns over the inappropriate behaviour of young people or presence of beggars and prostitutes – precisely the targets for contemporary ASB enforcement. There is also a long history of measures in place to deal with such ASB. For instance, when Robert Peel set up the 'New Police' in London in 1829, its main focus was stated as to prevent crime. One of the early instructions to the police was that every effort should be directed to enhancing 'the security of person and property, the preservation of public tranquillity, and all the other objects of a police establishment' (cited in Reith 1956). The phrase 'public tranquillity' is relevant here. Of course, preventing criminal activity contributes to this tranquillity; but similarly dealing with minor day-to-day irritations, anti-social behaviours or 'quality of life crimes'. According to Pearson (1983: 214) in the past a likely response from the police would have been 'the proverbial clip around the ear, or the dreaded flick of the Edwardian policemen's rolled cape'. 'Minor' crimes – including some assaults and gross disorder – were often treated informally and were not seen as 'the proper affairs of [a] criminal department' (1983: 214).

Additionally, in common law, there was the use of 'breach of the peace', something that dates back in legislation to the 1361 Justices of the Peace Act. According to Burney (2005: 46–7):

> '[B]reach of the peace' sometimes reveals situations which nowadays might attract the label 'anti-social' and be dealt with in ways that reflect that perspective ... The breach occurred through actions likely to evoke an angry response and stir up trouble, and people were often bound over to keep the peace for quite serious matters as well as private annoyances.

Breach of the peace can still be used. While it has no legislative definition, according to a judgement made in *Howell*[1] (1982), it is 'an act done or threatened to be done which either actually harms a person, or in his presence his property, or is likely to cause such harm or which puts someone in fear of such harm being done' (cited in Ramsay 2008). The modern bind-over order (1980 Magistrates' Courts Act) is not a conviction or penalty, but is meant to be preventative. Being bound over involves a person having to 'keep the peace' or 'be of good behaviour' for a specified period of time, for a specific sum, say, £1000 (known as a recognizance). If breached, the person returns to court to pay the sum. Refusal can lead to six months in prison. It is a simple practice that could be used much more quickly and cheaply than many enforcement measures introduced specifically to target ASB. Additionally, there are such things as parental bind-overs to ensure parental support when a child or young person has been convicted of an offence[2] (1991 Criminal Justice Act s.58, and 2000 Criminal Courts Act s.150). According to the 2000 Act, the aim is for the parent 'to take proper care of [the child] and exercise proper control over him' (see Dishley 2008).

Another example of early law that has been used to address anti-social issues is the 1847 Town Police Clauses Act. Included here were powers to control nuisance, making innkeepers liable for disorderly events and the power to block streets to control disorder. More frequent use has been made of local by-laws, specifically enacted to maintain and enforce respectability, usually with the threat of a fine. By-laws of relevance to the governance of ASB have included early pub closing arrangements or perhaps local littering fines. In nineteenth-century Middlesbrough, they were more encompassing: 'When Albert Park was opened in 1868 as an alternative and wholesome site of entertainment for working men and their families special by-laws not only forbade alcohol, swearing and brawling in the park but also made provision for the removal of persons 'offensively or indecently clad' (Taylor 2002, cited in Burney 2005: 52).

By-law powers can still be used today, although they have largely been over-taken by newer developments such as fixed penalty notices, a theme I shall return to. There is the question of whether such local arrangements are enforceable today – or for that matter, whether they were ever enforceable. But in setting standards of acceptability they had their uses and were often supplemented by more informal mechanisms of control – the 'please keep off the grass' sign of popular imagination, swiftly followed by a shouting and angry park keeper.

Developments immediately pre-New Labour

As already noted in Chapter 1, a lot of the current emphasis on ASB started with the Conservative government's 1986 Public Order Act. It was this legislation that introduced the concept of 'harassment, alarm or distress'. However, the focus here was on 'public disorder', such as causing a disturbance in a residential area, rowdy behaviour in a street late at night, throwing missiles or minor violence or threats of violence. The Conservatives also introduced with the 1994 Criminal Justice and Public Order Act various powers to stop outdoor 'raves', defined as:

> a gathering on land in the open air of 100 or more persons (whether or not trespassers) at which amplified music is played during the night (with or without intermissions) and is such as, by reason of its loudness and duration and the time at which it is played, is likely to cause serious distress to the inhabitants of the locality. (s.63(1))

The 1994 Act had other targets. According to John Muncie (1999: 158):

> For 'homeless' travellers and squatters, the 1994 Criminal Justice and Public Order Act had effectively limited their ability to live within the law. In 1994 John Major, then Prime Minister, launched an attack on 'offensive beggars', claiming that 'it is not acceptable to be out on the street' and 'there is no justification for it these days'.

Various forms of street people and youth have continued to be targeted by New Labour's legislation on ASB, in what Muncie saw as 'institutionalized intolerance'.

At a much more mundane level, the Conservatives introduced the 1996 Dogs (Fouling of Land) Act, which meant that in designated areas local authorities were able to issue fixed penalty notices to owners who did not clear up their dog's mess. You may not think dog mess, homeless people and ravers have much in common; however, what links them is a focus on 'quality of life' and an enforcement centred approach to dealing with these concerns – both themes continued by Labour in 1997. That said, what is possibly of most significance in the evolution of ASB sanctions was the various housing acts introduced by the Tories that focused on the control of anti-social tenants. The use of housing legislation is considered next.

Housing legislation

The behaviour of tenants has been a concern of social housing providers ever since the start of social housing (Cowen 1999; Haworth and Manzi 1999); as John Flint (2006b: 21) puts it, tenants are classified as 'deserving or undeserving based on moral assessments of their conduct in order firstly to ration access to housing, and secondly to secure conformity of a tenant's behaviour'. Prior to 1980, local authority tenants had no security of tenure and were excluded from protection under the 1977 Rent Act. Security of tenure came with the 1980 Housing Act, and could only be terminated by order of a county court. But with increasing concern about misbehaviour on council estates – and misbehaving youths in particular with, for example, the rise of joyriding – the 1996 Housing Acts shifted power back to the local authorities with the start of introductory tenancies (Card 2006; Hunter 2006). Repossessions were thought to be taking too long and so an introductory tenant does not have the same protection as someone on a secured tenancy. They can therefore be evicted more easily for unacceptable behaviour, such as nuisance and annoyance to neighbours, as well as more obviously for rent arrears. In the housing association sector, the 1988 Housing Act increased tenants' rights with the introduction of assured tenancies; yet, from 1995 some housing associations were given permission to use assured shorthold tenancies (referred to as *starter tenancies*) as a means of controlling ASB (Ruggieri and Levison 1998). For the whole social housing sector this was part of a noticeable shift to social (and crime) control (e.g. Cowen et al. 2001). The move was welcomed by many housing providers who were members of the 'Social Landlords Crime and Nuisance Group' – a powerful lobby that has had a definite influence on government policy on ASB.

The 1996 Housing Act (s.152) also saw the introduction of injunctions for anti-social tenants (or visitors). According to the Act a local authority can apply to the county or crown court for an injunction prohibiting a person from:

- Engaging in or threatening to engage in conduct causing or likely to cause a nuisance or annoyance to a person residing in, visiting or otherwise engaging in a lawful activity in residential premises to which this section applies or in the locality of such premises
- Using or threatening to use residential premises to which this section applies for immoral or illegal purposes
- Entering residential premises to which this section applies or being found in the locality of any such premises.

Under New Labour, the 2003 Anti Social Behaviour Act (s. 13) re-branded these injunctions to become Anti-Social Behaviour Injunctions (ASBIs),[3] with their use extended to housing action trusts and registered social landlords. The 2003 Act also introduced tenancy demotions, where a secured tenancy can be demoted to the less secure introductory tenancy for reasons of ASB.

Social landlords have certainly embraced the various enforcement measures open to them and by 2003 over half (58%) were employing specialist anti-social behaviour officers or teams (Nixon et al. 2003). And according to research conducted for the Housing Corporation by Pawson et al. (2005a) between 2005 and 2006 the majority of housing associations in England used either ASBIs or evictions for ASB (possession orders). ASBOs had been granted by 29 percent and demoted tenancies used by 11 percent.[4] An overview of the findings from this study is shown in Table 7.1.

Table 7.1 Housing associations in England using ASB powers in 2005–06

Action	Number	%
ASBOs granted	105	29.3
ASBIs granted	187	52.2
Evictions (for ASB)	231	64.5
Creation of demoted tenancies	38	10.6
None of the above	77	21.5

Note: Housing associations in England = 358.
Source: Pawson et al. 2005a.

A similar survey was conducted a year later by PA Consulting (2006), this time with 400 social landlords (a mixture of local authorities, housing associations and arms' length management organizations). This survey showed even greater use of ASB powers. For instance, in the year up to April 2006, 77 percent had used eviction powers, 58 percent ASBIs, and 30 percent demoted tenancies.

In another study, Pawson and colleagues (2005b) focused on the use of eviction/possession orders. There is a three stage process for possession: the first is the issuing of a notice seeking possession, then the action is entered in court and finally an eviction is implemented. According to results from a postal survey of local authority and housing association housing providers, the majority of evictions implemented during 2002/03 were for rent arrears (92.6%). That said, 5.6 percent of evictions were for ASB and a further 0.7 percent for ASB and rent arrears combined. This may seem a small proportion of the total, yet, according to Pawson et al. (2005b: 40), '[t]hese figures suggest that around 1,800 "anti-social" tenants will have been evicted in 2002/03 – of the order of one in every 3,000 tenants across England.'

While a number of studies have looked at how much ASB powers are being used by social landlords, there has not been any study so far that has evaluated the effectiveness of this enforcement approach. That said, few social landlords would rely entirely on these enforcement measures, preferring to balance these with neighbour mediation approaches or other preventative measures – more of which in Chapter 8. One major issue rising from ASB enforcement and housing is where the evicted tenant is meant to go. It may be to less popular estates – possibly exacerbating problems of ASB there and making them even less popular. Evicted tenants may find their only option is private rented accommodation and away from any support programmes available in the social housing sector. Anecdotally, some enforcement officers have commented that they may prefer the 'difficult' tenant to stay where they are, because at least they know where they are, unlike in the private rented sector where they can 'fall off' the officers' list.

Legislation to enforce 'better' parenting

While housing has been a major focus of tackling ASB, so too has parenting. In Chapter 4, evidence was presented that the pubic frequently equates youthful misbehaviour to inadequate parenting. The government has been quick to pick up on this. The use of Parenting Orders and Parenting Contracts has already been mentioned in Chapter 6 (see also Ministry of Justice 2007). However, to recap, Parenting Orders were introduced with the 1998 Crime and Disorder Act. They were strengthened in the 2003 Anti-Social Behaviour Act, which also saw the introduction of the less formal and voluntary Parenting Contracts.

A Parenting Order carries a maximum sanction of £1000 fine. Conditions attached to the order can be that the parent ensures control over the child (such as that the child is not allowed out of the house after a certain time) and that the parent attends specified counselling or guidance courses or programmes. These can last up to three months. Parenting Orders and Contracts can be sought if the child is on an ASBO. However, they are similarly available if the child has received a Child Safety Order[5] or Sexual Offences Prevention Order. They are also available if a child engages in more serious criminal activity or persistently truants from school. With the 2006 Education and Inspections Act (s.98–99) this was extended to include serious misbehaviour by a pupil not yet excluded. Parenting Orders can be applied for by a Youth Offending Team, local authority, registered social landlord or a 'relevant body' in education (the local education authority, head teacher or governing body).

The focus on parental responsibility certainly fitted with the Labour government's communitarian leanings – as influenced by Etzioni (1993a, b) – with its stated emphasis on 'respect and responsibility' (Home Office 2003c). According to Johnson (1999: 91–2): 'The emphasis of communitarianism is on duties and responsibilities rather than rights … Among the cures for a society dominated by selfishness, greed and materialism is a return to traditional family values, reversing the "parental deficit".' Thus, according to Charles Clarke, MP, speaking while Home Secretary (Respect website 2005):

> We recognise that parenting is a difficult job … Where people want help we will provide it. Where they are unwilling or unable to accept that help, we are not afraid to intervene. Ensuring that parents are supported or challenged to accept their responsibility is the right response where a child is disruptive in school or in the neighbourhood.

How much parents are truly responsible for their children's behaviour was an issue raised in Chapter 4. Just as important is how much the state should, or should not, be involved in family life. According to Article 8 of the European Convention on Human Rights everyone has a right to private and family life protected from arbitrary interference from the state. Yet, with its emphasis on *responsibility*, the Labour government has shown increased willingness to extend state intervention into family life (Labour would argue that this is far from arbitrary interference). By forcefully intervening the government has laid itself open to claims of being a 'nanny state'.[6] More specifically, according to Goldson and Jamieson (2002: 82), the state has tended to be interested in intervening in only *certain* types of family as, 'an extension of punitiveness underpinned by stigmatising and pathologising constructions of working class families'. In political and moral discourses this has the potential to create a simplistic divide between 'good' and 'bad' parents, and is similar to underclass thinking relating to 'deserving' and 'undeserving' poor (cf. Murray 1990; see also Chapter 3).

Of course, parenting classes in themselves can be a good thing, but should certain parents be made to attend them by law? An important study on coercive drug treatment by McSweeney et al. (2007) may help here. I am not suggesting these are the same clientele (although there may be overlap in some circumstances), only that the two approaches follow similar rationales. McSweeney and colleagues found that both court mandated clients and those who attended drug treatment voluntarily displayed sustained drug use reductions and improvements in offending outcomes. Perhaps coercion can work? However, the authors also observed that expectations should be realistic and court mandated programmes did not have superior client retention to voluntary schemes. The threat of censure in this case made little difference to the (albeit positive) outcome, although it may have made initial involvement more likely. If the same is true for parenting programmes – and it is a big 'if' – then there may be a place for Parenting Orders in extreme circumstances, but voluntary participation would be preferable. This is where Parenting Contracts, working in a similar fashion to ABCs, may have the advantage.

On-the-spot fines

The idea of an on-the-spot fine for anti-social 'yobs' has been an attractive one for the Labour government. Tony Blair, in particular, expressed his support for swift summary justice. For instance in a speech made in 2006, whilst acknowledging civil liberty concerns, he stated: '[H]ere's the rub. Without summary powers to attack ASB ... it won't be beaten ... The scale of what we face is such that, whatever the theory, in practice, in real every day street life, it can't be tackled without such powers' (Blair 2006a: 90).

As explored in Chapter 2, the scale of the problem (as claimed by Blair) can certainly be questioned. However, the government was also motivated by frustration at the slow speed and cost of criminal justice. In 2006 the government opted for a review of the criminal justice system in order to deliver '*simple, speedy, summary justice*' (DCA 2006). Along with the ASBO and various other orders discussed in this chapter, the on-the-spot fine is a classic piece of summary justice, what have become known as fixed penalty notices (FPNs). The alleged advantages is that they are 'simple' and 'speedy'. However, there are justice concerns. Blair had attempted to take things one step further, famously claiming the police should be able to take perpetrators to a cashpoint in order to pay their fine: 'A thug might think twice about kicking in your gate, throwing traffic cones around your street or hurling abuse into the night sky if he thought he might get picked up by the police, taken to a cashpoint and asked to pay an on the spot fine of, for example, £100' (Blair 2000). He had to withdraw this particular suggestion a week later after there was a lack of interest from the police, and a fair amount of mockery from the media and opposition politicians (e.g. BBC 2000). Instead, Labour decided simply to build on existing FPN provisions.

Rather than use historic by-law powers (as noted above), many local authorities have been enthusiastic in using FPNs to deal with minor anti-social behaviours. The key pieces of legislation are the 1990 Environmental Protection Act and the 2005 Clean Neighbourhoods and Environment Act[7] (Defra 2006a). FPNs are one-off penalties and can be issued on anyone from the age of ten. They tend to be for environmental ASB, for such things as dropping litter, fly posting, graffiti, noisy neighbours and licensed premises and not clearing up dog mess.[8] FPNs usually come with a £75 on-the-spot fine, and are not criminal sanctions. They can be issued by local authority and police personnel, including community support officers and other 'accredited persons'.

With the 2001 Criminal Justice and Police Act, Labour also introduced penalty notices for disorder (PNDs) for people aged 18 and over. After being used in pilot areas PNDs were introduced nationally in 2003. Following the 2003 Anti-Social Behaviour Act they were also made available to 16- and 17-year-olds. PNDs can be used for a huge range of offences, from dropping litter, being drunk and disorderly or breaching a fireworks curfew, through to buying alcohol for someone who is underage, trespass on a railway or even for shoplifting (up to a value of £200). The full list is given in Box 7.1 (correct at 2008). PNDs are mainly designed for use by the police (including British Transport Police, community support officers and other 'accredited persons') (see Home Office 2006e).

A potential issue with both FPNs and PNDs is that, just like ASBOs, they blur the line between criminal and non-criminal behaviour; for instance by treating shoplifting and dropping litter the same. There are also clear civil liberty concerns, as illustrated by the following quotation from an article in the *Daily Telegraph*:

> Last week, Mr Blair boasted that the Government had 'reversed the burden of proof' in anti-social behaviour cases. If you get a fixed penalty notice for loutish behaviour, the onus is on you to prove your innocence rather than on the police to prove your guilt. Yobs are not quite marched to cash points – they are given 30 days to pay a fine – but neither is the evidence against them weighed up in court. (Sylvester 2006)

Box 7.1   Offences liable to a fixed penalty for disorder (FPN)

Upper tier offences (£80 fine):

Anti-social behaviours

- Knowingly giving a false alarm to a person acting on behalf of a fire and rescue authority (England only)
- Knowingly giving a false alarm to a fire brigade (Wales only)
- Behaviour likely to cause harassment alarm or distress (1986 Public Order Act (s.5)
- Throwing fireworks in a thoroughfare
- Disorderly behaviour whilst drunk in public
- Criminal damage (under £500 value)
- Breach of fireworks curfew (11pm–7am)
- Possession of adult firework in public place by under 18
- Possession of category 4 firework
- Using a public electronic communications network in order to cause annoyance, inconvenience or needless anxiety.

Alcohol-related offences

- Sale of alcohol to a person under 18 (anywhere, not just in licensed premises)
- Purchase of alcohol by a person under 18
- Purchase or attempting to purchase alcohol on behalf of a person under 18 (includes licensed premises and off-licences)
- Consumption of alcohol by persons under 18 or allowing such consumption
- Delivery of alcohol to a person under 18 or allowing such delivery
- Selling or allowing alcohol to be sold to a drunken person on relevant premises (licensed premises, premises with club premise certificates and temporary activity premises)
- Obtaining alcohol for a person who is drunk.

Other offences

- Wasting police time or giving a false report
- Retail theft (under £200 value).

Lower tier offences (£50 fine):

Anti-social behaviours

- Throwing stones, etc., at trains or other things on railways
- Leaving/depositing litter.

Alcohol-related offences

- Being drunk in a highway, other public place or licensed premises
- Consuming alcohol in a designated public place, contrary to requirement by constable not to do so
- Consumption of alcohol by a person under 18 in a bar (1), or allowing this (2).

Other offences

- Trespassing on a railway.

Source: Government 'Respect' website, last updated Feb. 2008.

Both FPNs and PNDs have proved to be popular among those who issue them. For instance, in 2004 63,639 PNDs were issued by police forces in England and Wales. A year later there were 146,481 (Home Office 2007c). Using 2004 figures, the vast majority of PNDs were for the vaguely defined Public Order Act offence of 'causing harassment, alarm or distress', and for the more specific 'drunk and disorderly'. A breakdown of 2004 figures, giving the top ten offences, is provided in Table 7.2.

A crime fighting rationale has been suggested for FPNs, in that those given a notice may also be wanted for other more serious offences. That said, in trying to determine whether this was the case, Wellsmith and Guille (2005) came up against data collection issues. For instance, in their study, over half the FPNs issued by police were for vehicles without a current registered keeper. Whatever the rationale, there is a possibility that some police are using these notices as a quick and easy way of dealing with a problem, without recourse to the hassle of a criminal charge. According to Erol (2006: 2) the benefits to the police were 'reduced file preparation time, with reduced paperwork, meaning officers were able to spend more time out on patrol'. This is a good thing and, if used appropriately, there are clear advantages to a system of enforcement that is both simple and quick. However, there is also the danger that officers can hand out summary justice in the same way traffic wardens can hand out parking tickets. Clear guidance (and possibly restraint) are needed.

Table 7.2 PNDs issued by police in England and Wales, 2004

Offence	No.
Causing harassment, alarm or distress	24,840
Drunk and disorderly	22,644
Purchasing alcohol for consumption in bar of licensed premises for under 18	2116
Breach of fireworks curfew	1253
Theft (retail under £200)	1052
Wasting police time	813
Consuming alcohol in a designated public place	423
Throwing fireworks	161
Sending false messages	92
Throwing stones at trains	85
Other	338
Total	53,817 complete records (*actual total = 63,639*)

Source: Home Office 2005d.

Enforcing peace and order?

If the objective for tackling ASB is to improve people's quality of life, then unwanted and excessive noise would certainly fit within the auspices of ASB policy. Yet, deciding which noises can cause concern is not so clear. For instance, in a UK-wide survey by BRE (2002: 65), respondents were asked how much they thought noise spoilt their home life. While 75 percent said 'not at all' or 'not very much', 12 percent said 'a little', 7 percent 'quite a lot'; and 1 percent 'totally'. For the 8 percent affected quite a lot or totally, noise is clearly a serious issue. However, this noise nuisance can be *anything*, for example, including aircraft noise, traffic or police sirens (which, presumably are not the target of ASB enforcement), through to noisy neighbours and noisy businesses and entertainment venues (which are). Clearly, noise nuisance is not an issue for the vast majority of people. For the minority who do suffer, there are a range of enforcement powers that can be used. For instance, noise abatement notices (Taylor 2006) can be served following the 1990 Environmental Protection Act and 1996 Noise Act. Under these powers, local authorities can remove equipment that is the source of the nuisance. With the 2005 Clean Neighbourhoods Act (Defra 2006b) local authorities were given the power to serve noise abatement notices to dwellings and businesses if the noise is thought to be 'prejudicial to health or a nuisance' (a definition taken from the 1990 Environmental Protection Act) (see also CIEH

2006). A person or business issued an noise abatement notice is given a seven-day period in which to remedy the problem. If the problem persists it can then lead to a fine and summary conviction.

Closure notices and orders have been introduced to deal with noisy and disorderly premises. Closure notices, as introduced with the 2003 Anti-Social Behaviour Act, have a wide remit. For instance, the police – in consultation with the local authority – are given the power to close premises where class A drugs are being used or dealt and where 'the use of the premises is associated with the occurrence of disorder or serious nuisance to members of the public' (s.1(1b)) – a measure often sold as 'crack-house closures' (e.g. Peters and Walker 2005; Home Office 2007c).

If a closure notice is made, this must be taken to the magistrates' court in order to apply for a closure order, which can last up to three months. Additionally, local authorities and environmental health officers were granted the power to issue closure orders directly in order to close licensed premises for 24 hours due to 'noise nuisance'.[9]

Such enforcement powers have been popular among local authorities; however, most have used them alongside other preventative options and mediation services. Mediation, in particular, is thought to be effective for noisy neighbour disputes (Dignam et al. 1996). And as an approach, mediation fits perfectly with the notion of mutuality promoted by the government's 'Respect' agenda. Yet, like so much of the work to tackle ASB, this tends to come with the threat of censure. As for closure orders for 'crack houses', by including this within the remit of ASB measures again confuses the issue as to what is anti-social and what is criminal. Dealing and using class A drugs is clearly criminal. It may be helpful if policy literature on the subject avoided such confusion.

Area-based restrictions – including Dispersal Orders

Apart from the ASBO, the most significant ASB enforcement introduced by the Labour government has been the range of area-based restrictions, most notably the Dispersal Order. The key aim has been to restrict 'unwanted' people from certain public spaces – an idea that borrows from earlier curfew schemes and from the area restrictions attached to the ASBO. Young people, in particular, have been targeted, and can now find themselves excluded from certain public spaces at certain times (see Rogers and Coaffee 2005; Smithson and Flint 2006; Crawford and Lister 2007). Alongside the Dispersal Order there has been the introduction of Designated Public Place Orders designed to limit on-street drinking.

In terms of recent legislation such area-based restrictions originated with local child curfew schemes introduced with the 1998 Crime and

Disorder Act. Their objective was to: 'protect the local community from the alarm and distress caused by groups of young people involved in anti-social behaviour at night, and to protect children and young people from risks of being unaccompanied on the streets late at night'.

The intention was for local authorities to designate areas where the schemes would operate, placing restrictions on under tens. With the 2001 Criminal Justice and Police Act powers were extended to under 16s and the police could also apply for a curfew. The curfew could last for up to 90 days with the aim to 'protect the local community from anti-social behaviour instigated by groups of young people at night' (Home Office 2003e). Children found outside their homes after the curfew could be taken home. Officially, the curfews are not only to 'protect the local community', but also to protect the child. As such there is no penalty attached to them. And if anyone ten or under is found out after the curfew, they can be made subject to a child safety order.[10] Despite the protection rhetoric, removing children and young people from the streets is very much a punitive action. There are long established concerns about misbehaving young people in public places (e.g. Phillips and Cochrane 1988). Such fears that young people are 'up to no good', in conjunction with parental fears over child safety in public places – the conflicting views of children 'as risk' and 'at risk' (e.g. Kelly 2003; Valentine 2004; Woolley 2006) – has meant that young people and children are not meant to be seen on the streets and certainly not after dark.

There are obvious concerns with such an approach, as being disproportionate and targeting a particularly vulnerable age group. For instance, according to the Parliamentary Joint Committee on Human Rights (2001): '[G]iven the existence of other wide powers available to the police to protect young persons and to maintain public order, child curfews may be disproportionate interferences with rights ...' Although similar curfew schemes have proved popular elsewhere such as in the US (e.g. Walsh 2002), and have been tested in Scotland (Waiton 2001), the Local Child Curfew schemes have not been popular. According to the Youth Justice Board website (accessed April 2008), no local authority has applied for a curfew since introduction.

Dispersal Orders

Despite the lack of enthusiasm for child curfews, the Labour government had not given up on the idea of area or temporal exclusion and the 2003 Anti-Social Behaviour Act (s. 30)[11] saw the introduction of Dispersal Order powers. The police – working with the local authority – have the power to designate areas of heightened ASB concern as dispersal order zones, which can be in force for up to three months. Within a designated zone, groups may be dispersed if a police officer, or community support officer, 'has reasonable grounds for believing that the presence or behaviour of a group of two or more persons ... has resulted, or is likely to result, in any members of the public being intimidated, harassed, alarmed or distressed'. This emphasizes a problem with much ASB enforcement. Should it be proactive and target potential misbehaviour (in this case *presence*), or should it focus on *actual behaviour?* (Walsh 2003; Crawford and Lister 2007; Millie 2008a) A focus on presence has clear human rights concerns. Dispersal powers may be used more intelligently, but they run the risk of excluding all outsiders because, by their presence in public spaces, they *look* like they may cause problems. Within such a zone the police has the power to exclude for up to 24 hours. Refusal to cooperate can result in arrest and a summary charge. There are additional youth curfew-type powers attached to the order. Anyone aged under 16 found unsupervised in a designated zone between 9pm and 6am can be taken home by a police officer, who: 'may remove the person to the person's place of residence unless he has reasonable grounds for believing that the person would, if removed to that place, be likely to suffer significant harm (s.30(6b))'. This was, in effect, an attempt to revive the flagging fortunes of the child curfew schemes. However, this aspect of the Dispersal Order was challenged by the Divisional Court (2005) [12] stating that the power did not allow for reasonable force. The response by the police was to suspend use of this aspect of the order. However, a year later the decision was reversed by the Court of Appeal (2006). [13] It was found that, by 'removing' the person, the power is, by definition, coercive. As noted by Brotherton (2006): '[T]he word "remove" in s 30(6) of the 2003 Act carried with it a coercive power; and the word in its context naturally and compellingly meant "take away using reasonable force if necessary". However, a constable or CSO exercising the power given by s 30(6) was not free to act arbitrarily.' By not being an arbitrary power (like the child curfew scheme) it was also decided that the power was not a curfew. The Court of Appeal ruling gave conditions to the use of 'reasonable force' in that a young person could only be removed if they were at risk of ASB or crime or were causing, or there was a risk of them causing, ASB (Dobson 2006). So rather than removing all young people, the police could remove those perceived to be 'a risk' or 'at risk'. Therefore, although it is not an arbitrary power, the police could still enforce it in a subjective manner. However, according to Crawford and Lister (2007) many forces have been reluctant to use this particular power at all.

A Dispersal Order is often seen as a youth focused measure and a lot of police forces have used the main part of the order in this way, particularly on social housing estates to deal with 'youths hanging around'. In some market towns dispersal orders have also been used to deal with youth nuisance within the town centre (see Box 7.2). However, orders can also be targeted at *any* group deemed to be behaving anti-socially. Most often this will be within a city centre context. For instance, in 2004 the London Borough of Camden established a dispersal zone for the whole retail, pub and club area of Camden Town with a focus on drug and alcohol problems. Similarly in London's West End, in 2006 a dispersal order was in place that covered much of Soho, from Oxford Street down to Leicester Square, Piccadilly Circus and Trafalgar Square. A more targeted example is provided by Crawford and Lister (2007: 13) who report an order put in place in 2004 for just 24 hours on Hallowe'en (and repeated in 2005). The order covered a single street and was in force to protect an Asian family that had been subject to racial harassment and fireworks thrown at their premises on a previous Hallowe'en. A further example comes from Hodgkinson and Tilley (2007: 388), who report a Midlands city that used a Dispersal Order 'to tackle traffic and spectator problems caused by "boyracers" '.[14]

Box 7.2 Dispersal order notice, Melton Mowbray Police Station, Leicestershire, 2007

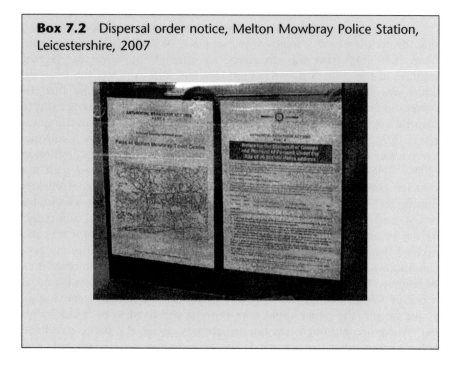

According to Home Office figures (2005e) over half of orders reported in surveys[15] between January 2004 and June 2005 were for residential areas (52%). A further 28 percent were in town/city centres and other shopping areas. A similar pattern emerged from analysis of Metropolitan Police data for April 2006 to March 2007 (Crawford and Lister 2007: 12). In London, 51 percent of all orders were in town/city centres or other shopping areas, and 34 percent were in residential areas. A few Dispersal Orders were in car parks,

bus or train stations, parks or particular 'beauty spots'. Orders were frequently renewed, with 36 percent in areas where there had been previous
orders.

Although the data did not indicate what types of residential areas were
targeted, anecdotally, they are more frequently in areas of social housing.
Despite the danger of stigmatizing such areas, it seems the police are using
these powers where ASB concerns *are* at their highest – in town and city
centres and poorer residential areas (as discussed in Chapter 2).

Nationally, the dispersal of groups powers have been popular among
police forces since being introduced in January 2004. In a survey of 214[16]
local partnerships (CDRPs), for the first full year of data (April 2004–March
2005) there were 610 orders reported in England and Wales. There was a wide
range in the number of orders across forces, ranging from two to 123 (Home
Office 2005e). However, after initial enthusiasm, 355 orders were reported in
2005–06 (Home Office 2007c; see also Crawford and Lister 2007).

Despite the high number of orders, there has so far been very little
assessment on how they operate. An early study was by Hannah Smithson
(2005) looking at the implementation of an order in East Manchester. In this
study, one practitioner justified the order because, '[y]oung people on these
estates have had a free rein in terms of [being] able to do what they want
when they want and cause distress to good residents, good people' (2005: 5).
The order ran for three months from September 2004. At the same time, I
was involved in monitoring progress with an order running on a social
housing estate in the Midlands.[17] The Midlands order ran for six months
from September 2004 and was similarly targeted at young people. A more
detailed assessment of Dispersal Order policy and implementation was
conducted in Leeds and Sheffield by Crawford and Lister (2007). Bringing
this evidence together a number of implementation issues can be identified
and are summarized in Box 7.3.

Other issues concerned possible displacement. For instance, Crawford
and Lister (2007) found that problems were sometimes shifted elsewhere for
the duration of the order. In the Midlands example, for the first night of the
order there was displacement *to* the dispersal zone, acting as an attractor to
youth from surrounding estates anxious to see what all the fuss was about
after seeing it mentioned on the local TV news.

More broadly, the use of dispersal orders can be seen as part of a process
of reclaiming public spaces from undesirables[18] (MacLeod 2002; Holden and
Iveson 2003; Rogers and Coaffee 2005). This would tie in with the regeneration rational for tackling ASB considered in Chapter 5. Questions need to be
asked as to the reasons Dispersal Orders are put in place; are they there to
tackle serious problems of disorder (in which case they may be justified
under strict controls) or are they used to tidy the streets and remove
unsightly groups of youths or street people because they are perceived as a

threat? In this case, dispersal would be a wholly disproportionate response. The concept of 'contested spaces' is relevant (e.g. Aitken 2001; Hubbard 2005; Hadfield 2006), that within any neighbourhood different groups can have different contested uses of public spaces. It is a question of whose use of the street is deemed more 'appropriate'.

Box 7.3 Implementing Dispersal Orders: some issues

1. *Setting up the order*: It is meant to be in response to a recognized problem and done in close cooperation with the local authority. In the Midlands example, although the local authority was consulted, this news had not filtered to all the relevant departments. The Youth Offending Team Manager commented, 'I'll tell you how I got to know about it, I had a phone call at my home at about 10 o'clock at night from one of my managers saying, "*have you seen Midlands Today?*" '[19]

2. *Maintaining initial enthusiasm and resources*: For both the Midlands study and the research in Leeds, initial agency enthusiasm was not always met by sustained police resources for the duration of the order. As a police manager in Leeds commented: 'Because what happens with a dispersal order is you do a lot of press, you put in extra resources to try and have an impact, but you can't maintain them. So you get a quick fix but it's not necessarily a long-term gain ... ' (Crawford and Lister 2007: 34). The Manchester example was better resourced having received specific funding as part of the New Deal for Communities.

3. *Dealing with local hostility*: This can come from the groups targeted, as reported in Smithson and Flint (2006: 36): 'Much of the hostility of young people in Manchester towards the police arose from the curfew aspect of the dispersal order which presupposes that young people's presence in specific locations at certain times is problematic or unacceptable'. In the Midlands study a youth services worker thought there was hostility from the whole community: 'This was fairly overblown by the newspapers, [they] referred to "floods of people on the streets" and then the police were called out to attend to them. Now I think really it was more a case of the police tried to enforce the curfews and the residents wouldn't have it. So in terms of the police, there's a big distance, there's no trust'.

4. *Managing expectations and keeping people informed*: According to Crawford and Lister (2007: 32) 'officers overseeing their implementation have become aware of their tendency to raise expectations

among the community. To address this, early consultation with the community is seem as crucial … ' In the Manchester study, it was thought that, 'efforts need to be made to publicise the implementation of the DO to ensure that residents are aware of its powers' (Smithson, 2005: 17).

5. *An exit strategy*: As Dispersal Orders are time limited, something needs to be in place so that any gains made are not lost. In the Midlands example, detached youth work was established during the order period, and this was to continue after the order finished – in something like a 'crackdown and consolidation'.[20] A common complaint in the Leeds and Sheffield study was that the order was just a 'sticking plaster'; as one resident put it, 'I think it gave people breathing space and disrupted the habits of some young people, but it is only a sticking plaster' (Crawford and Lister 2007: 73).

Designated Public Place Orders

Although the Dispersal Order is the main area-based restriction on ASB in Britain, it is not the only one. With the 2001 Criminal Justice and Police Act (s.13) [21] came the Designated Public Place Orders (DPPOs). These became active on 1 September 2006 and replaced existing local by-law provisions. Specific public spaces can be designated by local authorities as alcohol-free zones in an attempt to 'restrict anti-social drinking in designated public places' (Home Office 2007d). Enforcement of the DPPO allows the police to stop and confiscate alcohol, or give PNDs of £50, with failure to comply possibly leading to a fine of up to £500. Relatedly, the 1997 Confiscation of Alcohol (Young Persons) Act gave police the power to confiscate drink (and bottles, cans, etc.) from anyone under 18 in certain public places.

DPPO censure is attached to failure to comply with a police officer's[22] request and the officer's focus is meant to be on street drinkers thought to be causing a nuisance or annoyance or, more seriously, disorder. Clearly, the aim is to target certain kinds of anti-social or disorderly public drinker as it is not an offence to consume alcohol in a designated area. National and local policy has at the same time been encouraging more 'respectable' public drinking with its push for 'café culture' by encouraging pavement cafés and bars. The government has also introduced the notion of 24-hour drinking with the 2003 Licensing Act, in an attempt to encourage responsible drinking habits. However, this has not been the reality of drinking in British cities, dominated by a monoculture of youthful excess (e.g. Hadfield 2006; Norris and Williams 2008). For instance, according to research by Roberts and Eldridge (2007: 3):

By removing terminal hours [with the Licensing Act], it was anticipated consumers would adopt a more European and leisurely approach to alcohol consumption. Equally, it was anticipated that the
new regime would allow variety of premises to open at night.
Despite the Government and the media's ongoing discussion of café
culture, this study found no evidence of greater diversity in the
night-time economy.

The exclusionary nature of many urban centres at night in Britain
means DPPOs might be a useful measure in addresses some of the anti-social
excesses that come with the night-time economy. However, the orders need
to be part of a wider programme of preventative and other measures.

Concluding comments

In this chapter, excluding the ASBO, some of the major enforcement
measures that are available in Britain have been presented. What is clear is
the sheer range of enforcement options available to local authorities, housing
providers, the police and other agencies. However, enforcement can never be
the whole picture. Elsewhere (Millie et al. 2005a) a balance between enforcement and prevention is called for. And with the Respect Action Plan (Respect
Task Force 2006) the government called for 'a broader approach', promoting
both enforcement and prevention measures. However, *enforcing* standards of
behaviour was still the priority: 'We need to tackle root causes with the same
rigour and determination as we have taken with anti-social behaviour.
Everyone can change [but] if people who need help will not take it, we will
make them' (Tony Blair, cited in Respect Task Force 2006: 1). If ASB strategies
are to be rebalanced, then there needs to be greater use of a range of
prevention, mediation and support options. These are considered in the
following chapter.

Selected reading

In terms of non-ASBO enforcement measures, there has been a great deal of focus on the regulation of acceptable behaviour within a housing context. For this a great place to start is the edited volume by John Flint (2006). A high profile measure is the Dispersal Order, and Crawford and Lister have produced a very good appraisal of its use. This and selected other reading are listed below:

- Burney, E. (2000) Ruling out trouble: Anti-social behaviour and housing management, *The Journal of Forensic Psychology*, 11(2): 268–73.
- Crawford, A. and Lister, S. (2007) *The Use and Impact of Dispersal Orders: Sticking Plasters and Wake-up Calls*. Bristol: Policy Press.
- Flint, J. (2006b) Housing and the new governance of conduct, in J. Flint (ed.), *Housing, Urban Governance and Anti-social Behaviour: Perspectives, Policy and Practice*. Bristol: Policy Press.
- Hadfield, P. (2006) *Bar Wars: Contesting the Night in Contemporary British Cities*. Oxford: Oxford University Press.
- Home Office (2007c) *Tools and Powers to Tackle Anti-social Behaviour*. London: Home Office (Respect Task Force).
- Nixon, J., Blandy, S., Hunter, C., Reeve, K. and Jones, A. (2003) *Tackling Anti-social Behaviour in Mixed Tenure Areas*. London: ODPM.
- Norris, P. and Williams, D. (2008) 'The 2003 Licensing Act: the answer to 'binge drinking' and alcohol related disorder?, in P. Squires (ed.), *ASBO Nation: The Criminalisation of Nuisance*. Bristol: Policy Press.
- Respect Task Force (2006) *Respect Action Plan*. London: Home Office.

Notes

1   *R v. Howell* (1982) QB 416, 426.
2   Excluding referral orders.
3   Further amended with the 2006 Police and Justice Act (s.26).
4   Demotions were introduced just a year earlier on 30 June 2004.
5   Given to a child who has breached a local child curfew scheme. Despite enthusiasm from the government, no local authority has used these powers.

6   For instance, it has been suggested the government has refused to ban smacking for fear of being labelled a 'nanny state' (e.g. Lister 2006).

7   There is a range of other relevant legislation, including the 1978 Refuse Disposal (Amenity) Act; 1996 Noise Act; 2003 Local Government Act; and the 2003 Anti-Social Behaviour Act.

8   Section 59 of the 2005 Clean Neighbourhoods and Environment Act also introduced FPNs for persons who had committed an offence under a dog control order.

9   Similarly, under the 2001 Criminal Justice and Police Act (s.19–27) closure notices and closure orders can be used for unlicensed premises. With the 2007 Criminal Justice and Immigration Bill (s.103), the intention is to extend closure orders to cover all 'premises associated with persistent disorder or nuisance'.

10 'designed to help the child improve their behaviour and is likely to be used alongside work with the family and others to address any underlying problems. The orders were introduced by s,11 of the Crime and Disorder Act 1998 and amended by s.60 of the Children Act 2004' (Respect website accessed Apr. 2008).

11 The equivalent in Scotland were introduced with the 2004 Anti-Social Behaviour (Scotland) Act.

12 *R(W) v.* (1) *Commissioner of Police for the Metropolis*, (2) *London Borough of Richmond-upon-Thames*, (3) *Secretary of State for the Home Department* [2005] EWHC 1586.

13 The same case, but at the Court of Appeal: [2006] EWCA Civ 458. For a detailed explanation of the decision, see Dobson (2006).

14 Boyracers customize their cars, often to make them more 'sporty' or outrageous. They can sometimes cause problems for the police when unofficial meets are organized where people show off their cars. In Australia, the equivalent are 'hoons' who go 'hooning'.

15 Results from two surveys conducted of England and Wales police forces. Not all forces responded to both surveys.

16 214 CDRPs out of 373, a response rate of 57%.

17 Unpublished report, 2005.

18 A form of 'revanchism', an issue explored further in Chapter 9.

19 A local TV news programme.

20 A 'crackdown and consolidation' has an initial period of intense police activity to target a crime or disorder problem, but this is supported by preventative and other support programmes so that any gains made can be sustained. The crackdown and consolidation is then repeated in a cycle (see Millie 2005).

21 Slight amendments made with the 2006 Violent Crime Reduction Act (s.26).

22 Or community support officer.

8 Preventing anti-social behaviour

If a more balanced approach to ASB is to be promoted then there has to be greater emphasis on prevention; but how you attempt to prevent ASB will be dependent on what you think causes ASB (as well as what you think ASB *is*). Much that is discussed in this chapter relates to the discussion of possible causes in Chapter 4. For instance, there is a great deal of emphasis in policy on early intervention and parenting initiatives. Such programmes will be informed by psychosocial developmental thinking and assessment of risk and protective factors. People who believe a great deal of youthful ASB is caused by boredom will promote various diversionary activities. If ASB is down to a lack of respect for others, then programmes that encourage cooperation and intergenerational understanding, will be important in preventing future ASB. Similarly, mediation schemes can be implemented to encourage neighbourly trust and understanding and contributing to the development of collective efficacy and social capital, thereby improving mechanisms of informal social control.

As with discussion of enforcement measure, it is not possible to consider all things that may prevent ASB. Instead, this chapter focuses on some of the key approaches and developments: including, early intervention and work with parents; diversionary activities; community involvement schemes; mediation; and work focused on the night-time economy. The chapter also considers the possibility that design solutions may be able to contribute to a package of preventative measures.

Early intervention and parenting programmes

In line with a criminal careers perspective, there has been much interest from government in early intervention work in an attempt to promote pro-social behaviour *before* a child or young person moves onto anti-social and criminal activities. Emphasis is on working with the very young alongside providing

programmes of support and education for parents. As a community development worker has been quoted: 'If we are going to make a long-term
difference with young people, it doesn't start when they are 12; it's got to
start when they are two or three or four' (Millie et al. 2005a: 29). In the same
study, a local MP emphasized what he saw as the importance of early
intervention and working with parents or potential parents: 'The 0–5 group
needs to be really rigorously targeted in a constituency like mine. They need
to be targeted and their parents need to be targeted even before the kids are
born. Teenagers will be the mums and dads of tomorrow, teach them about
what the family is, what it means to have a family.'

When asked if early intervention risks stigmatizing certain populations,
the same MP replied, 'I don't care. I want to sort them out and give them
their life chance ... The stigma of being a criminal or being illiterate or not
having a job is far greater than intervening.' In Britain, the government has
been keen to promote the welfare and development of children via its 'Every
Child Matters' agenda and appointment of a children's commissioner (Chief
Secretary to the Treasury 2003); plus, possibly of most relevance here, the
'SureStart' programme (e.g. Tunstill et al. 2005, 2006; Belsky et al. 2007). As
previously noted, 'SureStart' was strongly influenced by the American High/
Scope Perry Pre-School programme that started in 1962. In an evaluation of
the lifetime effects of the High/Scope programme (Schweinhart et al. 2004)
some bold claims of effectiveness have been made:

> Adults at age 40 who participated in a high-quality preschool
> program in their early years have higher earnings, are more likely
> to hold a job, have committed fewer crimes, and are more likely to
> have graduated from High School. Overall, the study documented a
> return to society of more than $17 for every tax dollar invested in
> the early education program.

More specifically, it is claimed that those who received high quality
early education had fewer arrests than a non-programme control group. For
instance, 36 percent had been arrested five or more times compared to 55
percent of the control group. Similarly, 32 percent of those on the programme were later arrested for violent crime, compared to 48 percent of the
control (and 14% for drug crimes, compared to 34% of the control). A similar
American early intervention programme has been 'Head Start' which has
been running in various guises since 1965. Aimed at four-year-olds,[1] the
objective has been 'to bring about a greater degree of social competence in
children of low income families' (McKey et al. 1985: 2). It has been claimed
that the programme has positively influenced children's cognitive and
socio-emotional development, health, family and community life (McKey et
al. 1985; see also Zigler and Styfco 2004). With its emphasis on social
inclusion, these claims gained the attention of New Labour in Britain. Other

family-based programmes have been evaluated with many found to reduce later delinquency (although not all). However, an issue in evaluating effectiveness is that most programmes employ a range of interventions and, as a result, it is not easy to identify the specific ingredients that are successful (Farrington and Welsh 1999).

Nonetheless, the SureStart programme was launched by Labour in 1998 with a focus on the very young (under four) and parents living in deprived neighbourhoods. From the beginning, it was nothing if not ambitions; according to Norman Glass[2] of the Treasury (1999: 257): 'SureStart is a radical cross-departmental strategy to raise the physical, social, emotional and intellectual status of young children through improved services'. Glass also heralded the programme as an example of 'evidence-based policy making'. According to Smith (2006: 80), 'Glass's claim arguable errs on the side of optimism, since the relevant evidence came from a small number of studies conducted in the USA'; however, Smith does concede that this evidence has 'some substance'. In a SureStart programme implementation document (Tunstill et al. 2005: 13) the aims were stated as: 'to work with parents-to-be, parents and children, to promote the physical, intellectual and social development of babies and young children, particularly those who are disadvantaged' (see also DfES 2006). The full objectives are summarized in Box 8.1. Objective 4 is concerned directly with reducing future ASB and crime.

Box 8.1 SureStart objectives

1 *Be healthy:* Enjoying good physical and mental health and living a healthy lifestyle.
2 *Stay safe:* Being protected from harm and neglect and growing up able to look after themselves.
3 *Enjoy and achieve:* Getting the most out of life and developing broad skills for adulthood.
4 *Make a positive contribution:* To the community and to society and not engaging in anti-social or offending behaviour.
5 *Achieve economic well-being:* Not being prevented by economic disadvantage from achieving their full potential.

Source: As stated at www.surestart.gov.uk (accessed Apr. 2008).

By definition, many of the these aims, including to reduce ASB, are longer term objectives. However, early evaluation has been promising, although there have been issues with some people's ability or desire to join different schemes (Ormerod 2005; Anning and colleagues 2007). Access was similarly an issue with the US Head Start programme as there has not been enough funding for all poor families (Merrow 2004) Access problems for SureStart have been with attracting certain 'hard to reach' groups:

> [O]verall reach figures were disappointing. Those who used services often used several and reported satisfaction with them. But services offered at traditional times and in conventional formats did not reach many fathers, black and minority ethnic families and working parents. Providers found barriers to attracting 'hard to reach' families difficult to overcome. (Anning and colleagues 2007: 1)

As Sure Start has been targeted at deprived areas and families, there has been the additional possibility that some may have avoided the programme for fear of possible stigma. For instance, a recent study in the Midlands by Avis et al. (2007: 203) found: 'Parents' awareness of the targeted nature of SureStart can also lead to stigma and reluctance to use services'. The SureStart programme is currently being expanded to non-deprived areas, meaning such programme stigma may be reduced. It's a question of 'wait and see'.

The Dundee Families Project

A family-based intervention more specifically targeted at ASB was the Dundee Families Project, established in 1996 with its evaluation published in 2001 (Dillane et al. 2001; Scott 2006). The aim of the project was to work intensively with a small number of families at risk of eviction and becoming homeless as a result of ASB. The project received referrals from housing providers and from social services. As elsewhere (e.g. Atkinson et al. 2000) the project found the families tended to have multiple needs. For instance, in the Dundee project about a third were lone parent households and the vast majority were poor and in receipt of state benefits. Drug and alcohol problems were common and over half of adults had criminal convictions. Around half the children and women interviewed had suffered domestic abuse (Scott 2006: 204). In short, this was precisely the type of family that the SureStart initiative is having difficulty in reaching.

As the project focused on families 'deemed to have exhibited a range of anti-social behaviour' (Dillane et al. 2001: v), this could not be considered 'early intervention', in the strictest sense. A wide range of services was on offer including counselling, family support, after-school activities for young people, plus classes for adults in cookery, parenting, anger management and tenancy issues. Provision was via a residential 'core block' for severe cases, in dispersed tenancies and via outreach to existing tenancies (Dillane et al. 2001). Twenty-four-hour support was offered to all families on the project. According to the evaluation, 59 percent of cases were thought successful in that they completed the project. Longer term impacts are not easily measured, although the circumstances of many families did improve and eviction rates in Dundee fell following the start of the project (see Scott 2006: 215).

This apparent success led to the national introduction of 'intensive family support projects', largely based on the Dundee model (DCLG 2006b). These projects have since been rebranded as 'family intervention projects' (FIPs) (see Parr and Nixon 2008). According to the recent Youth Taskforce Action Plan (Youth Taskforce 2008: 11), FIPs are designed for, 'the most anti-social young people, making them improve their behaviour and take the help they need to turn their lives around'. Although support and prevention are integral to the projects, this clearly comes with the threat of censure for those who do not comply.

Super nannies

In an unusual move, Tony Blair, when Prime Minister, announced in the *Sun* newspaper, in November 2006, the introduction of 77 child psychologists (or 'super nannies') in some of Britain's more deprived neighbourhoods to give extra support to parents. Under the heading 'Tony Blair writes for the *Sun*', he stated:

> The 'nanny state' argument applied to this is just rubbish. No one's talking about interfering with normal family life. But life isn't normal if you've got 12-year-olds out every night, drinking and creating a nuisance on the street, with their parents not knowing or even caring. In these circumstances, a bit of nannying, with sticks and carrots, is what the local community needs, let alone the child.
> (Tony Blair 2006b)

According to the opposition, this was classic headline grabbing, coming as it did on the heals of a popular TV programme entitled *Supernanny*. Blair's differentiation between 'normal' family life and family life that 'isn't normal' is also interesting. It is certainly consistent with wider political discourse that distinguishes between a law abiding 'us' and an anti-social or criminal 'them'. It also blames parents for their children's ASB, labelling them as 'not knowing or even caring'.

Youth diversion

Beside parenting initiatives, there is a great deal of focus in policy on youth diversion; in simple terms, that young people become diverted from ASB and crime because they do not have the time or the inclination. As noted previously, youthful ASB is often seen as the result of boredom, and that 'kids will be kids' and will always push boundaries. There are a range of voluntary and state schemes available to tackle this boredom, ranging from boy scouts, youth clubs and various sporting organizations, through to more formal interventions for targeted populations thought to be at risk of ASB and crime. The government's approach to youth diversion is strongly influenced by the actuarial literature on risk and protective factors for ASB. For instance, it is stated in a recent report by HM Treasury and the Department for Children, Schools and Families (2007: 17):

> All children and young people are exposed to risk as they grow up. Where multiple risks combine – for example poor housing, lack of parental interest, irregular school attendance, or poor physical or mental health – there is an increased likelihood of poor outcomes. While the term 'risk' implies the possibility of negative outcome, young people experiencing risk factors are not inevitably on a pathway to exclusion in later life. This is because young people can develop resilience to risk through exposure to protective factors.

The recommendation of the report is involvement in 'positive activities' such as sport, the arts or other volunteering. One example is the 'Positive Futures' scheme using sport and leisure as a basis for reengaging young people living in deprived neighbourhoods (2007: 26). But it is questionable whether *all* activities need to be so structured as a great deal of youthful activity is naturally informal and yet still 'positive'. For instance, some young people will enjoy the informality of going skateboarding with their mates, or just 'hanging out' – and for the majority this will not lead to involvement in ASB or crime. Having said this, more formal activities do have their place and other young people are just as likely to prefer the structure that comes with belonging to a sport or youth club. A Youth Offending Team manager commented during a recent interview: '[W]e target in at low-level pre-criminal behaviours when we're concerned about them; get them involved in sports activities. We can do a lot with team building activities, you get all sorts of personal dynamics and skills acquisition.'[3] But a lot of official schemes are simply aimed at keeping young people busy; as one young person in a recent study described a programme: 'when there's nowt to do on the estate and everyone is bored, they just take you out to places where you can do stuff' (Mason and Prior 2008).

People have different views on the benefits of youth diversion and some perspectives are given in Box 8.2, all from practitioners interviewed in 2004. A clear need is identified for better provision, but there are concerns with *having* to occupy young people, that it can be seen as a reward for bad behaviour, and that, in some areas, kids have plenty to do anyway. More positively, the fourth respondent claims the solution is simply to ask the young people what they want (rather than assume they want what the state has on offer).

Box 8.2 Differing perspectives on youth diversion

1 *Do we really need to keep young people occupied?*

Don't get me wrong, I think we should have as much of that provision as we can get. I mean I will have as many youth workers as you can send to [the area] and as many youth clubs because clearly there is a need. But that then feeds the same circular argument. It's that you need all these facilities, you need to occupy these young people because if you don't occupy them then they are obviously going to get into trouble. And I think we have got a serious problem in society if we accept that it's true. (Community development worker 1)

2 *Is diversion a reward for bad behaviour?*

And I think it is a perception as well, [that] if you are a bad kid then you will get extra and you will be given diversion and support and everything else, and the good kids don't get anything. It is perceived that bad behaviour is rewarded and good behaviour is not rewarded and it is trying to kind of balance ... . The easiest way to change behaviour is if young people feel they are excluded from something they want to do. (Community development worker 2)

3 *Kids have plenty already (although they need more youth clubs)*

You have got your parks and you have got your football pitches, and in my area they have tennis court and football pitches, and you can play basketball. You have got your Play Stations and televisions. Even in the most deprived areas you have numerous televisions in the kids' bedrooms and it is part and parcel of life. What you should have more of I think is youth clubs. But mindless yobs are going to come in and vandalize it, because they will. (Local councillor)

4 *Ask them what they want*

I think the solution is, basically to find out. It's alright asking young people what they want. I've done it ... There's a tension, you know, where you provide things and they bore easy. Their attention if you like is so low, whereas it used to be football, cricket and stuff like that, they want IT and then, they crave something more. (Local authority worker)

Note: All interviewed during 2004 (for more from this study see Millie et al. 2005a).

A link between diversionary activities and preventing crime and ASB was also emphasized in government funding as part of the 'Children's Fund'.

Aimed at children aged 5–13, a quarter of all budgets had to be spent on youth crime prevention measures chosen from the following list of Youth Justice Board programmes (CYPU and YJB 2002; Mason and Prior 2008):

- Youth Inclusion Programmes (YIPs)
- Youth Inclusion and Support Panels (YISPs)
- Schools work, including Safer Schools Partnerships
- Restorative justice and mediation schemes
- Work with young victims of crime
- Services and activities aimed at preventing children aged 5–13 getting involved in crime.

Here I focus on YIPs and YISPs, plus some other state provisions. It is worth noting that, with such a large proportion of youth funding going to crime prevention, this whole approach can be seen as an example of the criminalization of social policy (Muncie 1999; Mason and Prior 2008).

Youth Inclusion Programmes (YIPs)

Youth Inclusion Programmes (YIPs) were established in 2000 and focused on 70 of the most deprived neighbourhoods in England and Wales. They were in part a response to an Audit Commission report into 'misspent youth' (1996). Participation is voluntary, but each scheme is targeted at the 50 13–16-year-olds in each area thought to be most 'at risk' of offending. Other young people are also encouraged to participate. The programme's initial targets were highly ambitious (Mackie et al. 2003: 4):

- To reduce arrests within the target group by 60 percent
- To cut truancy and school exclusions by a third
- To reduce recorded crime in the area by 30 percent.

The programme is based on youth *inclusion*, yet this inclusion is seen largely in terms of criminality. A wide range of activities has been on offer including education and training, sport, arts, group and personal development, family projects, health and drugs education, mentoring and motor projects. However, for phase one of the programme nearly a third (30%) of all provision was for sport (Mackie et al. 2003: 9). In the evaluation of phase one, there were successes in reducing offending in the targeted group, although truancy and crime in the area seemed to increase (Mackie et al. 2003). Rather than this indicating programme failure, it points toward the initial targets being unrealistic or overly ambitious for this type of intervention.

Youth Inclusion and Support Panels (YISPs)

Youth Inclusion and Support Panels (YISPs) were introduced in 2003 aimed at a younger clientele than YIPs, being focused on 8–13-year-olds in 70 of the most deprived neighbourhoods. Panels are led by local authorities and involve other relevant agencies. They were designed to be 'pre-crime at-risk panels' (Walker et al. 2007: ix) that provide support and services for children and families. The targeted children should not be known to the criminal justice system but be considered at high 'risk' of offending – again following an actuarial model of risk assessment (Smith 2006; Case 2007). According to Walker et al. (2007: xii): 'In order for children to be referred to a YISP, an assessment must indicate that four or more risk factors are present in their life. Furthermore, the child's behaviour should be of concern to two or more of the partner agencies and/or the child's parents/carers, all of whom consider that a multi-agency response is called for.'

As with YIPs, involvement in voluntary. The type of measures on offer include support services tailored to individual needs (via an Integrated Support Plan (ISP)); dedicated key workers for children and families, including mentoring; and, for some schemes, family group conferencing/restorative justice approaches to resolving familial difficulties. Some panels use a tiered approach, with those thought to have the greatest need receiving the greatest support (Walker et al. 2007).

According to Squires and Stephen (2005a: 205) an actuarial focus on risk is on dubious foundations, as 'while it is possible to identify predisposing factors with some degree of accuracy, we still have no certainties, no absolutes upon which we can "solve" the problem'. Furthermore, whole sub-populations may be identified as potentially anti-social or criminal – for instance, those on low income, coming from large families, having low IQ, or having experienced parental separation/divorce; as Walker et al. (2007: 47) have claimed in their evaluation of YISPs: 'Risk and protective factors are socially constructed concepts, subject to situational and contextual interpretation … It is clear from our evaluation of YISPs, children vary in respect of how they respond to risk, and even siblings who grow up in the same family show disparate patterns of adjustment.'

Additionally, if YISPs are truly targeted pre-crime then they would be very difficult to evaluate. For example, in an evaluation of the Children's Fund in Sheffield (Beirens et al. 2005: 21) it is claimed that 91 percent had not offended since involvement in the YISP. This looks great, but it is assumed that the right clientele were targeted in the first place (this 91 percent may not have gone on to offend anyway). In the same Sheffield evaluation, it is claimed that 86 percent of young people had decreased ASB since involvement and 62 percent had stopped behaving anti-socially. It seems that, while YISP involvement may be pre-crime, it is not necessarily pre-ASB.

Other diversionary schemes

The British government has introduced a whole range of other diversionary schemes for 'at-risk' young people. For instance summer activities have been funded to kerb school holiday boredom, including the 'Summer Splash' initiative in 2000 for 13–17-year-olds living on deprived estates (Loxley et al. 2002); and the 'Positive Activities for Young People' (PAYP) programme from 2003 to 2006 for young people aged 8–19 'at risk of social exclusion, committing crime or being the victim of crime' (CRG Research 2006: i). Much broader work that feeds into the government's focus on ASB and crime is the 'Connexions'[4] programme for 13–19-year-olds, set up to provide advice and services relating to opportunities in learning and employment. There is also the UK Youth Parliament[5] for 11–18-year-olds, designed to engender greater civic involvement (and interest). While not directly linked to work to prevent ASB, such initiatives are relevant as they tie in with notions of 'respect' and 'social capital'. The government's latest idea is for 'challenge and support projects' (Respect website 2008; Youth Taskforce 2008). These will provide funding for greater use of ISOs in 52 areas of England and Wales, and will also fund further preventative initiatives.

Some issues

While youth diversion can certainly be beneficial, both for the young people themselves and for local neighbourhoods, there are some issues with this approach. And following a 'risk' methodology, there is the possibility that young people will be labelled as potentially anti-social or criminal. Perhaps there is scope for provision that is *less* targeted?

Despite the proliferation of state diversion schemes, most youth provision is still in the hands of volunteers; for instance, there's the famous Salford Lads' Club[6] which has been running since 1903, or the scouting movement, which has existed since 1907; various religious or community groups have provided youth clubs; and most sporting clubs are run entirely by volunteers. Yet, if Putnam's (2000) view of a demise in social capital in America is true for Britain, then this would be reflected in a demise in volunteerism (see Chapter 4). Anecdotally, it seems that youth clubs, in particular, have found it difficult to recruit volunteers.

For preventative work more broadly, there is a need for 'local champions'. These can be agency workers or local volunteers but, as noted elsewhere, they are difficult to come by: 'We were repeatedly told that just one good worker can make all the difference, and that neighbourhood 'champions' were essential, whether they were local residents or professionals from agencies. People with these qualities are, of course, a scarce resource' (Millie et al. 2005a: 36).

A further issue concerns providing what the young people themselves actually want (as noted in Box 8.2). In this regard, the Youth Parliament is an interesting development; however, it may not be easy to involve those who are already marginalized (and perhaps more likely to commit ASB?). An example where youth consultation is imperative is in the design and location of 'youth shelters'. Shelters are designed as places where young people can 'hang out' and they tend to be located away from spaces of potential conflict with other groups. However, shelters are not always located where the young people want to congregate or, indeed, where they feel safe; as a community safety sergeant interviewed in 2003 commented:[7]

> Parks and facilities for youth are placed in areas that will not cause any concern to anybody else ... 'Stick them in an area where they're most likely to be vulnerable for crime' ... If you put them in an area where they're not going to be naturally overlooked by cars passing by, people walking by, they're in an isolated area, they become more easily vulnerable and victimised.

Ken Worpole (2006: 22) has similarly commented about youth shelters:

> Are they places of free expression – a generous public gesture to say that young people have the right to their own place in the neighbourhood or community – or is there a hidden agenda to suggest that they are like wasp jars, or miniature ghettos, where the young can be isolated and kept in their place?

Shelters are often built on the edge of playing fields and can be in fairly isolated locations. However, an example of a project that has attempted to get around this problem is shown in Box 8.3.

Box 8.3 The Youth Spaces project

The 'Youth Spaces' project was managed by *Midlands Architecture and the Designed Environment* (MADE 2006), based in the West Midlands. Local young people worked with artists and architects in the planning and design of youth shelters. The resulting shelters were each unique and the young people felt they had ownership of the final product. According to one of the architectural practices involved in the project (Sjölander da Cruz, Birmingham), the aim was to 'create a place that was part of an urban space, somewhere visible and not somewhere tucked away' (p. 24). Quotes from young people involved in the project included the following:

When you look at the shelter, I see it as like, our sort of zone and it's a place for me and my friends to hang around

It might as well just have a big neon sign saying 'skaters welcome' on here

Everyone has like a bad outlook on teenagers and everything, and we just want to prove them wrong, that not everybody's like that*

As diversionary activity, this type of approach has a lot of potential. However, like other schemes, there are issues around engaging those more marginalized. Also, the slow speed of the planning and development process can have repercussions for maintaining active involvement. Similarly, sustainability can be a problem as the next group of young people reach an age to want to 'hang out' and may not have the same 'ownership' of the shelters. Nonetheless, these are not problems that should stop such innovative approaches.

Shelter at Coleshill Skate Park, Warwickshire**

Shelter at Yardley Park, Stechford, Birmingham**

Notes: *Quotes taken from a DVD that accompanied the MADE (2006) publication.

**Photos kindly provided by MADE.

Neighbourhood-led prevention

So far in this chapter the focus has been on preventing youthful ASB. What I hope has been clear in this book is that young people are certainly not responsible for *all* ASB. In Chapter 4, it was noted that people living in areas most beset by ASB often feel powerless to do anything about it, largely for fear of receiving verbal abuse or more serious retaliation. Similarly, they can also feel the authorities are impotent to do anything meaningful to remedy local problems. The need for neighbourhood 'champions' has already been noted; however, it is possible that resident-led, or neighbourhood-led initiatives more broadly, can have greater effect at preventing ASB, with local people clearly taking the lead. Linked to this are issues of tolerance and acceptability of difference (and not labelling those outside neighbourhood norms as anti-social). Similarly of relevance are the linked concepts of social capital and collective efficacy, as well as the government's call for 'respect'. However, as has been noted elsewhere, solutions that are 'parachuted in' without taking account of local views are not likely to fully succeed (Hughes 2004). Similarly, if residents have been let down by agencies in the past, then they are less likely to buy into the latest state initiative (Purdue 2001). Clearly, there is a place for a neighbourhood governance of ASB, but how can disempowered people take control in this way?

Reassurance or neighbourhood policing

One possibility is that local views are canvassed more frequently and that these views are taken seriously. In this regard, lessons can be learnt from locally based policing as practised under the 'reassurance policing', or 'neighbourhood policing' banners (Home Office 2005a; Millie and Herrington 2005; Tuffin et al. 2006; see also Chapter 5). The key to a reassurance approach (Povey 2001) is that police officers are *visible* within the neighbourhood; they are *familiar* to local residents; and they are *accessible* – be that by being on patrol, at traditional police stations or through shop front services, by internet or even by mobile phone. Drawing on work on 'signal crimes' (Innes 2004a; see also Chapter 5), the aim is to build trust between the police and local residents, identify local concerns and priorities and then tackle these issues (making sure to deliver on any promises). The advantage is that the approach takes people's views seriously. The downside is that, like similar schemes elsewhere (e.g. Skogan and Hartnett 1997), some minority views may be missed. By being police led, there is also the prospect that suggested solutions may tend towards enforcement.

Mutual respect

It may be better if preventative solutions are led by local residents or users of public spaces, rather than by the police (in a classic bottom-up approach). Here; Richard Sennett's work on 'respect' is most relevant (as explored in Chapter 4). According to the government (Respect Taskforce 2006: 3) 'respect' has something to do with not 'dropping litter and queue jumping'; and not committing 'more serious anti-social behaviour like constant noise and harassment'. Sennett saw 'respect' in terms of understanding the needs of others in society, promoting a form of *mutual* respect or reciprocity. Writing about etiquette, Lynn Truss (2005, cited in Harris 2006c) has stated the following: 'Once you leave behind such class concerns as how to balance the peas on the back of a fork, all the important rules surely boil down to one: *remember you are with other people; show some consideration.*'

Consideration for others, understanding others' needs, reciprocity, and 'respect' will be good antidotes to anti-social behaviour. They will all contribute to improvements in social capital and collective efficacy, thereby potentially improving informal social control. Nonetheless, *how* these attitudes are encouraged and nurtured will be important; as Sennett warned (2003: 260): 'Treating people with respect cannot occur simply by commanding it should happen. Mutual recognition has to be negotiated.' Such mutuality needs to develop organically within and between different groups in a neighbourhood; for instance, across generations or particular interest groups. But, just as importantly, it needs to exist between the majority population and outsider groups, such as the young, the homeless or minority ethnic groups; as Putnam (2000) would see it, a need for 'bridging social capital'.

The government's view of 'respect' has had a greater focus on unacceptable behaviour; that 'ultimately every citizen has a responsibility to behave in a respectful way and to support the community around them in doing the same' (Respect Taskforce 2006: 3). Yet, mutual recognition is also vital between state and citizen. Following Tony Blair's launch of the Respect Action Plan, Sennett (2006) commented:

> Is it any surprise to you that a politician who elicits less and less respect from his public thinks that the public has a problem with respect. Blair wasn't worried about this in 1998. This Whitehall project is just the wrong end of the telescope. The issue isn't how individuals can behave better but how institutions can behave better.

When asked to comment on the government's proposals for 'respect', the Archbishop of York John Sentamu replied that: 'If we expect young people to be respectful, we should show respect. If they are not treated lovingly and forgivingly, they will be unforgiving. If we do not trust them, they will not trust us.' In terms of promoting respect (and perhaps preventing ASB), this is quite possibly the ideal. However, the government has been focused on instant results, on tackling ASB *now*; and so perhaps has not had the patience for such an approach.

The Archbishop of York's comments clearly reflect the need for tolerance. This is not a tolerance of ASB, but tolerance of others' behaviour that I may not understand and may find annoying; and also a recognition that people have different perspectives and conflicting expectations and uses of public space. This is a tricky business. According to Harris (2006d: 54) what is needed is neighbourliness, that he defined as 'mutual recognition among residents through repeated informal encounters over time'. Maybe, but the government has promoted *intolerance* of ASB (and by extension intolerance of those thought to be perpetrators of ASB); as Blair claimed in 2003: 'we cannot say we live in a just society, if we do not put an end to the anti-social behaviour, the disrespect, the conduct which we wouldn't tolerate from our own children and shouldn't have to tolerate from someone else's' (2003b).

From a perspective of intolerance, any attempt to promote respect could quite quickly become 'respect on my terms'. There will be a danger that neighbourliness could translate into good neighbourly relations with those I can relate to, people with similar values and interests – but not with the (perceived) anti-social 'other'. This intolerance could be, for instance, anti-youth (Squires and Stephen 2005a), anti-street people (Moore 2008), anti-prostitution (Scoular et al. 2007), or even anti-student (Hubbard 2008). The result is NIMBY-ism[8] or, worse, vigilantism (see e.g. Johnston 1996; Edwards and Hughes 2002).

This is a bleak outlook; however, it is not inevitable. As Sennett noted (2003: 260), 'mutual recognition has to be negotiated'; and this negotiation is somewhere where state agencies can intervene in providing intergenerational support or mediation services, in bringing people together to *negotiate* norms of acceptable behaviour. For such an approach to be effective *all* people within a given neighbourhood need to be involved and have ownership of the results. This would include perpetrators (perceived or actual), as well as outsider groups that are not usually consulted. Of course, in the vast majority of neighbourhoods such intervention will not be necessary. Also, in areas most beset by problems, such an approach will not stop all ASB. However, some behaviour currently misidentified as anti-social will be otherwise labelled as simply 'different' and tolerated. And perhaps actual ASB will be reduced as well (see Millie, forthcoming, for further discussion on respect).

Preventing ASB in the night-time economy

I want to shift attention now to preventing ASB within a city centre context and, more specifically, relating to the night-time economy. It is clear that a lot of ASB can occur in the city centre at night, and frequently related to too much alcohol or drugs. However, in trying to prevent night-time ASB, then there needs to be realization that some perceived misbehaviour will be just 'high spirits', while more serious problems of violence are *criminal* and ought to be treated as such. In Britain, there has been a major shake-up in the governance of the night following the implementation from November 2005 of the 2003 Licensing Act (Measham and Brain 2005; Hadfield 2006; Talbot 2006; Hough et al. 2008). Alongside various enforcement measures, the major focus of the Act was the liberalization of licensing hours. The media headline was that 24-hour licences were being introduced, although most bars and clubs have tended to apply for extensions rather than for the full 24 hours. However, the government's approach to drink-related ASB and violence has been confusing. According to Measham and Brain (2005: 278): 'On the one hand the government introduced the 2003 Licensing Act which promotes further deregulation of the night-time economy, on the other hand it released the Alcohol Harm Reduction Strategy for England'.[9] Yet the 2003 Act was intended as preventative. By removing the standard 11 o'clock closing time, it was meant to remove the pressure to 'get one more drink in' at last orders. Similarly, this was thought to stop the vast numbers of people leaving pubs and clubs at the same time (the 11.30pm peak for pubs and 2.30am for clubs). This would have further benefits at potential 'pinch points' for ASB and violent disorder – notably in queues for taxis or night buses and at food takeaways. One disadvantage of liberalization that did not receive so much attention from the government is that people will leave pubs and clubs at all hours into the early morning, making the night-time economy difficult to police (for instance, whether enough officers will be available to cover the early morning). Similarly, there will be an impact on paramedic and health provisions.

A Home Office report into the early impact of the Act (Hough et al. 2008) found that alcohol consumption had fallen slightly, but this consumption was extended longer into the night and early morning. The level of crime and disorder remained the same following the Act, as did the total alcohol-related demands on hospitals' accident and emergency departments. More positively, local residents were less likely to say drunk and rowdy behaviour was a problem after the implementation of the Act. This is one positive from these changes. In terms of having a preventative impact on ASB and violence, the licensing changes overall have had minimal impact and need to be seen as part of a wider picture.

Other preventative measures and campaigns that can plausibly have an impact include improved training for club doormen (Hobbs et al. 2003; Hadfield 2006) and better management practices within and between pubs and clubs. For instance, many pubs and clubs belong to local 'pub watch' or 'club watch' partnerships, where information on unwelcome customers is shared. Some clubs have also introduced cooling off periods at the end of an evening when free soft drinks are on offer and the club books taxis for customers. This should reduce potential conflict out on the street. For taxi queues, some cities have introduced 'taxi marshals' to help with getting people home and in reducing potential for ASB and violent disorder (see e.g. ODPM 2005a; DCLG 2007).

Other preventative measures have been put forward as part of the Alcohol Harm Reduction Strategy for England (Prime Minister's Strategy Unit 2004), including guidance on education and treatment. Wider restriction on the selling of alcohol may similarly contribute to preventing ASB; for instance the 2003 Licensing Act included stricter controls on selling alcohol on under-18s, as well as to people already drunk. All these measures together may contribute to reducing alcohol fuelled ASB. Yet, like earlier discussions of neighbourhood-led prevention, it is worth noting that concepts of 'respect', 'tolerance' and 'reciprocity' also apply to the night-time economy. Young people who go out drinking in city centres have been problematized as dangerous populations and labelled as 'binge drinkers'. While not denying that problematic behaviour does occur, a lot is misidentified as ASB. Any plan to prevent ASB ought to include all interested parties, including the users of the night-time economy – and other groups such as city centre residents.

Designing out ASB

In the broader crime prevention literature, there has been much written about the concept of 'crime prevention through environmental design' (e.g. Jeffery 1971; Taylor 2002; Cozens et al. 2005). Such design-led prevention is an area that seems to have been overlooked in much of the British policy literature on ASB.

Jane Jacobs (1961: 45) famously talked about the need for 'eyes upon the street', an idea taken forward by Oscar Newman (1972) among others in talking about 'natural surveillance'. According to this perspective, buildings can be designed to encourage users to have an interest in the goings-on outside. This can be within a residential setting by eliminating corners on a development that are unwatched; it can also be within a city centre, with cafés having on-street tables or retailers having on-street newsstands, both providing much needed 'natural surveillance'. Newman's related concept of 'territoriality' is relevant, that the street falls within people's sphere of influence. Newman's ideas of 'image' and 'environment' are also important here, that how an area is viewed has an impact on whether someone will intervene. However – and as noted – for someone to intervene in ASB there also needs to sufficient informal social control, as influenced by strong social capital or collective efficacy; or as Harris (2006c, 2007) has stated, 'neighbourliness'. In the city centre example, the waiter or shop worker has a vested interest in what is happening on the street. But in the residential setting, if the resident already feels disempowered, design alone is not going to be enough to encourage intervention; although the fact that an area is overlooked may be enough to prevent *some* ASB.

Design can be used also in alternative provisions for young people, away from areas of potential conflict (e.g. Scott 2002); although, as noted in the earlier 'youth shelter' example (see Box 8.3), these provisions need to be where young people want to be and where they are also safe themselves. Design can be used to tackle more mundane, everyday incivilities. The simplest is to provide a reasonable number of litter bins. Rumble-strips can be added to paving or steps to stop skateboarding in inappropriate locations. And climb-proof paint can be added to fencing or drainpipes to halt trespass and also to limit graffiti opportunities. In Westminster in London, urinals have been built that only emerge from the pavement during the evening and night in an attempt to stop people urinating in shop doorways or other equally inappropriate locations during a night out. At 6am the urinals telescope back into the pavement.[10] As Clarke and Eck (2003) would have it, such simple solutions 'remove excuses' for inappropriate behaviour.

At the more oppressive end of design, potential solutions include the creation of gated communities[11] and use of closed-circuit television (CCTV). There are certainly advantages to both. For instance, a gated community offers the promise of a 'sanitised residential cocoon' (Blandy 2006: 239), with all those from outside a particular street being excluded, including anyone who may be anti-social. Anyone from within, or those that are invited by residents, will be controlled by internal regulation (although according to Blandy (2006), knowledge of behavioural restrictions outlined in developers' covenants will be limited). A major disadvantage of a gated community is that it offers no protection to those outside its walls. It is an architecture of fear (e.g. Ellin 1997) that makes fear of the 'other' the defining discourse of urban living, something that can only reduce mutual respect and increase suspicion, literally, of 'outsiders' (see also Davis 1990; Caldeira 2001; Lemanski 2004).

In 2004 the government's 'Together' campaign[12] against ASB promoted a form of gating, through 'Operation Gate-it'. The aim was to enclose rear alleyways to some properties to exclude non-residents and to create communal spaces for residents that can be used as a combination of garden and play space. On this much smaller scale, the benefits of enclosing previously public space may outweigh the disbenefits; although longer term impacts need to be assessed.

As for the use of CCTV, this can have a role in supplementing natural surveillance (see Lyon 2007), although there are clear concerns over who precisely is being watched; as McLaughlin and Muncie (1999: 133) have claimed, this can be the 'usual suspects', including 'groups of young men, the poorly attired and visible ethnic minorities', as well as 'young women [who] are observed quite intensely, but voyeuristically, by male camera operators'. Better management and training should lessen *some* of these concerns. However, electronic surveillance's role in social control – as state panoptic, or as part of a wider dispersal of discipline (Foucault 1977; Cohen 1985; see Chapter 3) – has been a concern for some time. For instance, according to Bannister et al. (1998: 27), in the surveilled city, 'difference is not so much to be celebrated as segregated'. From this perspective, the objective is to control unwanted populations through exclusion. Keith Hayward (2004) has a different take, in that the social control purpose of CCTV is to control populations *within* controlled environments: 'For surveillance to manage its wayward subjects, to mould, shape and ultimately ensure conformity of conduct, those subjects must be *inside* the perimeter not *outside*.' (Hayward 2004: 139). Whichever, the impact is disproportionately on populations that are already marginalized as an anti-social 'other'. According to the Commission for Architecture and the Built Environment (CABE 2004a), turning to tough security such as gates and CCTV to solve ASB can in fact be counter productive. Instead, they propose greater emphasis on the *quality* of public places:

> [I]nvesting in the creation and care of high quality public spaces is more effective in tackling anti-social behaviour than the blanket use of tough security measures ... adopting measures such as CCTV and security gates without considering the overall design and care of public space will result in the creation of ugly, oppressive environments that can foster greater social problems. (CABE 2004a: 1)

The emphasis is one of 'place making' with greater investment in good design, attractive new facilities and good maintenance to create public spaces that people want to use and enjoy. These need to be *inclusionary* spaces. That said, a health warning is provided by Henry Shaftoe (2006):

> Even if we have the best of inclusive intentions, I don't believe we can just design convivial spaces from a standard blueprint. A number of public spaces have been designed and built in the past few years, to considerable critical acclaim from the design professions ... Yet in some cases they still haven't succeeded in attracting the heterogeneous range of uses and activities that indicate success.

Inclusionary urban design (and planning) can make an important contribution to preventing ASB; however, in common with other preventative approaches, this will not work in isolation.

Concluding comments

Just as there is with crime prevention, there is clearly a whole range of approaches to preventing ASB. All have the possibility of contributing to less ASB, but they will be more effective if part of a package of complementary measures. There are many other factors that can help nurture respect and lessen ASB. For instance, while there is a lot of policy focus on working with parents, there is also a role for education, that mutual respect can be an integral part of the school experience and explicitly taught as part of citizenship classes. Other areas to emphasize would be self-worth, aspiration and engagement.

Local and national agencies also need to lead by example, ranging from government through to local police officers, housing office workers and even street cleaners. For instance, in a recent focus group with London residents (Millie 2006) some participants complained about rude bus drivers – although, of course, bus drivers could give examples of rude passengers. Perhaps there is a place for training in manners (and patience) with customers? Similarly, police officers need to be civil and be seen to be fair.

In Chapter 4, I mentioned the law of unintended consequences, that some policy decisions have led by accident to conditions where ASB is more likely. If some form of 'ASB and crime impact assessment' was made for all policy decisions (in a similar way to environmental impact assessments) then such problems could be lessened. An example already mentioned is the introduction of charges for the disposal of trade waste, leading to some firms illegally dumping or fly tipping. If the ASB consequences had been considered, then the charge could have been set high enough to cover *some* costs, but low enough not to act as a disincentive to use the service. The same principle could apply to the drafting of legislation.

According to the government's Youth Taskforce Action Plan (Youth Taskforce 2008: 5) the latest development is the promotion of a 'triple track' approach to tackling ASB. This is detailed in Box 8.4.

> **Box 8.4** The Youth Taskforce Action Plan 'triple track' approach
>
> **1** *'Tough enforcement where behaviour is unacceptable or illegal'*
>
> Note the continuing ambiguity over the boundary of acceptable behaviour. Presumably tough enforcement should also be applied to legal activity, so long as it is 'unacceptable' – however defined?
>
> **2** *'Non-negotiable support to address the underlying causes of poor behaviour or serious difficulties'*
>
> An emphasis on support is encouraging; however, if this is 'non-negotiable' it simply continues the government's obsession with enforcement. After all, how do you make support 'non-negotiable'?
>
> **3** *'Better prevention to tackle problems before they become serious and entrenched, and to prevent problems arising in the first place'*
>
> This is perhaps the more promising and is aimed at 'at-risk' young people and families. Issues around stigma will need to be resolved.
>
> *Source*: Youth Taskforce 2008: 5.

Although 'tough enforcement' is still number one, it is encouraging that prevention is given such a profile. That said, it is clear that the preventative approach favoured by government is centred on actuarial risk assessment and all the problems of labelling that entails. Also, the idea of 'non-negotiable support' is a strange one and seems to have little in common with the idea of mutual respect. Enforcement certainly has its place, but the rhetoric and actions of government and the idea of 'non-negotiable support' possibly takes things too far down the punitive route. An approach that is truly balanced between enforcement and prevention will be more promising.

Selected reading

A list of selected further reading is included here that reflects the diversity of preventative options. The best place to start will be the government's latest policy drive, the 'Youth Taskforce Action Plan'. More information is also available on the government's 'Respect' website, www.respect.gov.uk:

- Belsky, J., Barnes, J. and Melhuish, E. (2007) *The National Evaluation of SureStart: Does Area-based Early Intervention Work?* Bristol: Policy Press.
- CABE (Commission for Architecture and the Built Environment) (2004a) *Policy Note: Preventing Anti-social Behaviour in Public Spaces, CABE Space,* Nov. 2004. London: CABE.
- DCLG (Department for Communities and Local Government) (2007) *How to Manage Town Centres.* London: DCLG.
- Dillane, J., Hill, M., Bannister, J. and Scott, S. (2001) *Evaluation of the Dundee Families Project.* Edinburgh: The Stationery Office.
- Harris, K. (2006c) *Respect in the Neighbourhood: Why Neighbourliness Matters.* Lyme Regis: Russell House Publishing.
- Mason, P. and Prior, D. (2008) The Children's Fund and the prevention of crime and anti-social behaviour, *Criminology and Criminal Justice,* 8(3): 279–296.
- Youth Taskforce (2008) *Youth Taskforce Action Plan: Give Respect, Get Respect – Youth Matters.* London: Department for Children, Schools and Families.

Notes

1   Early Head Start has been introduced for ages 0–3.
2   A civil servant closely associated with the introduction of SureStart (see Smith 2006).
3   See also Jacobson et al. (2005, 2008).
4   See www.connexions-direct.com.
5   See www.ukyouthparliament.org.uk.
6   Which now also accepts girls.
7   See Jacobson et al. (2005, 2008) for more from this study.
8   A common acronym for 'not in my back yard'.
9   See Prime Minister's Strategy Unit (2004).
10   Also, in what Westminster Council call 'Sat Lav', if you text TOILET to 80097, you will be given the location of the nearest public loo.

11 'A walled or fenced housing development to which public access is restricted' (see Atkinson et al. 2003: 3).

12 Working with the charity Groundwork UK.

9 Conclusions

According to Roger Matthews (2003: 5), '[A]lthough there is no certainty about what constitutes anti-social behaviour, we are reassured that it can occur everywhere and anywhere.' What this book has shown is that the precise limits to behaviour deemed to be anti-social are contested and in popular and political discourse, it can range from very minor irritations through to serious violent criminality. Yet when ASB is narrowed to the kind of repetitive non-criminal or minor criminal incivility that seems to be at the core of it all, then ASB is *not* the huge problem we have been told it is; that it does not occur 'everywhere and anywhere'. Instead, problems are concentrated in certain deprived and/or urban neighbourhoods and in town and city centre (but it should be noted that even here ASB can be misidentified or over-estimated). Where there are accentuated concerns, then some more serious forms of ASB do need to be tackled and there is then a place for enforcement; however, this needs to be balanced with preventative work. To be fair to the government, the rhetoric has shifted more to balance with the 'Respect' and 'Youth Taskforce' agendas. For instance, in the foreword to the Youth Taskforce Action Plan (Youth Taskforce 2008: 2) MP Ed Balls puts forward Labour's latest approach, still focusing on tough enforcement, but also on support and prevention: 'Focusing on just one of these is not enough; we need all three together if we are to improve young people's lives and successfully deal with the problems that concern communities.' That said, it is prevention with a big stick, with the Youth Taskforce promoting, for instance, 'non-negotiable support'; as Prime Minister Gordon Brown asserts elsewhere in the document, 'we want to see young people who get into trouble *made to* take the help they need to mend their ways' (2008: 34; emphasis added). This is a somewhat simplistic, authoritarian and moralistic perspective.

Although aspects of governmental responsibility have been shifted from department to department, it seems to be an agenda that is not going to disappear in a hurry. Also, it is not solely a Labour focus, with both the Liberal Democrats and Conservatives claiming they would tackle ASB if in power (Millie 2008b). In fact, on accepting the post of Mayor of London in

May 2008, Conservative, Boris Johnson, stated, 'I think there's a vital necessity to drive out so-called minor crime and disorder as a way of driving out more serious crime.' He did not directly refer to anti-social behaviour, but his perspective will be familiar. Very much like Tony Blair's vision for ASB, Johnson's view owes a lot to Wilson and Kelling's (1982) famous 'broken windows'. In fact, Johnson's first policy move was to ban the consumption of alcohol on public transport in the capital (*Daily Mail* 2008; Dawar 2008). And according to the *Daily Mail* (2008), Bill Bratton is now advising Johnson, 'on how "zero tolerance" of graffiti, fare-dodging and other minor crimes can prevent serious offending'.

In this chapter, I suggest possible alternative ways forward in dealing with ASB that are not enforcement heavy, but require buy-in from *all* users of public spaces. That ASB is seen as a stand-alone problem is also considered. Similarly, it is suggested that criminal policy may not be the best home for much that is currently regarded as anti-social. But first I want to go back to an assertion made in Chapter 3, that what is regarded as anti-social is essentially interpretative; that what in one situation is entirely acceptable or even celebrated, may be just tolerated elsewhere or deemed so unacceptable that it may lead to anti-social, or criminal, censure. This differential interpretation of behaviour is key to understanding how 'acceptable' behaviour can be negotiated, with a greater emphasis on tolerance, respect and reciprocity.

Behavioural expectations

A useful starting point here is to consider what it is about certain behaviours that makes them unacceptable to others. According to the legal philosopher Joel Feinberg (e.g. 1984, 1985) key determinants in criminality are 'harm' and 'offence'. If applied to ASB, then the behaviour is unacceptable because it causes genuine harm to others or is sufficiently offensive to warrant censure (see also von Hirsch and Simester 2006). Offensiveness, in particular, is a slippery concept with individuals being offended by very different things. As stated in Chapter 3, people can also interpret behaviour differently as acceptable, tolerable or anti-social, depending on situational factors – the temporal and spatial circumstances of the behaviour. Now add to this mix the cultural context of that behaviour. As has been noted, contemporary life in Britain has become increasingly individualistic and consumerist, which has fuelled demands for the behaviour of others to be controlled. Thus, what becomes acceptable or anti-social can be also largely dictated by a culture of consumption and the needs of a 'consuming majority' (cf. Bannister et al. 2006).

With the push for regeneration and urban renaissance (as explored in Chapter 5) there has been increasing demands to make towns and cities more attractive places to live and work in – and attractive to inward investment. There is certainly a logic of linking work to tackle ASB with regeneration strategies (Millie 2007b). Yet there is a danger that only the views of a consuming majority will be catered for, leading to a streetscape 'cleansed of difference' (Bannister et al. 2006: 924). A useful concept to use here is 'revanchism' (Smith 1996; MacLeod 2002; Holden and Iveson 2003). 'Revanchism' is a geo-political term for the reclaiming of territory. In the context of ASB and urban regeneration it has been used to describe the removal or dispersal of unwanted and *unsightly* outsiders who can be perceived as problematic populations, in effect to reclaim territory for consumerist consumption; for instance, according to Rogers and Coaffee (2005: 321–22): '[T]he impact of new "revanchist" urbanism on minority groups such as buskers, street entertainers, leafleters, beggars, skateboarders and the homeless ... [suggests] tensions between the "moving on", "displacement" and "dispersal" of legitimate, if un-aesthetic, users from public spaces.'

The place of aesthetics

A key determinate here is that such groups are perceived as 'un-aesthetic'. In simple terms, aesthetics can be seen as 'concerned with taste, with the subjective and emotive value attached to sensory encounters' (Millie 2008a: 386). MacLeod (2002: 605) similarly recognized the importance of aesthetics for determining behavioural acceptability, with surveillance in particular designed to promote, ' "acceptable" patterns of behavior commensurate with the free flow of commerce and the new urban aesthetics'. For instance, street people and the homeless can be perceived as a threat and as not fitting in with a 'new urban aesthetic'. Similarly, groups of young people congregating can be seen as threatening. This perception can be influenced by previous experience or reputation as formed by the reported experiences of others and the portrayal of young people in the media. But it can also be influenced by a youthful aesthetic that is seen as 'different' – including fashion, mannerisms and how young people talk. This difference is not understood by the majority and is thereby interpreted as threat and ASB. The revanchist response is to move them on or perhaps to use Dispersal Order powers to clear the area of young people who *may* become anti-social. As noted previously, provision for young people such as youth shelters and skate parks can be in out-of-the-way peripheral locations, hidden from the public gaze and less likely to upset the majority. Although providing for youth is a positive measure, if located out of sight then it can also be seen as revanchist. Yet, when youthful activities are catered for or tolerated in central locations then this 'difference' is not always threatening. For instance, at the South

Bank in London (see Chapter 3) the skateboarding, parcour and graffiti writing is something of a tourist *attraction*.

Graffiti writing is a behaviour regularly seen as anti-social, but also inherently tied up with understandings of aesthetics. According to Jeff Ferrell (1993: 160), '[G]raffiti writing stands doubly as a "crime of style"; for back alley graffiti writers and white-collar anti-graffiti campaigners alike, style matters.' Yet deciding how to respond to different forms of graffiti is not easy (Halsey and Young 2002). A contemporary example is the graffiti of Banksy (see Banksy 2005; Millie 2008a). His work has received wide media attention. For instance, an outdoor 'exhibition' of his and others' graffiti was recently given a slot on prime time news on the BBC (2 May 2008).[1] Like the youthful activities at the South Bank, his work has been credited as having tourist potential. But what makes his graffiti tolerated or celebrated while others can find their work censured as representing ASB or criminal damage? An example of Banksy's work is shown in Box 9.1, alongside more typical tagging graffiti.

Box 9.1   Banksy's graffito in Bristol compared to typical tagging graffiti

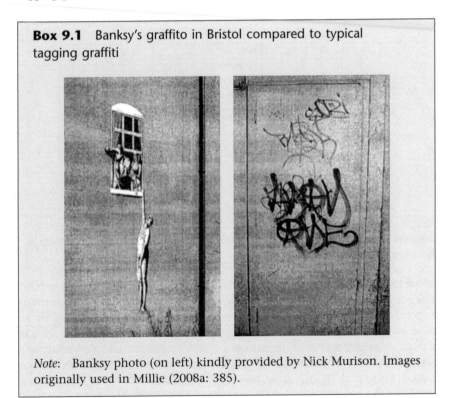

Note: Banksy photo (on left) kindly provided by Nick Murison. Images originally used in Millie (2008a: 385).

The Banksy work shown in Box 9.1 is on a building owned by Bristol City Council. The Council conducted an online poll to decide if it should be kept, with the results overwhelmingly in favour. The reasons given were that Banksy is from the city, that it has tourist potential and that 'there is a large difference between graffiti as vandalism (i.e. tagging) and street art of the kind created by Banksy' (Hayward 2006). Aesthetics clearly has a part in determining acceptability; but such subjective assessment can have important consequences as some graffiti taggers have ended up in jail (Millie 2008a). This differential interpretation of the same behaviour is something that is not easy to resolve; but basing it on something so transitory as taste and fashion means the law becomes differently applied to different people – depending on their ability and the particular aesthetic of their work.

The factors at play in determining whether a particular behaviour is celebrated, tolerated or censured are shown in a summary schematic in Figure 9.1.

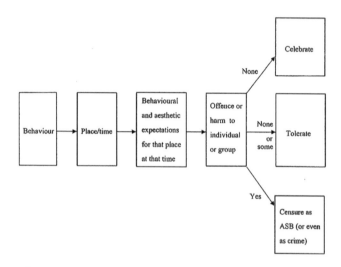

Source: Millie 2008a: 389.

Figure 9.1 A differential interpretation perspective on acceptable or anti-social behaviour

What this schematic demonstrates is that each behaviour occurs in a specific place and a specific time and that each of us has behavioural and aesthetic expectations for that place and time. For instance – and returning to an example used previously – loud and boisterous behaviour may be tolerated in a city centre pub and club district on a Friday night but not necessarily on a residential street the next day. Linked to these expectations are perceived and actual offence or harm caused by the behaviour. All these factors will contribute to whether the same behaviour is celebrated, tolerated or censured as ASB or even as crime. As previously noted, to go with the view of the majority as to what is celebrated and tolerated risks further marginalizing outsider populations and those with alternative uses of public space. What I suggest here is that, while some behaviours will always be anti-social, norms of acceptability need to be negotiated between *all* users of shared public spaces. Certainly not an easy thing to achieve; however, there are great benefits to such an approach.

A bottom-up governance of ASB

So how can *all* user groups be involved in setting standards of behaviour? With the Respect Action Plan (Respect Task Force 2006: 27) the government recognized the need to 'involve the community in setting standards and enforcing them'. But, returning to the origins of much contemporary discourse in ASB, this involvement was for social housing tenants working closely with their landlords. By only asking tenants then the views of others will invariably be missed – including many young people and other users of public space. And within tenant groups, there is a danger that only the most vocal will be heard, leading to further marginalization of minority tenant groups. What I suggest is a true bottom-up governance of ASB. This will involve consulting tenants; but also other groups including youths, street people and other minority and marginalized populations. Within the city centre it will involve consultation with business groups and retailers, shoppers, skateboarders, drinkers, street people, older people and anyone else who has a legitimate reason for using these shared public spaces. Granted, many will not want to be consulted – and it is always easier to hold a meeting with a pre-existing tenants' and residents' association or community group; but I believe taking the extra trouble to discover alternative perspectives on ASB will be rewarded.

This is somewhere where government agencies can have a job to do – not in dictating priorities, but instead in facilitating a negotiation of norms of acceptable and anti-social behaviour and in promoting related concerns of tolerance, respect and reciprocity. Reliance on just one method of consultation will always miss certain populations. For example, the Chicago Alternative Policing Strategy (Skogan and Hartnett 1997) found that when the police held large public meetings, Hispanic residents tended not to attend. Instead; combinations of meetings, focus groups, survey work, text and online consultation may be beneficial; but also taking the trouble of *going to* different user groups to seek their views. In such negotiations; the themes of tolerance and reciprocity will be key; but the main focus could be the statement put forward by Lynn Truss (2005), to 'remember you are with other people; show some consideration'. This consideration can be of minority interests as much as of the majority. The aim would be for state agencies to then take a back seat, with all users of shared public spaces (in residential areas and in urban centres) to develop a shared governance of ASB, turning to the state as a last resort where support, preventative work and enforcement are required. In Chapter 6, the four-step approach followed by the Safer Swansea Partnership was described, where a combination of warning letters, ABCs and ASBOs are used (with ASBOs as a last resort). A bottom-up governance of ASB could utilize such an approach, but with an extra step or two at the pre-warning stage utilizing and involving local people. This would have the benefit of improving local social capital and collective efficacy. And, by involving all users of shared public spaces, there may also be benefits for wider informal social control and in keeping unacceptable behaviour in check – without having to resort to formal intervention. There is the added benefit that the state could then focus its enforcement on tackling more serious criminality such as violence, street robbery or gang-related gun crime. For instance, in a focus group held in 2004 with 16–18-year-old women in North London,[2] I asked if guns were a problem locally. One response was: 'There's a lot of guns in this area that you don't know about, put it that way … and they feel it a need as well because they feel they've got to protect themselves, they feel they've got to have these guns.' In some neighbourhoods, these are clearly far more pressing criminal concerns than ASB that state agencies could be focusing on.

Admittedly, a bottom-up governance of ASB is something of a utopian vision. The state is not likely to want to take a back seat; and user groups may not be able to come to an agreement on behavioural acceptability. And, as noted, if people have been let down in the past, then it will take a lot more effort to gain their trust. As one male respondent in a focus group[3] with parents in London put it when asked about the introduction of police community support officers:

> Sorry for laughing, every six months you read about these ground breaking schemes to be brought into problem area X. It's a massive failure and they quietly go back to how things were before and they have probably wasted about £50k of money setting up something that everybody could have told them from day one that it isn't going to work.

This respondent certainly has a point. In areas most beset by problems of ASB, there is clearly the potential for intervention fatigue and any new approach to tackling ASB will need to have strong local buy-in. That said, this does not mean a new approach is not worth trying. The key is to earn the support and respect of local people. Then, areas of behavioural conflict will have to be *negotiated*. For example, where there is conflict between shoppers and skateboarders the solution could be as simple as allowing skateboarding at specific times of day. It may also be to provide specialist facilities for skateboarding; not in some out-of-the-way location, but instead within the city centre and somewhere where the skaters themselves can feel safe. For street people, it could be in allowing public drinking in certain areas; but also in providing support, accommodation and after-care (from other user groups as well as from state provision). For 'problem neighbours', it could be in offering mediation and conflict resolution, then support and enforcement or eviction as a last resort. The work of the Dundee Family Project and the more recent work with family intervention projects could be built on here.

But instead of labelling certain groups – the young, the homeless, the 'problem family', the night-time binge drinkers – it is important to recognize that *all* are capable of being anti-social. As a participant in a focus group with people who had experienced homelessness put it: 'It works both ways, like you can say you've been begging on the street and people come past and give it a bit, but then those people can say that they've walked down the street and they've been verbally abused by people that are drinking, you know what I mean. So you can't really say that one set of people is [worse].'

Finding an alternative home for ASB

In areas most beset by problems of ASB, the ideal would be to provide a package of complementary measures to deal with local problems. This would involve enforcement, but not as the main focus, instead emphasizing prevention and support. In fact, there is scope for shifting the control of ASB away from government agencies that are focused on enforcement. For instance, although much of the current Youth Taskforce Action Plan on ASB is managed through the Department for Children, Schools and Families, the Home Office 'retains responsibility for the overall response to anti-social behaviour' (Youth Taskforce 2008: 6). As ASB is such a contested concept, it could benefit from being effectively decriminalized and moved away from the Home Office entirely. As noted previously, much of the current focus on ASB can be seen as an example of the criminalization of social policy. Negotiating acceptable standards of (non-criminal) ASB could be handed to welfare oriented agencies working alongside local people. At a local partnership level, ASB strategies could be managed by new welfare partnerships rather than by the local Crime and Disorder Reduction Partnership; after all, much that is regarded as anti-social is not criminal. If the behaviour seriously breaches criminal standards, then it perhaps ought to be treated as such.

ASB also needs to be recognized as linked to a range of other policy agendas, rather than as a stand-alone problem. For instance, much preventative work focuses on parenting skills, tackling youth boredom and neighbourhood cohesion. Relatedly, work to improve young people's educational and employment aspirations could impact on levels of ASB. Agendas to tackle ASB have also been closely tied to regeneration programmes. But overall, rather than focusing on *controlling* 'unacceptable' behaviour, the focus could be shifted to one of *welfare* and therefore seeing much ASB as an issue of *social justice*. Here there is also scope to regard certain anti-social behaviours in terms of affecting 'environmental inequality' (see also Chapter 5); that people have differing access to 'quality' environments is itself an issue of social justice.

The potential impacts of wider policy decisions on ASB need to be also considered, so that the situation where the government tries to improve things on one hand, but makes them worse on the other, does not occur.

Concluding comments

When I started writing this book I thought I would be saying that ASBOs are a terrible thing, that ASB is exaggerated and that the government has used the ASB agenda as a device for the formal social control of marginalized or 'problematic' populations. Now that I've come to the end I still believe these statements to be more or less true; however, I don't reject enforcement out of hand. I can see that in specific circumstances where someone's repetitive ASB has become so intolerable that it causes serious harm and offence to the victim, then there is a place for giving the perpetrator an ASBO (or some other enforcement measure). That said, this would be in far fewer instances than is currently the case, and there would have to be stricter evidential tests for granting an ASBO in the first place. Similarly, there needs to be greater thought given to ASBO duration and the restrictions that accompany an order. There would also have to be better monitoring of the recipients of ASBOs – and other ASB enforcement measures – to ensure certain minority populations are not disproportionately targeted.

The second point that the extent of ASB has been exaggerated by the government is certainly true; although it is unlikely that politicians have been organized enough to have created ASB as a 'phantom menace'. In effect there has been a government, or politician-led 'moral panic' (cf. Cohen 1972). As noted back in Chapter 3, calling something a moral panic does not mean the concern does not exist, only that it is exaggerated. For example, while it is clear that much that is currently labelled as anti-social is not new, according to David Blunkett MP (2003b) there is a contemporary crisis, where ASB and disorder 'completely bedevils the community and under-mines trust and confidence'. This is perhaps over-selling it. More recently the government seems to have acknowledged that youthful ASB can be over-identified, although it is 'adults and the media' that are blamed and not the politicians: 'Young people are ... faced with the challenge of growing up in a culture that has widespread negative perceptions of youth. Adults and the media commonly associate young people with problems such as anti-social behaviour' (HM Treasury and DCSF 2007: 4).

As for the third claim that the ASB agenda has been used for the social control of marginalized populations, this also does seem to be the case. This is not a uniquely British problem (e.g. Beckett and Herbert 2008); but here youth in particular has been problematized, alongside other categories of 'them', including street people, homeless people and street sex workers, so that shared public spaces can be 'cleansed of difference' (cf. Bannister et al. 2006). As suggested, more inclusive policies based on respect and reciprocity – and leading to a shared bottom-up governance of ASB – may help in rebalancing systems of control, away from state control in favour of much more informal mechanisms of social control. This and the decriminalizing and tolerance of much that is regarded as anti-social (but is simply different) will be a positive way forward.

Finally, I want to conclude with the suggestion that some ASB can be good for you. This may seem like a daft thing to finish on; after all, the government believes ASB 'blights people's lives, undermines the fabric of society and holds back regeneration' (Home Office 2003c: 6). What I mean is that some behaviour currently labelled as anti-social, but that is only different or challenging, may be good for you. As Richard Sennett (1970: 108) suggested for mature urban living: [it is] a life with other people in which men (sic) learn to tolerate painful ambiguity and uncertainty. To counter the desire for slavery . . . [and] grow to need the unknown, to feel incomplete without a certain anarchy in their lives, to learn . . . to love the 'otherness' around them.

Fyfe and Bannister (1998: 264) have commented that without disorder and difference, people cannot learn how to deal with conflict. As a consequence, if more serious conflicts emerge the result is likely to be more confrontational, more violent. I would suggest that exposure to behaviour that we perceive to be anti-social or disorderly is beneficial as it challenges our cultural and moral understandings of social norms. So long as this behaviour does not cause us serious offence or harm and if we can accept the behaviour as challenging and different rather than threatening or anti-social, then such exposure can help in nurturing mutual respect and reciprocity. In urban areas in particular, shared public spaces are meant to places where our beliefs and expectations are challenged, rather than sanitized spaces where risk in minimized (CABE 2005b; Millie 2008a). To take a post-modern view, there exist plural norms of behavioural (and aesthetic) acceptability and so we should not be reliant solely on the normative expectations of the majority.

The government has not got it all wrong and there is still a place for ASB enforcement. But in order to engender a culture of tolerance, respect and reciprocity there needs to be an appreciation that some behaviour currently seen as anti-social *does not* take away one's own security (cf. Young 1999).

References

ADT Europe (2006) *Anti-social Behaviour Across Europe: An Overview of Research Commissioned by ADT Europe.* Sunbury: ADT Europe.

Ahmed, E., Harris, N., Braithwaite, J. and Braithwaite, V. (2001) *Shame Management Through Reintegration,* Cambridge: Cambridge University Press.

Aitken, S. (2001) *Geographies of Young People: The Morally Contested Spaces of Identity.* London: Routledge.

Allen, J., Lovbakke, J. and El Komy, M. (2005) Confidence and perceptions of the criminal justice system, in J. Allen, M. El Komy, J. Lovbakke and H. Roy (eds), *Policing and the Criminal Justice System – Public Confidence and Perceptions: Findings from the 2003/04 British Crime Survey.* Home Office Online Report 31/05. London: Home Office.

Ames, A., Powell, H., Crouch, J. and Tse, D. (2007) *Anti-social Behaviour: People, Places and Perceptions.* London: Ipsos Mori.

Anning, A. and colleagues (2007) *Understanding Variations in Effectiveness Amongst SureStart Local Programmes: Lessons for SureStart Children's Centres.* National Evaluation Summary. London: DFES.

Armitage, R. (2002) *Tackling Anti-social Behaviour: What Really Works?* NACRO Community Safety Practice Briefing. London: NACRO.

Arthur, R. (2005) Punishing parents for the crimes of their children, *Howard Journal of Criminal Justice,* 44(3): 233–53.

Arthurson, K. and Jacobs, K. (2006) Housing and anti-social behaviour in Australia, in J. Flint (ed.), *Housing, Urban Governance and Anti-social Behaviour: Perspectives, Policy and Practice.* Bristol: Policy Press.

Ashworth, A. (2004) 'Social control' and 'anti-social behaviour': The subversion of human rights? *Law Quarterly Review,* 120: 263–91.

Ashworth, A. (2005) *Sentencing and Criminal Justice,* 4th edn. Cambridge: Cambridge University Press.

Ashworth, A., Gardner, J., Morgan, R., Smith, A., von Hirsch, A. and Wasik, M. et al. (1998) Neighbouring on the oppressive: the government's 'Anti-Social Behaviour Order' proposals, *Criminal Justice,* 16(1): 7–14.

Atkinson, R., Blandy, S., Flint, J. and Lister, D. (2003) *Gated Communities in England.* London: Office of the Deputy Prime Minister.

Atkinson, R., Mullen, T. and Scott, S. (2000) *The Use of Civil Legal Remedies for Neighbour Nuisance in Scotland.* Edinburgh: Scottish Executive Central Research Unit.

Audit Commission (1996) *Misspent Youth: Young People and Crime.* London: Audit Commission.

Avis, M., Bulman, D. and Leighton, P. (2007) Factors affecting participation in SureStart programmes: A qualitative investigation of parents' views, *Health & Social Care in the Community*, 15(3): 203–11.

Baggini, J. (2006) Blair's philosophy, *Guardian*, 12 Jan. Available at: http://www.guardian.co.uk/society/2006/jan/12/publicservices.politics.

Bakalis, C. (2003) Anti-social behaviour orders – criminal penalties or civil injunctions?, *Cambridge Law Review*, 62: 583–6.

Baldwin, J., Bottoms, A. E. and Walker, M. A. (1976) *The Urban Criminal: A Study in Sheffield*. London: Tavistock Publications.

Banksy (2005) *Wall and Piece*. London: Century.

Bannister, J., Fyfe, N. and Kearns, A. (1998) Closed circuit television and the city, in C. Norris, J. Moran and G. Armstrong (eds), *Surveillance, Closed Circuit Television and Social Control*. Aldershot: Ashgate.

Bannister, J., Fyfe, N. and Kearns, A. (2006) Respectable or respectful? (In)civility and the city, *Urban Studies*, 435(6): 919–37.

Bannister, J. and Scott, S. (2000) Assessing the cost-effectiveness of measures to deal with anti-social neighbour behaviour: Discussion Paper No. 1, Department of Urban Studies University of Glasgow.

Barnardo's (2005) *Parliamentary Briefing Paper: Youth Justice*. Barkingside: Barnardo's.

Barnes, J. (2006) Networks, intervention and retaliation: informal social control in four English neighbourhoods, in K. Harris (ed.), *Respect in the Neighbourhood*. Lyme Regis: Russell House Publishing.

Baroness Linklater of Butterstone (2007) Lord's *Hansard*, 10 Jan.: col. 285. Available at: http://www.parliament.the-stationery-office.co.uk/pa/ld200607/ldhansrd/text/70110–0010.htm (accessed Feb. 2008).

Bauman, Z. (2000) *Liquid Modernity*. Cambridge: Polity Press.

Bauman, Z. (2007) *Liquid Times: Living in an Age of Uncertainty*. Cambridge: Polity Press.

BBC (2000) Blair backs down on fining 'louts', *BBC News Online*, 3 July. Available at: http://news.bbc.co.uk/1/hi/uk_politics/816949.stm.

BBC (2005) 'Asbo' and 'chav' make dictionary', *BBC Online*, 8 June. Available at: http://news.bbc.co.uk/1/hi/uk/4074760.stm.

BBC (2008) 'Tunnel becomes Banksy art exhibit', *BBC News Online*, 2 May. Available at: http://news.bbc.co.uk/1/hi/england/london/7377622.stm.

Beatty, C., Foden, M., Lawless, P. and Wilson, I. (2008) New Deal for Communities: a synthesis of new programme wide evidence: 2006–07. NDC National Evaluation Phase 2 Research Report No. 39. London: Department for Communities and Local Government.

Becker, H. (1963) *Outsiders: Studies in the Sociology of Deviance*. New York: The Free Press.

Beckett, K. and Herbert, S. (2008) Dealing with disorder: Social control in the post-industrial city, *Theoretical Criminology*, 12(1): 5–30.

Beinart, S., Anderson, B., Lee, S. and Utting, D. (2002) *Youth at Risk? A National Survey of Risk Factors, Protective Factors and Problem Behaviours Among Young People in England, Scotland and Wales*. London: Communities that Care.

Beirens, H., Coad, J., Mason, P., McCutcheon, M. and Prior, D. (2005) *Sheffield Children's Fund's Work to Address Crime and Anti-social Behaviour*. Sheffield: National Evaluation of the Children's Fund.

Belsky, J., Barnes, J. and Melhuish, E. (2007) *The National Evaluation of SureStart: Does Area-based Early Intervention Work?* Bristol: Policy Press.

BIBIC (British Institute for Brain Injured Children) (2005) *Ain't Misbehavin': Young People With Learning and Communication Difficulties and Anti-social Behaviour.* November Campaign Update. Bridgwater: BIBIC.

BIBIC (British Institute for Brain Injured Children) (2007) *BIBIC Research on ASBOs and Young People with Learning Difficulties and Mental Health Problems.* Bridgwater: BIBIC.

Blackman, O. (2007) Asbos are a failure, *Daily Mirror*, 27 July. Available at: http://www.mirror.co.uk/news/topstories/2007/07/27/asbos-are-a-failure-89520–19528541/

Blair, T. (1998) *The Third Way: New Politics for the New Century.* London: The Fabian Society.

Blair, T. (2000) Values and the power of community. Speech to the Global Ethics Foundation, University of Tübingen, 30 June. Available at:http://keeptony blairforpm.wordpress.com/.blair-speech-value-community-tubingen-30-june-2000/

Blair, T. (2001) Improving your local environment. Speech at Groundwork UK Seminar, Fairfield Hall, Croydon, 24 April. Available at: http://www.number-10.gov.uk/output/Page1588.asp.

Blair, T. (2003a) PM's speech on anti-social behaviour. QEII Centre, London. 14 October. Available at: http://www.pm.gov.uk/output/Page4644.asp.

Blair, T. (2003b) Speech to the Labour Party Conference. Bournemouth, 30 Sept. Available at http://www.guardian.co.uk/politics/2003/sep/30/labourconference.labour5.

Blair, T. (2004) PM's speech on anti-social behaviour. 28 October. Available at: http://www.number-10.gov.uk/output/Page6492.asp.

Blair, T. (2006a) Our nation's future: The criminal justice system. Speech reproduced in R. Garside and W. McMahon (eds), *Does Criminal Justice Work? The 'Right for the Wrong Reasons' Debate.* London: Crime and Society Foundation.

Blair, T. (2006b) Tony Blair writes for *The Sun* (alongside an article by A. Porter, Blair's super-nanny state), *The Sun*, 21 Nov. Available at: http://www.thesun.co.uk/sol/homepage/news/article72078.ece.

Bland, N. and Read, T. (2000) Policing anti-social behaviour. Police Research Series Paper No. 123. London: Home Office.

Blandy, S. (2006) Gated communities: a response to, or remedy for, anti-social behaviour? in J. Flint (ed.), *Housing, Urban Governance and Anti-social Behaviour: Perspectives, Policy and Practice.* Bristol: Policy Press.

Blears, H. (2005) House of Commons Select Committee on Home Affairs Minutes of Evidence. Q540, 8 Mar. Available at: http://www.publications.parliament.uk/pa/cm200405/ cmselect/cmhaff/80/5030803.htm#n1.

Blumstein, A., Cohen, J. and Farrington, D. (1988) Criminal career research: its value for criminology, *Criminology*, 26(1): 1–35.

Blunkett, D. (2003a) Civil renewal: a new agenda. The CSV Edith Kahn Memorial Lecture, 11 June.

Blunkett, D. (2003b) Speech to the Association of Police Authorities, 4 Nov. Available at: http://press.homeoffice.gov.uk/Speeches/speeches-archive/sp-hs-apa-1103?view=Binary.

Blunkett, D. (2004) Foreword, *One Year On: Together Tackling Anti-social Behaviour.* London: Home Office.

Blunkett, D. (2008) *The Inclusive Society? Social Mobility in 21st Century Britain.* London: Progress.

BMA (British Medical Association) (2006) *Child and Adolescent Mental Health: A Guide for Healthcare Professionals*. London: BMA Board of Science.

Bottoms, A. E. (2006) Incivilities, offence and social order in residential communities, in A. von Hirsch and A. P. Simester (eds), *Incivilities: Regulating Offensive Behaviour*. Oxford: Hart Publishing.

Boutellier, H. (2002) *Crime and Morality: The Significance of Criminal Justice in a Post-modern Culture*. Dordrecht. Kluwer Academic Publishers.

Bowling, B. (1999) The rise and fall of New York murder: Zero tolerance or crack's decline? *British Journal of Criminology*, 39(4): 531–54.

Braithwaite, J. (1989) *Crime, Shame and Reintegration*. Cambridge: Cambridge University Press.

Branigan, T. (2007) Every Asbo a failure, says Balls, in break with Blair era on crime, *Guardian*, 28 July, p. 13. Available at: http://www.guardian.co.uk/politics/2007/jul/28/ukcrime.immigrationpolicy.

Bratton, W. (1997) Crime is down in New York City: Blame the police, in N. Dennis (ed.), *Zero Tolerance: Policing a Free Society*. London: Institute of Economic Affairs.

BRE (2002) *The 1999/2000 National Survey of Attitudes to Environmental Noise: Volume 3 United Kingdom Results – Annex A*. Watford: BRE.

Bright, M., Asthana, A. and Thompson, L. (2005) Welcome to Asbo Nation, *The Observer*, 12 June. Available at: http://www.guardian.co.uk/humanrights/story/0%2C7369%2C1504684%2C00.html.

Brogan, D. and PA Consulting (2005) *Anti-social Behaviour Orders: An Assessment of Current Management Information Systems and the Scale of Anti-social Behaviour Breaches Resulting in Custody*. London: Youth Justice Board.

Bromley, R., Thomas, C. and Millie, A. (2000) Exploring safety concerns in the night-time city: Revitalising the evening economy, *Town Planning Review*, 71(1): 71–96.

Brotherton, M. (2006) R(W) v. Commissioner of Police of the Metropolis and another, Secretary of State for the Home Department, interested party [2006] EWCA Civ 458, *The WLR Daily*. Available at: http://www.lawreports.co.uk/WLRD/2006/CACIV/may0.7.htm.

Brown, A. (2004) Anti-social behaviour, crime control and social control, *Howard Journal of Criminal Justice*, 43(2): 203–11.

Brown, G. (2006) We will always strive to be on your side. Speech at the Labour Party Conference, 25 Sept. Available at: www.labour.org.uk.

Brown, K. (2007) Examining the introduction of legislation in Ireland to tackle juvenile anti-social behaviour, Probation Journal, 54(3): 239–250.

Bullock, K. and Jones, B. (2004) Acceptable Behaviour Contracts: Addressing antisocial behaviour in the London Borough of Islington, Home Office Online Report No. 02/04. London: Home Office.

Brown, P. (1999) Redefining acceptable conduct: Using social landlords to control behaviour, *Local Government Studies*, 25(1): 75–83.

Burke, R. H. (1998) *Zero Tolerance Policing*. Cambridge: Perpetuity Press.

Burney, E. (1999) *Crime and Banishment: Nuisance and Exclusion in Social Housing*. Winchester: Waterside Press.

Burney, E. (2000) Ruling out trouble: Anti-social behaviour and housing management, *The Journal of Forensic Psychology*, 11(2): 268–73.

Burney, E. (2002) Talking tough, acting coy: What happened to the anti-social behaviour order? *Howard Journal of Criminal Justice*, 41(5): 469–84.

Burney, E. (2005) *Making People Behave: Anti-social Behaviour, Politics and Policy.* Cullompton: Willan Publishing.

Burney, E. (2006) 'No spitting': Regulation of offensive behaviour in England and Wales, in A. von Hirsch and A. P. Semester (eds), *Incivilities: Regulating Offensive Behaviour.* Oxford: Hart Publishing.

Bursik, R. J. (1988) Social disorganization and theories of crime and delinquency, *Criminology*, 26: 519–51.

Butcher, A. (2007) Charges dropped against 'Bollocks to Blair' team chase rider, *Horse and Hound Magazine.* Available at: http://www.horseandhound.co.uk/news/article.php?aid=153463.

CABE (Commission for Architecture and the Built Environment) (2004a) Policy note: preventing anti-social behaviour in public spaces, *CABE Space*, Nov. London: CABE.

CABE (Commission for Architecture and the Built Environment) (2004b) *Raising the Standard: The Green Flag Award Guidance Manual.* London: CABE.

CABE (Commission for Architecture and the Built Environment) (2005a) *Decent Parks? Decent Behaviour? The Link Between the Quality of Parks and User Behaviour,* London: CABE.

CABE (Commission for Architecture and the Built Environment) (2005b) *What are We Scared Of? The Value of Risk in Designing Public Space.* London: CABE.

Caldeira, T. (2001) *City of Walls: Crime, Segregation and Citizenship in São Paulo,* Berkeley, CA: University of California Press.

Cameron, D. (2006) Making our country a safe and civilised place for everyone. Speech to the Centre for Social Justice, 10 July. Available at: www.conservatives.com.

Campbell, B. (1993) *Goliath: Britain's Dangerous Places.* London: Methuen.

Campbell, S. (2002) A review of anti-social behaviour orders, Home Office Research Study No. 236. London: Home Office.

Card, P. (2006) Governing tenants: From dreadful enclosures to dangerous places, in J. Flint (ed.), *Housing, Urban Governance and Anti-social Behaviour: Perspectives, Policy and Practice.* Bristol: Policy Press.

Carr, H. and Cowen, D. (2006) Labelling: Constructing definitions of anti-social behaviour? in J. Flint (ed.), *Housing, Urban Governance and Anti-social Behaviour: Perspectives, Policy and Practice.* Bristol: Policy Press

Carter, Lord (2007) *Securing the Future: Proposals for the Efficient and Sustainable Use of Custody in England and Wales.* London: Lord Carter of Coles.

Case, S. (2007) Questioning the 'evidence' of risk that underpins evidence-led youth justice interventions, *Youth Justice*, 7(2): 91–105.

Casey, L. (2005) Mob justice or yob control? Debate with Shami Chakrabarti *Society Guardian*, 19 March. Available at: www.society.guardian.co.uk.

Chakrabarti, S. (2006) Blurring the lines between civil and criminal law, in B. Shimshon (ed.), *Social Justice: Criminal Justice.* London: The Smith Institute.

Chartered Institute of Housing (1995) Neighbour nuisance: ending the nightmare, Good Practice Briefing No. 3. Coventry: Chartered Institute of Housing.

Chenery, S., Henshaw, C. and Pease, K. (1999) Illegal parking in disabled bays: a means of offender targeting, Policing and Reducing Crime Briefing Note No. 1/99. London: Home Office.

Chief Secretary to the Treasury (2003) *Every Child Matters*. Green Paper presented to Parliament, Sept. Cm5860. London: HMSO.

Christmann, K. and Rogerson, M. (2004) Crime, fear of crime and quality of life: Identifying and responding to problems. New Deal for Communities National Evaluation Research Report No. 35. Sheffield: Sheffield Hallam University.

CIEH (Chartered Institute of Environmental Health) (2006) *Neighbourhood Noise Policies and Practice for Local authorities: A Management Guide*. London: Chartered Institute of Environmental Health.

Clarke, C. (2000) House of Commons *Hansard*, 3 July: col.: 72W. Available at: http://www.publications.parliament.uk/pa/cm199900/cmhansrd/vo000703/text/00703w19.htm.

Clarke, C. (2005) We will reinforce a culture of respect. Speech at the Labour Party Conference, Brighton, 27 Sept.

Clarke, R. V. G. and Eck, J. (2003) *Become a Problem-solving Crime Analyst: In 55 Small Steps*. Cullompton: Willan Publishing.

Cloonan, M. (1995) 'I fought the law': Popular music and British obscenity law, *Popular Music*, 14(3): 349–63.

Coaker, Mr. (2007) Parliamentary written answer, *Hansard*, 25 June: col. 284A. Available at: http://www.publications.parliament.uk/pa/cm200607/cmhansrd/cm070625/text/70625w0063.htm.

Cobb, N. (2007) Governance through publicity: Anti-social behaviour orders, young people, and the problematization of the right to anonymity, *Journal of Law and Society*, 34(3): 342–73.

Cohen, A. K. (1955) *Delinquent Boys: The Culture of the Gang*. Glencoe, IL: The Free Press.

Cohen, S. (1971) Mods, rockers and the rest: Community reactions to juvenile delinquency, *The Howard Journal*, 12: 121–130. Reproduced in W. G. Carson and P. Wiles (eds), *Crime and Delinquency in Britain: Sociological Readings*. London: Martin Robertson and Company Ltd.

Cohen, S. (1972) *Folk Devils and Moral Panics: The Creation of Mods and Rockers*. London: MacGibbon and Kee Ltd.

Cohen, S. (1973) Property destruction: Motives and meanings, in C. Ward (ed.), *Vandalism*. London: The Architectural Press.

Cohen, S. (1985) *Visions of Social Control: Crime, Punishment, and Classification*. Cambridge: Polity Press.

Cohen, S. (2002) *Folk Devils and Moral Panics*, 3rd edn. London: Routledge.

Cole, I. and Nevin, B. (2004) *The Road to Renewal: The Early Development of the Housing Market Renewal Programme in England*. York: Joseph Rowntree Foundation.

Comedia (1991) *Out of Hours: A Study of Economic, Social and Cultural Lives in Twelve Town Centres across the UK*. London: Comedia.

Connolly, P. J. (2006) 'Heelgood factors: The role of the street environment in promoting or undermining informal social control', in K. Harris (ed.), *Respect in the Neighbourhood: Why Neighbourliness Matters*. Lyme Regis: Russell House Publishing.

Cook, D. (2006) *Criminal and Social Justice*. London: Sage.

Cowen, D. (1999) *Housing Law and Policy*. Basingstoke: Macmillan.

Cowen, D., Pantazis, C. and Gilroy, R. (2001) Social housing as crime control: An examination of the role of housing management in policing sex offenders, *Social & Legal Studies*, 10(4): 435–57.

Coyne, I., Chesney, T., Logan, B. and Madden, N. (forthcoming) *Cyber-bullying in a Virtual Community: Perceptions and Experiences of Residents*. Nottingham: University of Nottingham.

Cozens, P. M., Saville, G. and Hillier, D. (2005) Crime prevention through environmental design (CPTED): A review and modern bibliography, *Property Management*, 23(5): 328–56.

Crawford, A. (1997) *The Local Governance of Crime: Appeals to Community and Partnerships*. Oxford: Clarendon Press.

Crawford, A. (2003) ''Contractual governance' of deviant behaviour, *Journal of Law and Society*, 30(4): 479–505.

Crawford, A. and Lister, S. (2007) *The Use and Impact of Dispersal Orders: Sticking Plasters and Wake-up Calls*. Bristol: Policy Press.

CRG Research (2006) *Positive Activities For Young People: National Evaluation – Final Report*. Cardiff: CRG Research Ltd.

Curtis, A. (2004) *The Power of Nightmares*. Broadcast on BBC, from 20 Oct.

CYPU (Children and Young People's Unit) and YJB (Youth Justice Board) (2002) *Use of Children's Fund Partnership Funding for Crime Prevention Activities Jointly Agreed with Youth Offending Teams*. London: CYPU and YJB.

Daily Mail (2008) Boris bans alcohol on Tubes and buses in first attack on ASBO culture, *Daily Mail*, 7 May. Available at: http://www.mailonsunday.co.uk/pages/live/articles/news/news.html?in_article_id=564550&in_page_id=1770.

Davis, M. (1990) *City of Quartz: Excavating the Future in Los Angeles*. London: Verso.

Dawar, A. (2008) Johnson bans alcohol on London's public transport, *Guardian*, 7 May. Available at: http://www.guardian.co.uk/politics/2008/may/07/london.drugsandalcohol.

DCA (Department for Constitutional Affairs) (2006) Delivering simple, speedy, summary justice, DCA Report No. 37/06. London: DCA.

DCLG (Department for Communities and Local Government) (2006a) Joining up for safer neighbourhoods: A theme report from the Neighbourhood Management Pathfinder Programme National Evaluation, Research Report No. 31. London: DCLG.

DCLG (Department for Communities and Local Government) (2006b) Anti-social behaviour intensive family support projects, Housing Research Summary No. 230. London: DCLG.

DCLG (Department for Communities and Local Government) (2007) *How to Manage Town Centres*. London: DCLG.

DCSF (Department for Children, Schools and Families) (2008) *Young People's Views on Their Portrayal and Anti-social Behaviour Enforcement*. London: DCSF.

Defra (Department for Environment, Food and Rural Affairs) (2005) *Securing the Future: Delivering UK Sustainable Development Strategy*, London: Defra.

Defra (Department for Environment, Food and Rural Affairs) (2006a) *Fixed Penalty Notices: Guidance on the Fixed Penalty Notice Provisions of the Environmental Protection Act 1990, the Clean Neighbourhoods and Environment Act 2005 and Other Legislation*, London: Defra.

Defra (Department for Environment, Food and Rural Affairs) (2006b) *Noise: Guidance on Sections 69 to 81 and Section 86 of the Clean Neighbourhoods and Environment Act 2005*. London: Defra.

Dennis, F. (2006) Our children run wild – but it's the police who are in handcuffs, *Daily Telegraph*, 5 Nov. Available at: http://www.telegraph.co.uk.

DfES (Department for Education and Skills) (2006) *Implementing SureStart Local Programmes: An Integrated Overview of the First Four Years*, London: DfES.

DfT (Department for Transport) (2004) *National Travel Survey: 2003, Final Results*. London: DfT.

Dignam, J., Sorsby, A. and Hibbert, J. (1996) *Neighbour Disputes: Comparing the Cost Effectiveness of Mediation and Alternative Approaches*. Sheffield: University of Sheffield Centre for Criminological and Legal Research.

Dillane, J., Hill, M., Bannister, J. and Scott, S. (2001) *Evaluation of the Dundee Families Project*. Edinburgh: The Stationery Office.

Dishley, D. (2008) *An Introduction to Jurisdiction in Magistrates Youth Court*. London: Your Life You Choose.

Dixon, D. and Maher, L. (2005) Policing, crime and public health: Lessons for Australia from the 'New York miracle', *Criminal Justice*, 5(2): 115–43.

Dobson, N. (2006) Government: Anti-social behaviour – removing young persons, Pinsent Masons Update, June. Available at: http://www.pinsentmasons.com/media/244814425.pdf.

Donoghue, J. (2007) The judiciary as a primary definer on anti-social behaviour orders, *Howard Journal of Criminal Justice*, 46(4): 417–30.

Donovan, T. (2004) Youth justice: Antisocial orders come under fire, *Young People Now*, 28 Apr.

Downes, D. (1966) *The Delinquent Solution: A Study in Subcultural Theory*. London: Routledge & Kegan Paul.

Downes, D. (1979) Praxis makes perfect, in D. Downes and P. Rock (eds), *Deviant Interpretations: Problems in Criminological Theory*. Oxford: Martin Robertson Publishing.

Downes, D. and Rock, P. (1982) *Understanding Deviance: A Guide to the Sociology of Crime and Rule Breaking*. Oxford: Oxford University Press.

Downes, D. and Rock, P. (2007) *Understanding Deviance*, 5th edn. Oxford: Oxford University Press.

Duff, R. A. and Marshell, S. E. (2006) How offensive can you get? in A. von Hirsch and A. P. Simester (eds), *Incivilities: Regulating Offensive Behaviour*. Oxford: Hart Publishing.

Dunn, P. (2004) *Acceptable Behaviour Contracts*. London: Metropolitan Police. Available at: http://www.met.police.uk/saferneighbourhoods/asbo/training/abc_training.pdf.

Durkheim, E. (1984) *The Division of Labour in Society* (trans. W. D. Halls). Basingstoke: Macmillan.

Durkheim, E. (2003) The normal and the pathological, in E. McLaughlin, J. Muncie and G. Hughes (eds), *Criminological Perspectives: Essential Readings*, 2nd edn. London: Sage.

DWP (Department of Work and Pensions) (2007) *Housing Benefit Guidance on Housing Benefit Anti Social Behaviour Sanction for Local Authorities Participating in the Pilot Scheme*. London: DWP.

Eames, M. and Adebowale, M. (eds) (2002) *Sustainable Development and Social Inclusion: Towards an Integrated Approach to Research*. York: Joseph Rowntree Foundation/YPS.

Eck, J. E. and Maguire, E. R. (2000) Have changes in policing reduced violent crime? An assessment of the evidence, in A. Blumstein and J. Wallman (eds), *The Crime Drop in America*. Cambridge: Cambridge University Press.

Economist (2005) Enemies of the state, *Economist*, 5 Feb.

Edwards, A. and Hughes, G. (2002) Introduction: The community governance of crime, in A. Edwards and G. Hughes (eds), *Crime Control and Community: The New Politics of Public Safety*. Cullompton: Willan Publishing.

Ekblom, P. (1979) Police truancy patrols, in J. Burrows, P. Ekblom and K. Heal (eds), *Crime Prevention and the Police*, Home Office Research Study No. 55. London: Home Office.

Elias, N. (1978) *The Civilising Process, Volume 1: The History of Manners* (trans. E. Jephcott). Oxford: Blackwell.

Elias, N. and Scotston, J. L. (1965) *The Established and the Outsiders: A Sociological Enquiry into Community Problems*. London: Frank Cass & Co. Ltd.

Ellin, N. (1997) *Architecture of Fear*. New York: Princeton Architectural Press.

Engineer, R., Phillips, A., Thompson, J. and Nicholls, J. (2003) Drunk and disorderly: A qualitative study of binge drinking among 18- to 24-year-olds, Home Office Research Study No. 262. London: Home Office.

Erikson, K. (1964) Notes on the sociology of deviance, in H. Becker (ed.), *The Other Side: Perspectives on Deviance*. New York: The Free Press.

Erikson, K. (1966) *Wayward Puritans*. New York: Wiley.

Erol, R. (2006) *Alcohol Misuse Enforcement Campaign: Guidance on Problem Profiles*. London: UCL Jill Dando Institute.

Etzioni, A. (1993a) *The Spirit of Community: Rights, Responsibilities and the Communitarian Agenda*. New York: Crown Publishers.

Etzioni, A. (1993b) *The Parental Deficit*. London: Demos.

Eysenck, M. W. (1994) *Individual Differences: Normal and Abnormal*. Hove: LEA Ltd.

Farrall, S. (2004) Can we believe our eyes? A response to Mike Hough, *International Journal of Social Research Methodology*, 7(2): 177–9.

Farrell, G. and Pease, K. (1993) Once bitten, twice bitten: Repeat victimisation and its implications for crime prevention, Crime Prevention Unit Series Paper No. 46. London: Home Office.

Farrington, D. P. (1992) Criminal career research in the United Kingdom, *British Journal of Criminology*, 32(4): 521–36.

Farrington, D. P. (1995a) The challenge of teenage antisocial behaviour, in M. Rutter (ed.), *Psychosocial Disturbances in Young People: Challenges for Prevention*. Cambridge: Cambridge University Press.

Farrington, D. P. (1995b) The development of offending and anti-social behaviour from childhood: key findings from the Cambridge Study in Delinquent Development, *Journal of Child Psychology and Psychiatry*, 36: 929–64.

Farrington, D. P. (2000) Psychosocial predictors of adult antisocial personality and adult convictions, *Behavioral Sciences & the Law*, 18(5): 605–22.

Farrington, D. P., Coid, J. W., Hartnett, L. M., Jolliffe, D., Soteriou, N., Turner, R. E. and West, D. J. (2006) Criminal careers up to age 50 and life success up to age 48: New findings from the Cambridge Study in Delinquent Development. Home Office Research Study No. 299. London: Home Office.

Farrington, D. P. and Welsh, B. C. (1999) Delinquency prevention using family-based interventions, *Children & Society*, 13(4): 287–303.

Fassenfelt, J. (2006) Use of individual support orders (ISOs), *Magistrate*, 62(3): 70.

Feinberg, J. (1984) *Harm to Others: The Moral Limits of the Criminal Law, Volume 1*. New York: Oxford University Press.

Feinberg, J. (1985) *Offence to Others: The Moral Limits of the Criminal Law, Volume. 2*. New York: Oxford University Press.

Felson, R. B. and Staff, J. (2006) Explaining the academic performance-delinquency relationship, *Criminology*, 44(2): 299–320.

Ferrell, J. (1993) *Crimes of Style: Urban Graffiti and the Politics of Criminality*. New York and London: Garland Publishing.

Ferrell, J. (1998) Against the law, *Social Anarchism*, 25. Available at: http://www.socialanarchism.org/mod/magazine/display/67/index.php.

Ferrell, J. (2004) Boredom, crime and criminology, *Theoretical Criminology*, 8(3): 287–302.

Ferrell, J. (2006) The aesthetics of cultural criminology, in B. A. Arrigo and C. R. Williams (eds), *Philosophy, Crime and Criminology*. Chicago, IL: University of Illinois Press.

Field, F. (1989) *Losing Out: The Emergence of Britain's Underclass*. Oxford: Blackwell.

Field, F. (2002) How to tame the Barbarians, *Sunday Times*, 16 June.

Field, F. (2003) *Neighbours from Hell*. London: Politico's.

Finch, E. (2002a) Stalking the perfect stalking law: an evaluation of the efficacy of the Protection from Harassment Act 1997, *Criminal Law Review*, Sept. 703–18.

Finch, E. (2002b) Stalking: A violent crime or a crime of violence? *Howard Journal of Criminal Justice*, 41(5): 422–33.

FitzGerald, M., Hough, M., Joseph, I. and Qureshi, T. (2002) *Policing for London*. Cullompton: Willan Publishing.

Fletcher, H. (2005) *ASBOs: An Analysis of the First 6 Years*, 20 July. London: NAPO.

Flint, J. (2002) Social housing agencies and the governance of anti-social behaviour, *Housing Studies*, 17(4): 619–37.

Flint, J. (2004) The responsible tenant: Housing governance and the politics of behaviour, *Housing Studies*, 19(6): 893–909.

Flint, J. (2006a) *Housing, Urban Governance and Anti-social Behaviour: Perspectives, Policy and Practice*. Bristol: Policy Press.

Flint, J. (2006b) Housing and the new governance of conduct, in J. Flint (ed.), *Housing, Urban Governance and Anti-social Behaviour: Perspectives, Policy and Practice*. Bristol: Policy Press.

Flint, J. and Nixon, J. (2006) Governing neighbours: anti-social behaviour orders and new forms of regulating conduct in the UK, *Urban Studies*, 43(5/6): 939–55.

Foucault, M. (2003) *Discipline and Punish: The Birth of the Prison* (trans. A. Sheridan). London: Allen Lane. Excerpt reprinted as The carceral, in E. McLaughlin, J. Muncie and G. Hughes (eds), *Criminological Perspectives: Essential Readings*, 2nd edn. London: Sage.

France, A. (2008) Risk factor analysis and the youth question, *Journal of Youth Studies*, 11(1): 1–15.

France, A. and Utting, D. (2005) The paradigm of 'risk and protection-focused prevention' and its impact on services for children and families, *Children & Society*, 19(2): 77–90.

Fyfe, N. and Bannister, J. (1998) 'The eyes upon the street': Closed circuit television surveillance and the city, in N. Fyfe (ed.), *Images of the Street: Planning, Identity, and Control in Public Space*. London: Routledge.

Gardner, J., von Hirsch, A., Smith, A. T. H., Morgan, R., Ashworth, A. and Wasik, N. (1998) Clause 1: The hybrid law from hell? *Criminal Justice Matters*, 31: 25–7.

Garland, D. (2001) *The Culture of Control: Crime and Social Order in Contemporary Society*. Oxford: Oxford University Press.

Garland, D. (2002) Of crimes and criminals: The development of criminology in Britain, in M. Maguire, R. Morgan and R. Reiner (eds), *The Oxford Handbook of Criminology*, 3rd edn. Oxford: Oxford University Press.

Garofalo, J. and Laub, J. (1978), The fear of crime: Broadening our perspective, *Victimology*, 3: 242–53.

Gelsthorpe, L. (1999) Parents and criminal children, in A. Bainham, S. Day Sclater and M. Richards (eds), *What is a Parent? A Socio-legal Analysis*. Oxford: Hart Publishing.

Gill, O. (1977) *Luke Street: Housing Policy, Conflict and the Creation of the Delinquent Area*. London: Macmillan.

Gil-Robles, A. (2005) Report by Mr Alvaro Gil-Robles, Commissioner for Human Rights, on his visit to the United Kingdom, 4th–12th November 2004, Office of the Commissioner for Human Rights, 8 June, CommDH(2005)6. Strasbourg: Council of Europe.

Girling, E., Loader, I. and Sparks, R. (2000) *Crime and Social Change in Middle England: Questions of Order in an English Town*. London: Routledge.

GLA (Greater London Authority) (2005) *The London Anti-Social Behaviour Strategy 2005–2008*. London: GLA.

Glass, N. (1999) SureStart: The development of an early intervention programme for young children in the United Kingdom, *Children & Society*, 13(4): 257–64.

Goldson, B. (1997) Children in trouble: State responses to juvenile crime, in P. Scraton (ed.), *Childhood in Crisis*. London: UCL Press.

Goldson, B. and Jamieson, J. (2002) Youth crime, the 'parenting deficit' and state intervention: A contextual critique, *Youth Justice*, 2(2): 82–99.

Goss, J. (1993) The 'magic of the mall': An analysis of form, function, and meaning in the contemporary retail built environment, *Annals of the Association of American Geographers*, 83(1): 18–47.

Green, H., McGinnity, A., Meltzer, H., Ford, T. and Goodman, R. (2005) *Mental Health in Children and Young People in Great Britain*, Office for National Statistics. Basingstoke: Palgrave Macmillan.

Greenhalgh, L. and Worpole, K. (1995) *Park Life: Urban Parks and Social Renewal*. London: Comedia and Demos.

Greenwood, P., Model, K. E., Rydell, C. P. and Chiesa, J. (1996) *Diverting Children from a Life of Crime: Measuring Costs and Benefits*. Santa Monica, CA: RAND.

Griffiths, K. (2006) Asbo saved my son from crime, *Telegraph & Argos* (Bradford), 3 Nov.

Guardian (2005) An evening with Louise Casey: Excerpts from an after-dinner speech given by the government's 'yob tsar', *Guardian*, 7 July. Available at: http://politics.guardian.co.uk/whitehall/story/0,9061,1522714,00.html.

Hadfield, P. (2006) *Bar Wars: Contesting the Night in Contemporary British Cities*. Oxford: Oxford University Press.

Halpern, D. (2005) *Social Capital*. Cambridge: Polity Press.

Halsey, M. and Young, A. (2002) The meanings of graffiti and municipal administration, *The Australian and New Zealand Journal of Criminology*, 35(2): 165–86.

Halsey, M. and Young, A. (2006) 'Our desires are ungovernable': Writing graffiti in urban space, *Theoretical Criminology*, 10(3): 275–306.

Hancock, L. (2001) *Community, Crime and Disorder: Safety and Regeneration in Urban Neighbourhoods*. Basingstoke: Palgrave.

Hancock, L. (2006) Urban regeneration, young people, crime and criminalisation, in B. Goldson and J. Muncie (eds), *Youth Crime and Justice*. London: Sage.

Hancock, L. (2007) Is urban regeneration criminogenic?; in R. Atkinson and G. Helms (eds), *Securing an Urban Renaissance: Crime, Community, and British Urban Policy*. Bristol: Policy Press.

Harcourt, B. E. (1998) Reflections on the subject: A critique of the social influence conception of deterrence, the broken windows theory, and order-maintenance policing New York style, *Michigan Law Review*, 97(2): 291–389.

Harcourt, B. E. (2001) *Illusion of Order: The False Promise of Broken Windows Policing*. Cambridge, MA: Harvard University Press.

Harcourt, B. E. and Ludvig, J. (2006) Broken windows: New evidence from New York City and a five-city social experiment, *University of Chicago Law Review*, 73: 271–320.

Harradine, S., Kodz, J., Lernetti, F. and Jones, B. (2004) Defining and measuring anti-social behaviour, Home Office Development and Practice Report No. 26. London: Home Office.

Harris, K. (2006a) To doff my cap: Talking about respect, in K. Harris (ed.), *Respect in the Neighbourhood: Why Neighbourliness Matters*. Lyme Regis: Russell House Publishing.

Harris, K. (2006b) Formalising the informal? Policy and local social relations, in K. Harris (ed.), *Respect in the Neighbourhood: Why Neighbourliness Matters*. Lyme Regis: Russell House Publishing.

Harris, K. (2006c) *Respect in the Neighbourhood: Why Neighbourliness Matters*. Lyme Regis: Russell House Publishing.

Harris, K. (2006d) 'Do you live on 'ere?' Neighbourhood and respect, in K. Harris (ed.), *Respect in the Neighbourhood: Why Neighbourliness Matters*. Lyme Regis: Russell House Publishing.

Harris, K. (2007) Respect in the neighbourhood: Neighbourliness and narratives of decline, *Community Safety Journal*, 6(4): 34–41.

Haworth, A. and Manzi, T. (1999) Managing the 'underclass': Interpreting the moral discourses of housing management, *Urban Studies*, 36(1): 153–66.

Hayes, B. (1998) Applying Bratton to Britain: The need for sensible compromise, in M. Weatheritt (ed.), *Zero Tolerance Policing: What Does it Mean and is it Right for Policing in Britain?* London: The Police Foundation.

Hayward, C. (2006) Banksy: Graffiti or street art? Ask Bristol Consultation Report, prepared for Councillor Gary Hopkins, 17 July. Available at: www.bristol.gov.uk/ccm/cms-service/download/asset/?asset_id=22160100.

Hayward, K. J. (2004) *City Limits: Crime, Consumer Culture and the Urban Experience*. London: Glasshouse.

Hayward, R. and Sharp, C. (2005) Young people, crime and antisocial behaviour: Findings from the 2003 Crime and Justice Survey. Home Office Research Findings 245, London: Home Office.

Hearnden, I. and Millie, A. (2004) Does tougher enforcement lead to lower reconviction? *Probation Journal*, 51(1): 48–58.

Hebdige, D. (1979) *Subculture: The Meaning of Style*. London: Methuen.

Herbert, D. T. (1993) Neighbourhood incivilities and the study of crime in place, *Area*, 25(1): 45–54.

Herrington, V. and Millie, A. (2006) Applying reassurance policing: Is it 'business as usual'? *Policing and Society*, 16(2): 146–63.

Heseltine, M. (1983) *Reviving the Inner Cities*. London: Conservative Political Centre.

Hewitt, D. (2007) Bovvered? A legal perspective on the ASBO, *Journal of Forensic and Legal Medicine*, 14(6): 355–63.

Hill, J. and Wright, G. (2003) Youth, community safety and the paradox of inclusion, *Howard Journal of Criminal Justice*, 42(3): 282–97.

HM Treasury and DCSF (2007) *Aiming High for Young People: A Ten Year Strategy for Positive Activities*. London: HM Treasury.

Hobbs, D., Hadfield, P., Lister, S. and Winlow, S. (2003) *Bouncers: Violence and Governance in the Night-time Economy*. Oxford: Oxford University Press.

Hodgkinson, S. and Tilley, N. (2007) 'Policing anti-social behaviour: Constraints, dilemmas and opportunities, *Howard Journal of Criminal Justice*, 46(4): 385–400.

Holden, A. and Iveson, K. (2003) Designs on the urban: New Labour's urban renaissance and the spaces of citizenship, *City*, 7(1): 57–72.

Holt, A. (2008) 'Room for resistance? Parenting orders, disciplinary power and the production of 'the bad parent', in P. Squires (ed.), *ASBO Nation: The Criminalisation of Nuisance*. Bristol: Policy Press.

Home Office (1991) *Safer Communities: The Local Delivery of Crime Prevention Through the Partnership Approach* (The Morgan Report). Standing Conference on Crime Prevention. London: Home Office.

Home Office (1997) Community safety order: a consultation paper, Sept. London: Home Office.

Home Office (1999) *Crime and Disorder Act: Guidance on Anti-Social Behaviour Orders*, London: Home Office.

Home Office (2000) *Anti-Social Behaviour Orders: Guidance on Drawing up Local ASBO Protocols*. London: Home Office.

Home Office (2003a) *Together Tackling Anti-social Behaviour: Action Plan*. London: Home Office.

Home Office (2003b) *The One-day Count of Anti-social Behaviour*, Sept. London: Home Office.

Home Office (2003c) Respect and responsibility – taking a stand against anti-social behaviour, Cm 5778. London: Home Office.

Home Office (2003d) *A Guide to Anti-Social Behaviour Orders and Acceptable Behaviour Contracts*. London: Home Office.

Home Office (2003e) Local child curfews guidance document working draft. Last updated 15 Sept. Available at: http://www.crimereduction.homeoffice.gov.uk/youth/youth18.htm.

Home Office (2004a) *Anti-social Behaviour: A Collection of Published Evidence*. London: Home Office ASB Research Section, RDS Crime and Policing Group.

Home Office (2004b) *Anti-social Behaviour Orders: A Guide*. London: Home Office.

Home Office (2005a) *Neighbourhood Policing: Your Police; Your Community – Our Commitment*. London: Home Office.

Home Office (2005b) *Publishing Anti-social Behaviour Orders*. Home Office Guidance, Mar. London: Home Office.

Home Office (2005c) Sentencing statistics 2004, Home Office Statistical Bulletin No. 15/05. London: Home Office.

Home Office (2005d) Penalty notices for disorder statistics 2004: England and Wales, Home Office Online Report No. 35/05 (additional tables). London: Home Office.

Home Office (2005e) *Use of Dispersal Powers*. London: Home Office.

Home Office (2006a) *A Guide to Anti-Social Behaviour Orders*; London: Home Office.

Home Office (2006b) Anti-social behaviour orders: Statistics, Home Office Crime Reduction website, Last updated 17 Oct. Available at: http://www.crimereduction. homeoffice.gov.uk/asbos/asbos2.htm.

Home Office (2006c) Anti-social behaviour orders continue to bring respite to communities, Home Office Press Release, 8 Dec. Available at: http://press.homeoffice. gov.uk/press-releases/asbos-bring-communities-respite.

Home Office (2006d) Guidance for local authorities on the operation of section 20 of the Drugs Act 2005, 27 Sept. London: Home Office.

Home Office (2006e) *Penalty Notices for Disorder: A Guide*. London: Home Office (Respect Taskforce). Available at: www.respect.gov.uk.

Home Office (2007a) ASBO breaches from June 2000 to December 2005 (following a Freedom of Information Request). Available at: http://www.homeoffice.gov.uk/ about-us/freedom-of-information/released-information/foi-archive-crime/ 5577-asbos-breached-00–05?version=1.

Home Office (2007b) Sentencing statistics 2005: England and Wales, Home Office Statistical Bulletin 03/07. London: Home Office.

Home Office (2007c) *Tools and Powers to Tackle Anti-social Behaviour*. London: Home Office (Respect Taskforce).

Home Office (2007d) The local authorities (alcohol consumption in designated public places) regulations 2007, Circular No. 013/2007. London: Home Office.

Home Office (2008) *Crime Reduction Toolkits: Anti-social Behaviour*. Available at: http:// www.crimereduction.homeoffice.gov.uk/toolkits/as00.htm.

Hope, T. and Hough, M. (1988) Area, crime and incivilities: A profile from the British Crime Survey, in T. Hope (ed.), *Communities and Crime Reduction*. London: HMSO.

Horse and Hound Magazine (2005) Girl arrested over 'Bollocks to Blair' shirt, 22. Sept. Available at: http://www.horseandhound.co.uk/competitionnews/392/68779.html.

Hough, M. (2004) Worry about crime: Mental events or mental states? *International Journal of Social Research Methodology*, 7(2): 173–6.

Hough, M., Hunter, G., Jacobson, J. and Cossalter, S. (2008) The impact of the Licensing Act 2003 on levels of crime and disorder: an evaluation, Home Office Research Report No. 04. London: Home Office.

Hough, M. and Jacobson, J. (2004) Getting to grips with antisocial behaviour, in J. Grieve and R. Howard (eds), *Communities, Social Exclusion and Crime*. London: The Smith Institute.

House of Commons (2003) ODPM: Housing, planning, local government and the regions committee. Living places: cleaner, safer, greener. Eleventh report of session 2002–03, vol. 1. HC 673–1, London: The Stationery Office.

House of Commons (2005) Fifth report from the Home Affairs Committee Session 2004–05. Available at: http://www.publications.parliament.uk/pa/cm200405/cmselect/ cmhaff/80/8002.htm.

Howard League for Penal Reform (2004) Select Committee on Home Affairs written evidence, 20. Memorandum submitted by the Howard League for Penal Reform, 21 Dec.

Howard League for Penal Reform (2005) Abolish ASBOs for children. News release 5 Apr. Available at: http://www.howardleague.org/index.php?id=222.

Hubbard, P. (2005) Spaces on the margin: The spatiality of exclusion, in M. Phillips (ed.), *Contested Worlds: An Introduction to Human Geography*. Chichester: Ashgate.

Hubbard, P. (2008) Regulating the social impacts of studentification: A Loughborough case study, *Environment and Planning A*, 40(2): 323–41.

Hughes, G. (1996) Communitarianism and law and order, *Critical Social Policy*, 16: 17–41.

Hughes, G. (2001) Crime and disorder reduction partnerships: The future of community safety?, in G. Hughes, E. McLaughlin and J. Muncie (eds), *Crime Prevention and Community Safety: New Directions*. London: Sage.

Hughes, G. (2004) The community governance of crime, justice and safety: Challenges and lesson-drawing, *British Journal of Community Justice*, 2(3): 7–20.

Hughes, G. and Follett, M. (2006) Community safety, youth and the 'anti-social', in B. Goldson and J. Muncie (eds), *Youth Crime and Justice*. London: Sage.

Hulsman, L. H. C. (1986) Critical criminology and the concept of crime, *Contemporary Crises*, 10(1): 63–80.

Hunter, A. (1978) Symbols of incivility. Paper presented to the American Society of Criminology Conference.

Hunter, C. (2006) The changing legal framework: From landlords to agents of social control, in J. Flint (ed.), *Housing, Urban Governance and Anti-social Behaviour: Perspectives, Policy and Practice*. Bristol: Policy Press.

Hunter, C. and Nixon, J. (2001) Taking the blame and losing the home: Women and anti-social behaviour, *Journal of Social Welfare and Family Law*, 23(4): 395–410.

Innes, M. (1999) 'An iron fist in an iron glove?' The zero tolerance policing debate, *Howard Journal of Criminal Justice*, 38(4): 397–410.

Innes, M. (2003) *Understanding Social Control: Deviance, Crime and Social Order*. Maidenhead: Open University Press.

Innes, M. (2004a) Signal crimes and signal disorders: Notes on deviance as communicative action, *British Journal of Sociology*, 55(3): 335–55.

Innes, M. (2004b) Reinventing tradition? Reassurance, neighbourhood security and policing, *Criminal Justice*, 4(2): 151–71.

Innes, M. (2005) Why 'soft' policing is hard: On the curious development of reassurance policing, how it became neighbourhood policing and what this signifies about the politics of police reform, *Journal of Community and Applied Social Psychology*, 15(3): 156–69.

Innes, M. and Fielding, N. (2002) From community to communicative policing: 'Signal crimes' and the problem of public reassurance', *Sociological Research Online*, 7(2). Available at: www.socresonline.org.uk/7/2/innes.html.

Innes, M., Fielding, N. and Langan, S. (2002) Signal crimes and control signals: towards an evidence-based conceptual framework for reassurance policing. A report for Surrey Police. Guildford: University of Surrey.

Irving, B. (2002) *Fear of Crime: Theory, Measurement and Application*. London: Police Foundation.

Ipsos Mori (2005) Public concern about ASB and support for ASBOs, 10 June. Available at: http://www.ipsos-mori.com/polls/2005/asbo-top.shtml.

Ipsos Mori (2006) Public attitudes to parenting, 21 Nov. Available at: http://www.ipsos-mori.com/polls/2006/respect.shtml.

Isal, S. (2006) *Equal Respect: ASBOs and Race Equality*. London: Runnymede Trust.

Jacobs, J. (1961) *The Death and Life of Great American Cities*. New York: Vintage Books.

Jacobson, J., Millie, A. and Hough, M. (2005) *Tackling Anti-social Behaviour: A Critical Review*. London: Institute for Criminal Policy Research, King's College London.

Jacobson, J., Millie, A. and Hough, M. (2008) Why tackle anti-social behaviour?, in P. Squires (ed.), *ASBO Nation: The Criminalisation of Nuisance*. Bristol: Policy Press.

Jeffery, C. R. (1971) *Crime Prevention through Environmental Design*. London: Sage.

Johnson, B. (2008) Speech on winning the london mayoral contest. City Hall, London, 3 May, BBC News.

Johnson, J. G., Smailes, E., Cohen, P., Kasen, S. and Brook, J. S. (2004) Anti-social parental behaviour, problematic parenting and aggressive offspring behaviour during adulthood: A 25-year longitudinal investigation, *British Journal of Criminology*, 44(6): 915–30.

Johnson, N. (1999) The personal social services and community care, in M. Powell (ed.), *New Labour, New Welfare State? The 'Third Way' in British Social Policy*. Bristol: Policy Press.

Johnston, C. and Mooney, G. (2007) 'Problem' people, 'problem' places? New Labour and council estates', in R. Atkinson and G. Helms (eds), *Securing an Urban Renaissance: Crime, Community and British Urban Policy*. Bristol: Policy Press.

Johnston, L. (1996) What is vigilantism? *British Journal of Criminology*, 36(2): 220–36.

Johnston, P. (2005) She boasted about binge drinking and 'decking' officials in crude outburst. Now Blair promotes her to respect tsar, *Telegraph*, 3 Sep. Available at: http://www.telegraph.co.uk/news/main.jhtml?xml=/news/2005/09/03/ncasey03.xml.

Johnstone, C. and MacLeod, G. (2007) New Labour's 'broken' neighbourhoods: Liveability, disorder, and discipline, in R. Atkinson and G. Helms (eds), *Securing an Urban Renaissance: Crime, Community, and British Urban Policy*. Bristol: Policy Press.

Jones, C. and Murie, A. (1998) *Reviewing the Right to Buy*. Birmingham: University of Birmingham and Joseph Rowntree Foundation.

Jones, H. and Sager, T. (2001) Crime and Disorder Act 1998: Prostitution and the anti-social behaviour order, *Criminal Law Review*, Nov.: 873–85.

Jones, T. and Newburn, T. (2001) Widening access: improving police relations with hard to reach groups, Police Research Series Paper No. 138. London: Home Office.

Jones, T. and Newburn, T. (2002) The transformation of policing? Understanding current trends in policing systems, *British Journal of Criminology*, 42(1): 129–46.

Jones, T. and Newburn, T. (2007) *Policy Transfer and Criminal Justice: Exploring US Influences over British Crime Control Policy*. Maidenhead: Open University Press.

JRF (Joseph Rowntree Foundation) (2002) *A National Survey of Problem Behaviour and Associated Risk and Protective Factors Among Young People: Findings*. York: JRF.

Judicial Studies Board (2007) *Anti-social Behaviour Orders: A Guide for the Judiciary*, 3rd edn. London: Judicial Studies Board.

Kelling, G. (1998) The evolution of broken windows, in M. Weatheritt (ed.), *Zero Tolerance Policing: What Does it Mean and is it Right for Policing in Britain?* London: The Police Foundation.

Kelling, G. and Coles, C. (1995) *Fixing Broken Windows*. New York: The Free Press.

Kelly, P. (2003) Growing up as risky business? Risks, surveillance and the institutionalized mistrust of youth, *Journal of Youth Studies*, 6(2): 165–80.

Labour Party (1995) *A Quiet Life: Tough Action on Criminal Neighbours*. London: Labour Party.

Labour Party (2005) Britain forward not back. General election manifesto, Labour Party, London.

La Grange, R. L., Ferraro, K. and Supancic, M. (1992) Perceived risk and fear of crime: The role of social and physical incivilities, *Journal of Research in Crime and Delinquency*, 29(3): 311–34.

Lane, D. A. (1987) Personality and antisocial behaviour: A long-term study, *Personality and Individual Differences*, 8(6): 799–806.

Lemanski, C. (2004) A new apartheid? The spatial implications of fear of crime in Cape Town, South Africa, *Environment and Urbanization*, 16(2): 101–11.

Lemert, E. M. (1951) *Social Pathology*. London: McGraw-Hill.

Lemert, E. M. (1967) *Human Deviance, Social Problems, and Social Control*. Englewood Cliffs, NJ: Prentice-Hall.

Lemetti, F. and Parkinson, S. (2005) The cost of anti-social behaviour orders, Home Office Summary Report, Mar. London: Home Office.

Levi, R. (2008) Loitering in the city that works: On circulation, activity and police in governing urban space, in M. D. Dubber and M. Valverde (eds), *Police and the Liberal State*. Stanford, CA: Stanford University Press.

Levitt, S. D. and Dubner, S. J. (2005) *Freakonomics*. London: Penguin Books.

Lewis, M. (2007) *States of Reason: Freedom, Responsibility and the Governing of Behaviour Change*. London: Institute for Public Policy Research.

Lister, R. (1996) *Charles Murray and the Underclass: The Developing Debate*. London: IEA Health and Welfare Unit.

Lister, R. (2006) Children (but not women) first: New Labour, child welfare and gender, *Critical Social Policy*, 26(2): 315–35.

London Borough of Camden (2004) Meeting of the Anti-Social Behaviour Scrutiny Panel, 21 Apr. Available at: http://www3.camden.gov.uk/templates/committees/showHTML.cfm?file=11629.htm.

Loukaitou-Sideris, A. (1993) Privatisation of public open space: The Los Angeles experience, *Town Planning Review*, 64(2): 139–67.

Lovbakke, J. (2007) Public perceptions, in S. Nicholas, C. Kershaw and A. Walker, Home Office Statistical Bulletin, 4th edn. (eds) *Crime in England and Wales 2006/07*, London: Home Office.

Loxley, C., Curtin, L. and Brown, R. (2002) Summer Splash schemes 2000: Findings from six case studies, Crime Reduction Research Series Paper No.12. London: Home Office.

Lucus, K., Walker, G., Eames, M., Fay, H. and Poustie, M. (2004) Environment and social justice: rapid research and evidence review, final report, 8 Dec. London: Policy Studies Institute.

Lund, B. (1999) 'Ask not what your community can do for you': Obligations, New Labour and welfare reform, *Critical Social Policy*, 19(4): 447–62.

Lyon, D. (2007) *Surveillance Studies: An Overview*. Cambridge: Polity Press.

MacDonald, R. (1997) *Youth, the 'Underclass' and Social Exclusion*. London: Routledge.

Macdonald, S. (2003) The nature of the anti-social behaviour order: R (McCann & Others) v. Crown Court at Manchester, *The Modern Law Review*, 66(4): 630–9.

Macdonald, S. (2006) A suicidal woman, roaming pigs and a noisy trampolinist: Refining the ASBO's definition of 'anti-social behaviour', *Modern Law Review*, 69(2): 183–213.

Mackie, A., Burrows, J. and Hubbard, R. (2003) *Evaluation of the Youth Inclusion Programme: End of Phase One Report*. London: Morgan Harris Burrows.

MacLeod, G. (2002) From urban entrepreneurialism to a 'revanchist city'? On the spatial injustices of Glasgow's renaissance, *Antipode*, 34(3): 602–24.

MADE (Midlands Architecture and the Designed Environment) (2006) *Youth Space: A Collaborative Youth Shelter Project Connecting Young People, Architects and Artists*, Birmingham: MADE.

Maguin, E. and Loeber, R. (1996) Academic performance and delinquency, *Crime and Justice: A Review of Research*. 20: 145–264.

Mannheim, H. (1948) *Juvenile Delinquency in an English Middletown*. London: Kegan Paul, Trench, Trubner and Co. Ltd.

Mannheim, H. (1965) *Comparative Criminology*. London: Routledge Kegan Paul.

Manzo, J. (2004) The folk devil happens to be our best customer: Security officers' orientation to 'youth' in three Canadian shopping malls, *International Journal of the Sociology of Law*, 32(3): 243–61.

Margo, J., Dixon, M., Pearce, N. and Reed, H. (2006) *Freedom's Orphans: Raising Youth in a Changing World*. London: Institute for Public Policy Research. Available at: http://www.ippr.org.uk/pressreleases/?id=2388.

Mason, P. and Prior, D. (2008) The Children's Fund and the prevention of crime and anti-social behaviour, *Criminology and Criminal Justice*, 8(3): 279–296.

Matthews, H., Taylor, M., Percy-Smith, B. and Limb, M. (2000) The unacceptable flaneur: The shopping mall as a teenage hangout, *Childhood*, 7(3): 279–94.

Matthews, R. (2003) Enforcing respect and reducing responsibility: A response to the white paper on anti-social behaviour, *Community Safety Journal*, 2(4): 5–8.

Matthews, R. (2005) Policing prostitution: Ten years on, *British Journal of Criminology*, 45(6): 877–95.

Matthews, R. (2006) Reintegrative shaming and restorative justice: Reconciliation or divorces?, in I. Aertsen, T. Daems and L. Robert (eds), *Institutionalizing Restorative Justice*. Cullompton: Willan Publishing.

Matthews, R., Easton, H., Briggs, D. and Pease, K. (2007) *Assessing the Use and Impact of Anti-social Behaviour Orders*. Bristol: Policy Press.

Matza, D. (1969) *Becoming Deviant*. Englewood Cliffs, NJ: Prentice-Hall.

Mawby, R. I. and Simmonds, L. (2004) Feelings of security in the city: Anxiety over crime as spatially defined, *Security Journal*, 17(2): 73–85.

May, D. (1975) Truancy, school absenteeism and delinquency, *Scottish Educational Studies*, 7: 97–107.

Mays, J. B. (1954) *Growing Up in the City: A Study of Juvenile Delinquency in an Urban Neighbourhood*. Liverpool: Liverpool University Press.

McCarthy, P. and Walker, J. (2006) R-E-S-P-E-C-T, find out what it means to me: The connection between respect and youth crime, *Crime Prevention and Community Safety*, 8(1): 17–29.

McKey, R. H., Condelli, L., Ganson, H., Barrett, B. J., McConkey, C., Plants, M. C. and Smith, A. N. (1985) *The Impact of Head Start on Children, Families and Communities: Head Start Synthesis Project Final Report*. Washington, DC: US Department of Health and Human Services.

McLaughlin, E. and Muncie, J. (1999) Walled cities: Surveillance, regulation and segregation, in S. Pile, C. Brook and G. Mooney (eds), *Unruly Cities? Order/Disorder*. Buckingham: Open University Press.

McNulty, T. (2007) Antisocial behaviour orders and individual support orders, House of Commons *Hansard Written Answers*, 29 Jan.: col. 121W.

McSweeney, T., Stevens, A., Hunt, N. and Turnbull, P. J. (2007) Twisting arms or a helping hand? Assessing the impact of 'coerced' and comparable 'voluntary' drug treatment options, *British Journal of Criminology*, 47(3): 470–90.

Mead, G. H. (1918) The psychology of punitive justice, *American Journal of Sociology*, 23(5): 577–602.

Mead, L. (1986) *Beyond Entitlement: The Social Obligations of Citizenship*. New York: The Free Press.

Measham, F. and Brain, K. (2005) 'Binge' drinking, British alcohol policy and the new culture of intoxication, *Crime, Media, Culture*, 1(3): 262–83.

Merrow, J. (2004) The 'failure' of Head Start, in E. Zigler and S. J. Styfco (eds), *The Head Start Debates*. Baltimore, MD: Brookes Publishing.

Merton, R. K. (1938) Social structure and anomie, *American Sociological Review*, 3(5): 672–82.

Merton, R. K. (1996) *On Social Structure and Science*. Chicago, IL: University of Chicago Press.

Michael, A. (1998) Standing Committee B, Crime and Disorder Bill (House of Lords), 30 Apr. Available at: http://www.publications.parliament.uk/pa/cm199798/cmstand/b/st980430/am/80430s02.htm.

Michael, A. (2005) House of Commons Standing Committee G: Clean Neighbourhoods and Environment Bill, clause 12, col. 90, 20 Jan. Available at: http://www.publications.parliament.uk/pa/cm200405/cmstand/g/st050120/am/50120s01.htm.

Millie, A. (1997) Crime in the city centre: Patterns and perception of risk. A case study of Swansea. Unpublished PhD thesis, University of Wales Swansea.

Millie, A. (2005) Reducing burglary by crackdown and consolidation, *Policing: An International Journal of Police Strategies and Management*, 28(1): 174–88.

Millie, A. (2006) Anti-social behaviour: Concerns of minority and marginalised Londoners, *Internet Journal of Criminology*. Available at: http://www.internetjournalofcriminology.com.

Millie, A. (2007a) Looking for anti-social behaviour, *Policy & Politics*, 35(4): 611–27.

Millie, A. (2007b) Tackling anti-social behaviour and regenerating neighbourhoods, in R. Atkinson and G. Helms (eds), *Securing an Urban Renaissance: Crime, Community and British Urban Policy*. Bristol: Policy Press.

Millie, A. (2008a) Anti-social behaviour, behavioural expectations and an urban aesthetic, *British Journal of Criminology*, 48(3): 379–94.

Millie, A. (2008b) Crime as an issue during the 2005 UK general election, *Crime, Media, Culture*, 4(1): 101–11.

Millie, A. (2008c) Vulnerability and risk: Some lessons from the UK Reducing Burglary Initiative, *Police Practice and Research*, 9(3): 183–198.

Millie, A. (forthcoming) Securing Respect: Behavioural Expectations and Anti-Social Behaviour in the UK, Bristol: Policy Press.

Millie, A. and Herrington, V. (2005) Bridging the gap: Understanding reassurance policing, *Howard Journal of Criminal Justice*, 44(1): 41–56.

Millie, A., Jacobson, J. and Hough, M. (2003) Understanding the growth in the prison population in England and Wales, *Criminal Justice*, 3(4): 369–87.

Millie, A., Jacobson, J., Hough, M. and Paraskevopoulou, A. (2005b) *Anti-social Behaviour in London: Setting the Context for the London Anti-Social Behaviour Strategy*. London: Greater London Authority.

Millie, A., Jacobson, J., McDonald, E. and Hough, M. (2005a) *Anti-social Bbehaviour Strategies: Finding a Balance*. Bristol: Policy Press.

Millon, T., Simonsen, E., Davis, R.D. and Birket-Smith, M. (1998) *Psychopathy: Antisocial, Criminal, and Violent Behaviour*. New York: Guilford Press.

Ministry of Justice (2007) *Parenting Contracts and Orders Guidance*. London: Ministry of Justice with the Department for Children Schools and Families and the Youth Justice Board.

Misztal, B. A. (2000) *Informality: Social Theory and Contemporary Practice*. London: Routledge.

Mori (2003) *Survey of Public Confidence in Criminal Justice*; London: Mori.

Mooney, J. and Young, J. (2006) The decline in crime and the rise of anti-social behaviour, *Probation Journal*, 53(4): 397–407.

Moore, L. and Yeo, H. (2004) *Crime in England and Wales 2003/2004: London Region*. London: Home Office.

Moore, S. (2008) Street life, neighbourhood policing and 'the community', in P. Squires (ed.), *ASBO Nation: The Criminalisation of Nuisance*. Bristol: Policy Press.

Moore, S. and Statham, E. (2006) Can intergenerational practice offer a way of limiting anti-social behaviour and fear of crime?, *Howard Journal of Criminal Justice*, 45(5): 468–84.

Morris, L. (1994) *Dangerous Classes: The Underclass and Social Citizenship*. London: Routledge.

Muncie, J. (1999) Institutionalized intolerance: Youth justice and the 1998 Crime and Disorder Act, *Critical Social Policy*, 19(2): 147–75.

Muncie, J. (2001) The construction and deconstruction of crime, in J. Muncie and E. McLaughlin (eds), *The Problem of Crime*, 2nd edn. London: Sage.

Murray, C. (1990) *The Emerging British Underclass*. London: Institute of Economic Affairs.

NAO (National Audit Office) (2006) The Home Office: Tackling anti-social behaviour. Report by the Comptroller and Auditor General HC 99 Session 2006–2007 (corrected version). London: NAO.

Newburn, T. (2007) *Criminology*. Cullompton: Willan Publishing.

Newburn, T. and Jones, T. (2005) Symbolic politics and penal populism: The long shadow of Willie Horton, *Crime, Media, Culture*, 1(1): 72–87.

Newman, O. (1972) *Defensible Space: People and Design in the Violent City*. London: The Architectural Press.

Newman, O. (1996) *Creating Defensible Space*. Washington, DC: US Department of Housing and Urban Development.

Nixon, J., Blandy, S., Hunter, C., Reeve, K. and Jones, A. (2003) *Tackling Anti-social Behaviour in Mixed Tenure Areas*. London: Office of the Deputy Prime Minister.

Nixon, J., Hodge, N., Parr, S., Willis, B. and Hunter, C. (2008) Anti-social behaviour and disability in the UK, *People, Place & Policy Online*, 2(1): 37–47.

Nixon, J. and Parr, S. (2006) Anti-social behaviour: Voices from the front line, in J. Flint (ed.), *Housing, Urban Governance and Anti-social Behaviour: Perspectives, Policy and Practice*. Bristol: Policy Press.

Norris, P. and Williams, D. (2008) The 2003 Licensing Act: The answer to 'binge drinking' and alcohol related disorder?, in P. Squires (ed.), *ASBO Nation: The Criminalisation of Nuisance*. Bristol: Policy Press.

ODPM (Office of the Deputy Prime Minister) (2005a) *How to Manage Town Centres*. London: ODPM.

ODPM (Office of the Deputy Prime Minister) (2005b) New Deal for Communities 2001–2005: An interim evaluation. Research Report No.17. London: ODPM and Sheffield Hallam University.

ODPM (Office of the Deputy Prime Minister) (2005c) *Planning Policy Statement 1: Delivering Sustainable Development*. London: ODPM.

ODPM (Office of the Deputy Prime Minister) (2005d) *Defining Sustainable Communities*. London: The Stationery Office.

Olweus, D. (1999) Sweden, in P. K. Smith, Y. Morita, J. Junger-Tas., D. Olweus, R. Catalono and P. Slee (eds), *The Nature of School Bullying: A Cross-national Perspective*. New York: Routledge.

Ormerod, P. (2005) The impact of SureStart, *The Political Quarterly*, 76(4): 565–7.

Osborne, G. (2008) Sincerest flattery: David Blunkett's views on social mobility show Conservative thinking is driving the agenda, *Guardian*, 10 Jan. Available at: http://www.guardian.co.uk/comment/story/0,,2238152,00.html

PA Consulting (2006) Priority review of the uptake by social landlords of legislative powers to tackle anti-social behaviour, Department of Communities and Local Government (DCLG) Housing Research Summary No. 232. London: DCLG.

Paling, C. (2006) Bagged and tagged three times for … er, doing nothing, in *Two's Company, Three's Antisocial?* The Times online, 3 Aug. Available at: http://www.timesonline.co.uk/tol/life_and_style/article697845.ece?token=null&offset=12.

Palmer, G., Kenway, P. and Wilcox, S. (2006) *Housing and Neighbourhoods Monitor*. York: Joseph Rowntree Foundation.

Papps, P. (1998) Anti-social behaviour strategies – individualistic or holistic? *Housing Studies*, 13(5): 639–56.

Parliamentary Joint Committee on Human Rights (2001) *Parliamentary Joint Committee on Human Rights – First report*, Session 1999–2000. Available at: http://www.publications.parliament.uk/pa/jt200001/jtselect/jtrights/69/6901.htm

Parr, S. and Nixon, J. (2008) Rationalising family intervention projects, in P. Squires (ed.), *ASBO Nation: The Criminalisation of Nuisance*. Bristol: Policy Press.

Pawson, H., Davidson, E. and Lederle, N. (2005a) *Housing associations' use of anti-social behaviour powers*, Housing Corporation Sector Study No. 59. London: Housing Corporation.

Pawson, H., Flint, J., Scott, S., Atkins, R., Bannister, J., McKenzie, C. and Mills, C. (2005b) *The Use of Possession Actions and Evictions by Social Landlords*. London: Office of the Deputy Prime Minister.

Pawson, H. and McKenzie, C. (2006) Social landlords, anti-social behaviour and countermeasures, in J. Flint (ed.), *Housing, Urban Governance and Anti-social Behaviour: Perspectives, Policy and Practice*. Bristol: Policy Press.

Pearson, G. (1983) *Hooligan: A History of Respectable Fears*. Basingstoke: Macmillan.

Pearson, G. (1989) 'A Jekyll in the classroom, a Hyde in the street': Queen Victoria's hooligans, in D. Downes (ed.), *Crime and the City: Essays in Memory of John Barron Mays*. Basingstoke: Macmillan.

Pearson, G. (1994) Youth, crime and society, in M. Maguire, R. Morgan and R. Reiner (eds), *Oxford Handbook of Criminology*, 1st edn. Oxford: Clarendon Press.

Pearson, G. (2006) Disturbing continuities: 'Peaky blinders' to 'hoodies', *Criminal Justice Matters*, Autumn 65: 6–7.

Pearson, G. (2006) Hybrid law and human rights: Banning and behaviour orders in the appeal courts, *Liverpool Law Review*, 27(2): 125–45.

Peters, L. and Walker, R. (2005) Rapid assessment of powers to close 'crack houses', Home Office Development and Practice Report No. 42. London: Home Office.

Phillips, Lord (2007) How important is punishment? Howard League for Penal Reform Cripps Lecture, 15 Nov. Available at: http://www.judiciary.gov.uk/docs/speeches/lcj_howardleague151107.pdf

Phillips, S. and Cochrane, R. (1988) Crime and nuisance in the shopping centre: A case study in crime prevention, Crime Prevention Unit Paper No. 16. London: Home Office.

Pheonix, A. (1996) Social constructions of lone motherhood, in E. B. Silva (ed.), *Good Enough Mothering? Feminist Perspectives on Lone Motherhood*. London: Routledge.

Povey, K. (2001) *Open All Hours: A Thematic Inspection Report on the Role of Police Visibility and Accessibility in Public Reassurance*. London: Her Majesty's Inspectorate of Constabulary.

Pratt, J. D. (1983) Folk-lore and fact in truancy research: Some critical comments on recent developments, *British Journal of Criminology*, 23(4): 336–53.

Prime Minister's Strategy Unit (2004) *Alcohol Harm Reduction Strategy for England*. London: Prime Minister's Strategy Unit.

Prior, D. and Paris, A. (2005) Preventing children's involvement in crime and anti-social behaviour: A literature review, Research Report No. 623, Nottingham: Department for Education and Skills.

Pullen, D. (1973) Community involvement, in C. Ward (ed.), *Vandalism*. London: The Architectural Press.

Purdue, D. (2001) Neighbourhood governance: Leadership, trust and social capital, *Urban Studies*, 38(12): 2211–24.

Putnam, R. D. (2000) *Bowling Alone: The Collapse and Revival of American Community*. New York: Simon & Schuster.

Quinney, R. (1970) *The Social Reality of Crime*. Boston, MA: Little, Brown and Co.

Quinton, P. and Morris, J. (2008) Neighbourhood policing: the impact of piloting and early national implementation, Home Office Online Report No. 01/08. London: Home Office.

Raco, M. (2007) The planning, design, and governance of sustainable communities in the UK, in R. Atkinson and G. Helms (eds), *Securing an Urban Renaissance: Crime, Community, and British Urban Policy*. Bristol: Policy Press.

Ramsay, P. (2004) What is anti-social behaviour?, *The Criminal Law Review*, Nov.: 908–25.

Ramsay, P. (2008) Vulnerability, sovereignty, and police power in the ASBO, in M. Dubber and M. Valverde (eds), *Police in the Liberal State*. Palo Alto, CA: Stanford University Press.

Ramsey, M. (1989) Downtown drinkers: The perceptions and fears of the public in a city centre, Crime Prevention Unit Paper No. 19. London: Home Office.

Reid, K. (2002) Anti-social behaviour orders: Some current developments, *Journal of Social Welfare and Family Law*, 24(2): 205–22.

Reith, C. (1956) *A New Study of Police History*. Edinburgh: Oliver and Boyd.

Respect Taskforce (2006) *Respect Action Plan*. London: Home Office.

Respect website (2005) Parents must take responsibility for children's behaviour, *Respect Website News*, 2 Sept. Available at: http://www.respect.gov.uk/members/news/article.aspx?id=8522.

Respect website (2007a) Types of anti-social behaviour, *Respect Website News*. Available at: http://www.respect.gov.uk/article.aspx?id=9068.

Respect website (2007b) ASBOs and human rights (last updated 11 June 2007). Available at: http://www.respect.gov.uk/members/article.aspx?id=7838.

Respect Website (2008) Tackling anti-social behaviour £13m to help prevent anti-social behaviour, 5 Mar. Available at: http://www.respect.gov.uk/members/news/article.aspx?id=12096.

Rhodes, J., Tyler, P. and Brennan, A. (2005) Assessing the effect of area based initiatives on local area outcomes: Some thoughts based on the national evaluation of the Single Regeneration Budget in England, *Urban Studies*, 42(11): 1919–46.

Rhodes, J., Tyler, P., Brennan, A., Stevens, S., Warnock, C. and Otero-Garcia, M. (2002) *Lessons and Evaluation Evidence from Ten Single Regeneration Budget Case Studies: Mid-term Report*. London: Department for Transport, Local Government and the Regions.

Roberts, J. and Hough, M. (2005) *Understanding Public Attitudes to Criminal Justice*. Maidenhead: Open University Press.

Roberts, J., Stalans, L., Indermaur, D. and Hough, M. (2002) *Penal Populism and Public Opinion*. Oxford: Oxford University Press.

Roberts, M. (2004) *Good Practice in Managing the Evening and Late Night Economy: A Literature Review from an Environmental Perspective*. London: Office of the Deputy Prime Minister.

Roberts, M. and Eldridge, A. (2007) *Expecting 'Great Things'? The Impact of the Licensing Act 2003 on Democratic Involvement, Dispersal and Drinking Cultures.* London: University of Westminster.

Roberts, P. (2006) Penal offence in question: some reference points for interdisciplinary conversation, in A. von Hirsch and A. P. Simester (eds), *Incivilities: Regulating Offensive Behaviour.* Oxford: Hart Publishing.

Robinson, W. S. (1950) Ecological correlations and the behavior of individuals, *American Sociological Review*, 15(3): 352–7.

Rodger, J. J. (2006) Antisocial families and withholding welfare support, *Critical Social Policy*, 26(1): 121–43.

Rodger, J. J. (2008) *Criminalising Social Policy: Anti-social Behaviour and Welfare in a De-civilized Society.* Cullompton: Willan Publishing.

Rogers, P. and Coaffee, J. (2005) Moral panics and urban renaissance: Policy, tactics and youth in public space, *City*, 9(3):321–40.

Rose, N. (2000) Community, citizenship, and the third way, *American Behavioral Scientist*, 43(9): 1395–411.

Roseneil, S. and Mann, K. (1996) Unpalatable choices and inadequate families: Lone mothers and the underclass debate, in E. B. Silva (ed.), *Good Enough Mothering? Feminist Perspectives on Lone Motherhood.* London: Routledge.

Rubin, J., Rabinovich, L., Hallsworth, M. and Nason, E. (2006) *Interventions to Reduce Anti-social Behaviour and Crime: A Review of Effectiveness and Costs.* Cambridge: RAND Europe.

Ruggieri, S. and Levison, D. (1998) *Starter Tenancies and Introductory Tenancies: An Evaluation.* London: The Housing Corporation.

Rutherford, A. (2000) An elephant on the doorstep: Criminal policy without crime in New Labour's Britain, in P. Green and A. Rutherford (eds), *Criminal Policy in Transition.* Oxford: Hart Publishing.

Safer Swansea Partnership (2007) Safer Swansea Partnership Anti-Social Behaviour Progress Report 2005–2006, Internal project document, Safer Swansea Partnership, Swansea.

Sampson, R. J. and Grove, W. B. (1989) Community structure and crime: Testing social-disorganization theory, *American Journal of Sociology*, 94(4): 774–802.

Sampson, R. J. and Laub, J. H. (1992) Crime and deviance in the life course, *Annual Review of Sociology*, 18: 63–84.

Sampson, R. J. and Raudenbush, S. W. (1999) Systematic social observation of public spaces: A new look at disorder in urban neighbourhoods, *American Journal of Sociology*, 105(3): 603–51.

Sampson, R. J., Raudenbush, S. W. and Earls, F. (1997) Neighborhoods and violent crime: A multilevel study of collective efficacy, *Science*, 277(5328): 918–24.

Sanders, T. (2005) *Sex Work: A Risky Business.* Cullompton: Willan Publishing.

Scarman, Lord (1981) *The Brixton Disorders 10–12 April, 1981*, Cmnd. 8427. London: HMSO.

Scarman, Lord (1984) An epilogue, in J. Benyon (ed.), *Scarman and After: Essays Reflecting on Lord Scarman's Report, the Riots and their Aftermath.* Oxford: Pergamon Press.

Schur, E. M. (1971) *Labelling Deviant Behaviour: Its Sociological Implications.* London: Harper & Row.

Schweinhart, L. J., Barnes, H. V. and Weikart, D. P. (1993) *Significant Benefits: The High/Scope Perry Pre-School Study Through Age 27*. Ypsilanti, MI: High/Scope Educational Research Foundation.

Schweinhart, L. J., Montie, J., Xiang, Z., Barnett, W. S., Belfield, C. R. and Nores, M. (2004) Lifetime Effects: The High/Scope Perry Preschool Study Through Age 40, Research summary, Ypsilanti, MI: High/Scope Press.

Scott, M. S. (2002) Disorderly youth in public places, Problem-Oriented Guides for Police Series No. 6. Washington, DC: US Department of Justice.

Scott, S. (2006) Tackling anti-social behaviour: An evaluation of the Dundee Families Project, in J. Flint (ed.), *Housing, Urban Governance and Anti-social Behaviour: Perspectives, Policy and Practice*. Bristol: Policy Press.

Scoular, J., Pitcher, J., Campbell, R., Hubbard, P. and O'Neill, M. (2007) What's anti-social about sex work? The changing representation of prostitution's incivility, *Community Safety Journal*, 6(1): 11–18.

Scraton, P. (2005) The denial of children's rights and liberties in the UK and the north of Ireland, European Civil Liberties Network Essay No. 14. Available at: http://www.ecln.org/essays/essay-14.pdf.

Sellin, T. (1938) *Culture, Conflict and Crime*. New York: Social Science Research Council.

Sennett, R. (1970) *The Uses of Disorder: Personal Identity and City Life*. New York and London: W. W. Norton.

Sennett, R. (2003) *Respect: The Formation of Character in an Age of Inequality*. London: Penguin Books.

Sennett, R. (2006) Views on respect: Richard Sennett, *BBC News Online*, 9 Jan. Available at: http://news.bbc.co.uk/1/hi/uk/4589616.stm.

Sentamu, J. (Archbishop of York) (2006) Views on respect: Archbishop of York, *BBC News Online*, 9 Jan. Available at: http://news.bbc.co.uk/1/hi/uk/4589636.stm

Sentencing Advisory Panel (2007) Consultation paper on breach of an anti-social behaviour order (ASBO), 16 Aug. Available at: http://www.sentencing-guidelines.gov.uk/docs/ASBO%20consultation%20paper%202007-08-8-Final.pdf.

SEU (Social Exclusion Unit) (1999) *Bridging the Gap: New Opportunities for 16–18 Year Olds Not in Education, Employment or Training*. London: Social Exclusion Unit.

SEU (Social Exclusion Unit) (2000a) *Report of Policy Action Team 8: Anti-social Behaviour*. London: SEU.

SEU (Social Exclusion Unit) (2000b) *National Strategy for Neighbourhood Renewal: A Framework for Consultation*. London: SEU (Cabinet Office).

SEU (Social Exclusion Unit) (2000c) *Report of Policy Action Team 4: Neighbourhood Management*, London: SEU.

SEU (Social Exclusion Unit) (2001) *A New Commitment to Neighbourhood Renewal: National Strategy Action Plan*. London: SEU.

Shaftoe, H. (2006) Behaving badly in public spaces, *Urban Design*, No. 97, Winter.

Shaw, C. and Mackay, H. (1942) *Juvenile Delinquency in Urban Areas*. Chicago, IL: University of Chicago Press.

Simester, A. P. and von Hirsch, A. (2006) Regulating offensive conduct through two-step prohibitions, in A. von Hirsch and A. P. Simester (eds), *Incivilities: Regulating Offensive Behaviour*. Oxford: Hart Publishing.

Skogan, W. G. (1990) *Disorder and Decline: Crime and the Spiral of Decay in American Neighborhoods*. New York: The Free Press.

Skogan, W. and Hartnett, S. M. (1997) *Community Policing, Chicago Style*. New York: Oxford University Press.

Smith, D. (2006) Youth crime and justice: Research, evaluation and 'evidence', in B. Goldson and J. Muncie (eds), *Youth Crime and Justice*. London: Sage.

Smith, D. J. (1992) *Understanding the Underclass*. London: Policy Studies Institute.

Smith, N. (1996) *The New Urban Frontier: Gentrification and the Revanchist City*. London: Routledge.

Smith, P. K., Cowie, H., Olafsson, R. F. and Liefooghe, A. P. D. (2002) Definitions of bullying: A comparison of terms used, and age and gender differences, in a fourteen–country international comparison, *Child Development*, 73(4): 1119–33.

Smith, R. (2006) Actuarialism and early intervention in contemporary youth justice, in B. Goldson and J. Muncie (eds), *Youth Crime and Justice*. London: Sage.

Smith, R. (2007) *Youth Justice: Ideas, Policy, Practice*, 2nd edn. Cullompton: Willan.

Smithson, H. (2005) Effectiveness of a dispersal order to reduce ASB among young people: A case study approach in east Manchester, New Deal for Communities National Evaluation Research Report No. 48, Sheffield: Sheffield Hallam University.

Smithson, H. and Flint, J. (2006) Responding to young people's involvement in anti-social behaviour: A study of local initiatives in Manchester and Glasgow, *Youth and Policy*, 93: 21–39.

Social Justice Policy Group (2006) *Breakdown Britain: Interim Report on the State of the Nation*. London: Social Justice Policy Group.

Solanki, A., Bateman, T., Boswell, G. and Hill, E. (2006) *Anti-Social Behaviour Orders*. London: Youth Justice Board.

Sparks, R., Girling, E. and Loader, I. (2001) Fear and everyday urban lives, *Urban Studies*, 38(5–6) 885–98.

Squires, P. (2006) New Labour and the politics of antisocial behaviour, *Critical Social Policy*, 26(1): 144–68.

Squires, P. (2008) *ASBO Nation: The Criminalisation of Nuisance*. Bristol: Policy Press.

Squires, P. and Stephen, D. E. (2005a) *Rougher Justice: Anti-social Behaviour and Young People*. Cullompton: Willan Publishing.

Squires, P. and Stephens, D. E. (2005b) Rethinking ASBOs, *Critical Social Policy*, 25(4): 517–28.

Stephen, D. and Squires, P. (2003) *Community Safety, Enforcement and Acceptable Behaviour Contracts: An Evaluation of the Work of the Community Safety Team in the East Brighton 'New Deal for Communities' Area*. Brighton: Health and Social Policy Research Centre, University of Brighton.

Stinchcombe, A. (1964) *Rebellion in a High School*. Chicago, IL: Quadrangle Books.

Stone, N. (2004) Orders in respect of anti-social behaviour: Recent judicial developments, *Youth Justice*, 4(1): 46–54.

Straw, J. (1996) Speech By Shadow Home Secretary, Jack Straw, Speech To The NACRO AGM. Available at: http://www.prnewswire.co.uk/cgi/news/release?id=19432.

Straw, J. and Michael, A. (1996) *Tackling Youth Crime: Reforming Youth Justice. A Consultation Paper on an Agenda for Change*. London: Labour Party.

Sutherland, E. (1940) 'White-collar criminality, *American Sociological Review*, 5(1): 2–10.

Sylvester, R. (2006) Tony Blair's 'instant justice' will make criminals of us all, *Daily Telegraph*, 16 Jan. Available at: http://www.telegraph.co.uk/opinion/main.jhtml?xml=/opinion/ 2006/01/16/do1601.xml.

Talbot, D. (2006) The Licensing Act 2003 and the problematization of the night-time economy: Planning, licensing and subcultural closure in the UK, *International Journal of Urban and Regional Research*, 30(1): 159–71.

Tannenbaum, F. (1938) *Crime and the Community*. New York: Columbia University Press.

Taub, R. P., Garth Taylor, D. G. and Dunham, J. D. (1984) *Paths of Neighbourhood Change: Race and Crime in Urban America*. Chicago, IL: University of Chicago Press.

Taylor, D. (2002) *Policing the Victorian Town: The Development of the Police in Middlesbrough c.1840–1914*. Basingstoke: Palgrave Macmillan.

Taylor. I. and Walton, P. (1973) Hey, mister, this is what we really do … , in C. Ward (ed.), *Vandalism*. London: Architectural Press.

Taylor, L. (1971) *Deviance and Society*. London: Thomas Nelson & Sons Ltd.

Taylor, R. B. (1999a) The incivilities thesis: Theory, measurement, and policy, in R. H. Langworthy (ed.), *Measuring What Matters: Proceedings from the Policing Research Institute meetings*. Washington, DC: National Institute of Justice.

Taylor, R. B. (1999b) Crime, grime, fear, and decline: a longitudinal look, National Institute of Justice Research in Brief. Washington, DC: National Institute of Justice.

Taylor, R. B. (2001) *Breaking Away from Broken Windows: Baltimore Neighborhoods and the Nationwide Fight Against Crime, Grime, Fear, and Decline*. Boulder, CO: Westview Press.

Taylor, R. B. (2002) Crime prevention through environmental design (CPTED): Yes, no, maybe, unknowable, and all of the above, in R. B. Bechtel, A. Churchman (eds), *Handbook of Environmental Psychology*. New York: John Wiley & Sons.

Taylor, R. (2006) *Review of Use of Noise Abatement Notices Served Under Section 80 of the Environmental Protection Act 1990*. Fairwarp: Rupert Taylor Acoustics and Vibration Consultants.

Thompson, L. (2007) *The Respect Drive: The Politics of Young People and Community. A Study Based in the London Borough of Hackney*. London: Goldsmiths, University of London.

Thorp, A. (1998) Anti-social behaviour, in A. Thorp, J. Fiddick and E. Wood (eds). *The Crime and Disorder Bill [HL], Bill 167 of 1997–98: Anti-social Neighbours, Sex Offenders, Racially Motivated Offences and Sentencing Drug-dependent Offenders*. House of Commons Research Paper 98/44, 6 Apr. London: House of Commons.

Thorpe, K., Robb, P. and Higgins, N. (2007) Extent and trends, in S. Nicholas, C. Kershaw and A. Walker (eds), *Crime in England and Wales 2006/07*. Home Office Statistical Bulletin 11/07. London: Home Office.

Thorpe, K. and Wood, M. (2004) in S. Nicholas and A. Walker (eds), *Crime in England and Wales 2002/2003. Supplementary Volume 2: Crime, Disorder and the Criminal Justice System – Public Attitudes and Perceptions*. Home Office Statistical Bulletin 02/04. London: Home Office.

Thrasher, F. M. (1927) *The Gang: A Study of 1,313 Gangs in Chicago*. Chicago, IL: University of Chicago Press.

Thrift, N. (2005) But malice aforethought: Cities and the natural history of hatred, *Transactions, Institute of British Geographers*, 30(2): 133–50.

Times, (2006) Stallholders fined for offensive Blair T-shirts, *The Times Online,* July 4. Available at: http://www.timesonline.co.uk/tol/news/uk/article682521.ece (accessed Dec. 2007).

Tonry, M. (2004) *Punishment and Politics: Evidence and Emulation in the Making of English Crime Control Policy.* Cullompton: Willan Publishing.

Tremblay, R., Hartup, W. and Archer, J. (2004) *Developmental Origins of Aggression.* New York: Guilford Press.

Truss, L. (2005) *Talk to the Hand: The Utter Bloody Rudeness of Everyday Life (or Six Good Reasons to Stay Home and Bolt the Door).* London: Profile Books.

Tuffin, R., Morris, J. and Poole, A. (2006) An evaluation of the impact of the National Reassurance Policing Programme, Home Office Research Study No. 296. London: Home Office.

Tunstill, J., Meadows, P., Akhurst, S., Akhurst, S., Chrysanthou, J., Garbers, C., Morley, A. and van de Velde, T. (2006) *Implementing SureStart Local Programmes: An Integrated Overview of the First Four Years.* London: DFES.

Tunstill, J., Meadows, P., Allnock, D., Akhurst, S., Chyrsanthou, J., Garbers, C. and Morley, A. (2005) *Implementing SureStart Local Programmes: An In-depth Study.* London: DFES.

Urban Task Force (1999) *Towards an Urban Renaissance.* London: DETR.

Urban Parks Forum (2002) *Public Parks Assessment: A Survey of Local Authority Owned Parks Focusing on Parks of Historic Interest.* Reading: Urban Parks Forum.

URBED (Urban and Economic Development of the Environment) and DoE (Department of the Environment) (1994) *Vital and Viable Town Centres: Meeting the Challenge.* London: HMSO.

Upson, A. (2006) Perceptions and experience of anti-social behaviour: Findings from the 2004/05 British Crime Survey, Home Office Online Report 21/06. London: Home Office.

Valentine, G. (2004) *Public Space and the Culture of Childhood.* Aldershot: Ashgate.

Vitale, A. S. (2008) *City of Disorder: How the Quality of Life Campaign Transformed New York Politics.* New York: NYU Press.

Vold, G. B., Bernard, T. J. and Snipes, J. B. (2002) *Theoretical Criminology,* 5th edn. Oxford: Oxford University Press.

von Hirsch, A., Ashworth, A., Wasik, M., Smith, A. H., Morgan, R. and Gardner, J. (1995) Overtaking on the right, *New Law Journal,* 145: 1501–1516.

von Hirsch, A. and Simester, A. P. (2006) *Incivilities: Regulating Offensive Behaviour.* Oxford: Hart Publishing.

Wain, N. (2007) *The ASBO: Wrong Turning Dead End.* London: Howard League for Penal Reform.

Waiton, S. (2001) *Scared of the Kids? Curfews, Crime and the Regulation of Young People.* Sheffield: Sheffield University Press.

Waiton, S. (2005) The politics of antisocial behaviour, in C. O'Malley and S. Waiton (eds), *Who's Antisocial? New Labour and the Politics of Antisocial Behaviour.* Institute of Ideas Occasional Paper No. 2. London: Academy of Ideas Ltd.

Walker, J., Thompson, C., Laing, K., Raybould, S., Coombes, M., Procter, S. and Wren, C. (2007) *Youth Inclusion and Support Panels: Preventing Crime and Antisocial Behaviour.* Research Report No. DCSF-RW018. London: Department for Children, Schools and Families.

Walklate, S. and Evans, K. (1999) *Zero Tolerance or Community Tolerance? Managing Crime in High Crime Areas*. Aldershot: Ashgate.

Walklate, S. and Mythen, G. (2008) How scared are we?, *British Journal of Criminology*, 48(1): 209–25.

Walsh, C. (2002) Curfews: No more hanging around, *Youth Justice*, 2(2): 70–81.

Walsh, C. (2003) Dispersal of rights: A critical comment on specified provisions of the Anti-Social Behaviour Bill, *Youth Justice*, 3(2): 104–11.

Walters, R. and Woodward, R. (2007) Punishing 'poor parents': 'Respect', 'responsibility' and parenting orders in Scotland, *Youth Justice*, 7(1): 5–20.

Ward, C. (1978) *The Child in the City*. London: The Architectural Press.

Warpole, K. (2006) The youth shelter, in *Youth Space: A Collaborative Youth Shelter Project Connecting Young People, Architects and Artists*. Birmingham: Midlands Architecture and the Designed Environment, p. 22.

Wellsmith, M. and Guille, H. (2005) Fixed penalty notices as a means of offender selection, *International Journal of Police Science and Management*, 7(1): 36–43.

West, D. J. and Farrington, D. P. (1973) *Who Becomes Delinquent?* London: Heinemann.

White, S. (1999) 'Rights and responsibilities': A social democratic perspective, *The Political Quarterly*, 70(1): 166–80.

Whitehead, C. M. E., Stockdale, J. E. and Razzu, G. (2003) *The Economic and Social Costs of Anti-Social Behaviour*. London: London School of Economics.

Wikström, P-O. (2003) *Individual Risk, Life-style Risk, and Adolescent Offending: Findings from the Peterborough Youth Study*. Available at: http://www.scopic.ac.uk/documents/Peterborougharticle_000.pdf.

Williams, N. (2004) Three-year vice ban for Asbo prostitute, *Wandsworth Borough News*, 26 Mar:

Wilson, J. Q. (1975) *Thinking About Crime*. New York: Basic Books.

Wilson, J. Q. and Kelling, G. L. (1982) Broken windows: The police and neighbourhood safety, *The Atlantic Monthly*, Mar, 249(3): 29–38.

Wood, M. (2004) Perceptions and experience of antisocial behaviour: findings from the 2003/4 British Crime Survey, Home Office Online Report No. 49/04. London: Home Office.

Woolley, H. (2006) Freedom of the city: Contemporary issues and policy influences on children and young people's use of public open space in England, *Children's Geographies*, 4(1): 45–59.

Young, J. (1999) *The Exclusive Society: Social Exclusion, Crime and Difference in Late Modernity*. London: Sage.

Young, J. (2002) Critical criminology in the twenty-first century: Critique, irony and the always unfinished, in R. Hogg and K. Carrington (eds), *Critical Criminology: Issues, Debates, Challenges*. Cullompton: Willan Publishing.

Young, J. (2007) *The Vertigo of Late Modernity*. London: Sage.

Young, T., Hallsworth, S., Jackson, E. and Lindsey, J. (2006) *Crime Displacement in King's Cross: A Report for Camden Community Safety Partnership*. London: London Metropolitan University.

Youth Justice Board (2006) *Individual Support Orders (ISO) Procedure: A Protocol to be Used and Adapted by YOTs When Managing ISOs*. London: Youth Justice Board.

Youth Taskforce (2008) *Youth Taskforce Action Plan: Give Respect, Get Respect – Youth Matters*. London: Department for Children, Schools and Families.

Zigler, E. and Styfco, S. J. (2004) *The Head Start Debates*. Baltimore, MD: Brookes Publishing.

Zimbardo, P. G. (1973) A field experiment in auto shaping, in C. Ward (ed.), *Vandalism*. London: The Architectural Press.

INDEX

UNDERSTANDING YOUTH AND CRIME 2e

Listening to Youth?

Sheila Brown

Reviewers' comments on the first edition

"This is an excellent introductory textbook on youth and crime. It is excellent not only in its analysis of criminological questions about youthful offending, but also because it positions the debate within a wider context of the relationship between young people and society."
Young People Now

"The style is lively and readable, and the reader is pointed unobtrusively within the text towards the work of the leading authors in the field ... a thorough and thoughtful introduction to the subject."
Social Policy

"... a critical and scholarly summary of the state of research and theorizing around 'youth and crime' ... This book provides a useful and challenging overview of the topic for undergraduate students."
The Times Higher Education Supplement

This book is an accessible introduction to the subject of youth and crime. The author explores the social construction of childhood and youth, and looks at the role of the media in creating a strong association of young people with crime and disorder, which sustains processes of marginalization and exclusion and leads to frequent 'panics' about youth crime. The importance of media representations of race and gender in these processes are also explored.

The second edition is substantially revised and updated to take account of new political events and legislative developments, including:

● A new chapter on the phenomenon of 'cybercrime'
● A critical examination of recent developments in youth justice policy
● A new chapter on the impact of globalization on young people, which raises major issues around poverty, war and the commercial exploitation of children

This is a key text for students in criminology, sociology, social policy, and cultural studies.

Contents: Series editor's foreword – Acknowledgements – Introduction to the second edition – Constructing the other: Childhood and youth – Problem youth meets criminology: The formative decades – Representing problem youth: The repackaging of reality – In whose interests? Politics, policy and UK youth justice – 'Punishing youth': Victims or villains? – Youth and crime: Beyond the boy zone – Netdangers: Cyberkids and cybercrimes – Beyond boundaries: Understanding global youth and crime – Conclusion: Listening to youth? – Glossary – References – Index.

2005 272pp
978-0-335-21678-9 (Paperback) 978-0-335-21679-6 (Hardback)

RESEARCHING CRIMINOLOGY

Iain Crow and Natasha Semmens

'... what makes the book stand out is the inclusion of real research into various criminal justice institutions that have actually been undertaken by the authors. In doing so, what is produced is a book that stimulates interest and injects research passion, as well as offering research 'know how' into what can often be a difficult and sometimes dry area of research.'

Tina Patel, Liverpool John Moores University

'This book provides an essential tool for undergraduate students embarking upon their own research projects in Criminology. It provides clear and informative guidance on a range of research methods and designs to assist students in their own criminological endeavours.'

Jacki Tapley, University of Portsmouth

- How do criminologists go about studying crime and its consequences?
- How are programmes for offenders and communities evaluated?
- How can you collect and analyse criminological material?

Research on crime and criminality is often referred to by the media, policy makers and practitioners, but where does this research come from and how reliable is it?

Designed especially for students on criminology and criminal justice courses, and professionals working in the field, *Researching Criminology* emphasises the importance of research as an integrated process. It looks at the ways in which a mixture of investigative methods can be used to analyze a criminological question.

Written by two experienced researchers and lecturers *Researching Criminology* is a comprehensive introduction to the aims, principles and methods of doing criminological research. The book covers all the key topics that you will encounter when researching crime. Individual chapters include material on:

- The research process
- Principles of researching criminology
- How to design criminological research
- Evaluation research
- Researching ethically
- A glossary of essential key concepts

Structured in three parts, addressing the principles of criminological research, how to collect and analyse material and providing detailed examples of real world research, *Researching Criminology* will be of benefit to all students of criminology and criminal justice, for practitioners interested in criminological research, and for those undertaking criminological research for the first time.

Contents: Part one: The principles of criminological research – The research process – The principles of researching criminology – Designing criminological research – Criminological evaluation – Part two: Collecting and analysing material – Researching by reading – Researching by looking – Researching by asking and listening – Analysing criminological research – Part three: Real world research – Researching offenders and employment – Researching the youth court – Researching a community safety programme – Researching the fear of crime.

2007 312pp
978-0-335-22140-0 (Paperback) 978-0-335-22141-7 (Hardback)

THE END OF MULTICULTURALISM?

Terrorism, Integration and Human Rights

Derek McGhee

*'... the book is a brave and authoritative analysis of multicultural-
ism ... McGhee successfully locates his subject in the context of recent
developments in both community cohesion and human rights and
shows with great skill how differing impulses within government and
the wider community pull multiculturalism in various different directions ... With this book, McGhee manages to be both topical and
well-informed: it deserves a wide readership.'*

Professor Conor Gearty, LSE

This topical book provides a thorough examination of debates on multiculturalism, in the context of current discussions on security, integration and human
rights.

Recent debates on national identity and the alleged failure of multiculturalism
have focused on the social disorder in Oldham, Burnley and Bradford in the
summer of 2001 and the bombings and attempted bombings in London in July
2005. Derek McGhee assesses how these events and the events that have
occurred outside Britain, especially the attacks on the USA on 11th September
2001, have resulted in the introduction of a number of high profile debates in
Britain with regards to immigration, integration, citizenship, 'race' inequality
and human rights.

McGhee examines these debates on multiculturalism and terrorism in light of
enduring questions regarding 'Muslim integration' and 'Muslim loyalty' in
contemporary Britain. He also explores the nature of a diverse range of
inter-related areas of public policy, including anti-terrorism, immigration, integration, community cohesion, equality and human rights, critically examining
many of the Government's key strategies in recent years.

The End of Multiculturalism? will appeal to a wide readership of students and
academics in sociology, politics, international relations and law.

*Contents: Acknowledgments – Preface – Introduction – Deportation, detention & torture
by proxy: Foreign national terror suspects in the UK – In between allegiance and
evilization: The Muslim question post 7/7 – Counter terrorism, community relations,
radicalisation and 'Muslim grievances' – Cohesion, citizenship and integration (beyond
multiculturalism?) – Culture change: The Commission for Equality and Human Rights:
Future proofing the nation – Shared values, Britishness and human rights – Afterword
– Notes – Bibliography – Index.*

2008 208pp
978-0-335-22392-3 (Paperback) 978-0-335-22391-6 (Hardback)